CITIZENS AND SOLDIERS KEEPING INDIA'S TRYST WITH DESTINY

Paradigm for National Security and Resurgence

Brigadier Deepak Sethi, PhD (Veteran)

Deepak Sethi

ISBN:1983575682
ISBN-13:9781983575686

Dedicated to my Parents
Late Sri Ram and Kamala Sethi

To My Family...

.....and to my Professor Late Steve Guisinger

Citizens and Soldiers Keeping India's Tryst with Destiny

CONTENTS

Citizens and Soldiers Keeping India's Tryst with Destiny

PREFACE

The fact that *National security* affects us all, sounds like a self-evident cliché. However, often forgotten is the fact that we all are its stakeholders; not only as beneficiaries but also as *citizens* we have a duty to safeguard it too. Thus, all of us are *soldiers* in this mission as farmers, workers, businesspersons, administrators, defence personnel, and politicians.

Military power alone cannot guarantee National security. National will, internal stability, and economic strength have to back it. Also imperative is visionary leadership to formulate an integrated *National Security Doctrine and Policy* that will ensure security in the external and internal environments. This book will therefore cover a wide canvas to embrace both dimensions.

The book addresses primarily all citizens – the *aam aadmi,* to highlight their stake and role in the Nation's security. It will also interest policy makers, strategic thinkers, and diplomatic, military and economic experts. Given the wide audience, I have struck a balance between *breadth* and *depth* of coverage, to retain interest at both ends of the continuum.

Genesis of the *National Security Paradigm* proposed in this book is my dissertation, *Impact of Internal Security Environment on our Armed Forces.* I had submitted it to the College of Defence Management in 1991, and got the *'Best Dissertation Award'.*

I wrote it at a time of intense political and social turmoil in our country. Caste and communal passions had been unleashed along with high political instability and economy slowdown. The Armed Forces had restored order at trouble spots across the Nation.

National Security Paradigm in that dissertation had focused mainly on the *internal environment.* After taking early retirement in 1997, and then earning PhD in International Business Strategy and Management from the *University of Texas at Dallas* in 2001, I developed the model further. It is now a more comprehensive framework that integrates both *internal* and *external* security.

While my academic discipline is *International Business* (IB), I also conduct research on the cusp of IB and IR (*International Relations*). I have published papers in several top-tier US and European journals wherein I have drawn insights from both fields. Hence, I have tried to meld those insights while formulating the new *National Security Paradigm.*

Born six months before India's independence, I have seen firsthand our 71-year history. Though uprooted from our home and hearth due to partition, there was never a sense of despair. That was an era of optimism, and people contributed to Nation-building with boundless enthusiasm.

India's industrial and economic development and her military fascinated me right from childhood. It was because of the oft-repeated phrase that India used to be a *sone ki chidiya* – much craved for her riches, but which was left impoverished by invaders and colonial masters. They had wantonly destroyed India's indigenous skills and crafts, and *even a pin had to be imported.*

So, everyone felt extremely proud about the *Temples of Modern India*, as per Pandit Nehru's characterization. The Bhakra dam, Durgapur, Bhilai and Rourkela steel plants, BHEL, HMT, Chitaranjan locomotive factory, Apsara nuclear reactor, Gnats and HF24 flying out of HAL, or tanks rolling out of Avadi; they all were spectacular milestones. There was anger too when USA denied us F-104s, and rewarded Pakistan with them since it had joined CENTO and SEATO. The 1962 war with China struck a big blow to the Nation's esteem and many like me joined the Armed Forces.

During my military career, I closely followed the *guns vs. butter* debate, and penned articles how at 3.2% of GDP our defence budget was inadequate. I did not realize then that it would go down to 1.5% of GDP by 2018, despite our two-front confrontation with China and Pakistan. We are yet to *catch-up* with China, which has a 25-year lead in modernizing its Armed Forces and building military infrastructure in Tibet.

Regrettably, the post-independence optimism now seems to have given way to cynicism, loss of faith in institutions, religious, caste and class polarization, declining standards of probity, and a sense of despair. Those who are corrupt among our politicians and bureaucrats are to blame. But, are we not responsible too for letting them have their way?

The *National Security Paradigm* is generic, and can analyze any country's security environment. However, to illustrate its application I have discussed its dimensions in the Indian context.

I have written mainly in *third person* and provided extensive citations and statistics to support the analyses. However, at places I have also included anecdotes, observations, and personal views to illustrate some of the aspects.

In format and style, the book can best be described as *hybrid*. I have tried an *easy-to-read,* conversational style instead of drab academic writing. I have avoided technical jargon to the extent possible keeping in view the audience of common citizens.

Chapters in Part 1 essentially lay the groundwork of the geopolitical context of any country's security environment. They enable a better understanding of the rights and obligations of a *Westphalia Nation-state*. Only these chapters focus on some academic aspects to explain the conceptual basis of the *paradigm*.

Chapters in Part 2 discuss at length various dimensions in India's internal security environment. The opening chapter of Part 3 surveys the Global geopolitical environment, with special emphasis on China and India. Remaining chapters in this part discuss different dimensions of external security, such as *National Security Doctrine,* military power, economic strength, diplomacy and soft power.

In Part3, I also discuss how by ensuring internal cohesion and stability, and by harnessing the citizens' will and enthusiasm it is possible to enhance the paradigm for *National Security* to attain the higher goal of *National Resurgence.*

There is some overlap in elements of the external and internal environments. Discussion on those elements might appear repetitive, though I have tried to restrict it as much as possible.

I have consciously chosen to underplay the emotive issues that are causing widespread angst and frustration in the Armed Forces, both among veterans and serving soldiers. Contentious issues such as the raw deal to the Armed Forces in grades, designations, pay, allowances, disability awards, NFU, and OROP, and their deliberate denigration have been discussed *ad infinitum* in the public domain. I am not reiterating all those details, as that may shift the focus away from the overall theme of the book.

Undoubtedly, financial inequities are important, but more critical and anguishing to our *soldiers* is the deliberate onslaught on their pride and honour. That is creating a dangerous chasm, but the politico-bureaucratic dispensation seems oblivious and even apathetic towards it.

I feel it is more important to underscore the disastrous effects of such a rift to the *aam aadmi*. Soldiers are emotional beings and *izzat aur iqbal* is their driving force. Their hurt pride and pent up angst can be terrible for our military power and National security.

I have chosen *qualitative analysis* over *quantitative analysis* to keep the narrative simple and avoid statistical modelling. Since *qualitative analyses* can be *subjective,* I have cited extensively statistical data from well-regarded global and national sources to support those observations.

Citations from the vast body of work in relevant disciplines have been included to make the case that my observations are not just *off-the-cuff*. However, my intent is not to pass judgements on many of the events and statistics used to illustrate the application of the *National Security Paradigm*. I leave that to the wisdom of the readers.

Living in the United States for past 20 years has provided me deep insights into its society, institutions, and the security milieu. This has provided me with a wider perspective about National security issues. However, some might believe that I am *out of touch* with ground realities in India, while analyzing the paradigm in the Indian context.

That is not true. I closely follow events in India and am in constant touch with my *matrbhoomi*. Distance, in any case, is no bar to information and knowledge in the highly interconnected world. Distance, in fact is an advantage since it enables me to take a detached view of the changes, during my annual trips back home.

Given the ethos of *plain speaking* imbibed from 20 years of teaching and research in US academia, I might seem *not-too-diplomatic* in my observations. However, I have been careful not to hurt sensibilities of people of different political persuasions.

Here is my analysis therefore, about India's National security challenges in the internal as well as external environments, discussed within the framework of the proposed *National Security Paradigm*.

FOREWORD

India faces a host of national security challenges; traditional as well non-traditional. Many external and internal challenges are old. Some are of a relatively recent vintage. Others have begun to appear on the horizon. Our preparedness to meet all of them is an imperative that cannot and must not be understated. All this demands a clear understanding of the security challenges, a comprehensive approach to confront them, and an unwavering leadership to guarantee comprehensive security, particularly the defence of the country.

Although national security is the most talked about subject amongst India's strategic community, it is also the weakest link in India's governance. Till date, there is no official document on national security strategy or doctrine. Nor is there any other document, or white paper, which discusses matters related to national security comprehensively.

Why? There can be three reasons:

First, India's strategic culture remains weak. There is lack of strategic awareness amongst the Indian elite and political leaders.

George Tanham in his interpretive essay on 'India's Strategic Thought' had stated "India does not admit easily to broad generalizations. It is an extraordinarily complex and diverse society. The lacunae and ambiguities seem compatible with a culture that encompasses and accommodates readily to complexity and contradictions; more confusing to Westerners but not to Indians who accept such complexity and contradictions as part of life."

Strategic culture is defined as the 'ability of the people and society to generate power; and to have the social will and ability for a full and effective use of that power'. In our long history, there is little record of strategic thinking ever since that ancient classic, Arthashastra, written by Kautilya in 320 BC.

India was a powerful and rich nation during the Maurya dynasty in 305 BC, the Gupta dynasty in 400-600 AD, the Mogul rule from 1526-1761 AD. And then came the British who ruled India from early 18th century to mid-20th century. The last two came from outside. The Moguls chose to be absorbed within India.

Why were outsiders able to conquer and rule? It was because Indian rulers followed an insular perspective. They did not think strategically, or consider themselves as a nation. India was a house divided with rulers fighting among ourselves.

When the British ruled India, they did not permit Indian political leaders or civil and military officers to deal with strategic issues. Strategic planning and organisational affairs of the armed forces were kept away from public view.

Ever since independence in 1947, we have had to deal with a number of security challenges-three and half wars with Pakistan and one with China. The number of insurgencies, militancy and terrorist activities has been numerous. We have made many strategic errors, primarily due to our strategic inexperience and neglect of a strategic mind-set. (However, one major achievement has been integration of over 600 states within the Indian Union and a constitutionally controlled federal system that exists today.)

Although this situation is changing gradually and we now have a large number of strategic forums and think tanks, but for strategic thinking and culture to sink in the elite, particularly the political class, will take more time.

Second, India's politics over the years has become more and more polarised and divisive. There is no political consensus in the country on national security issues. For instance, even now, there is no consensus on how to treat security challenges from Pakistan and China. The government policies on these issues have fluctuated. To give another example, there is little agreement on how to deal with Maoists. The views of political parties on Jammu and Kashmir and insurgencies in the North East differ widely. There is no clarity as to how the government would deal with major terror attacks today or in the future.

Third, no government has been able to address the crucial issue of coordination required to formulate and address the issues of national security. The National Security Council exists more on paper. It has neither adequate resources nor the authority to enforce anything. The departmental interests are very strong with tendency to work in silos and there is little common understanding among various segments of the government on

(a) what national security constitutes, or (b) what are India's strategic perspectives and how to pursue them collectively?

In the interdependent world of today, India's security is predicated on many components. The divisions between internal and external, and traditional and non-traditional security, are no longer valid. Infrastructure, political cohesiveness, economic strength, technology, an equitable society, and deterrent military capability are important for defining the security concerns of India.

At the same time, India's geographical location, size, demography, economic strength, defence capabilities and rich heritage make it an influential player on the global stage. In the coming years, India will be expected to assume a greater role in regional and global affairs. This underlines the imperative of building consensus on a national security strategy, enhancing institutional competencies and strengthening our strategic culture.

In the years to come, many security challenges will emerge from a complex interplay of economic, technological, social and ideological forces. Such a scenario requires consideration of security in a holistic manner and a comprehensive security strategy.

Like in most other democratic countries, India needs a documented national security strategy, which should be reviewed periodically, say every 3 to 5 years. In the absence of a coherent policy and strategy, the government's responses will remain ad hoc and partial, which may prove costly.

Currently, we also need an institutionalised mechanism, which can enable us to build broad political and public consensus on important national security issues.

'Citizens and Soldiers Keeping India's Tryst with Destiny: A Paradigm for National Security and Resurgence' is a comprehensive, much readable book on India's national security and strategy. Its approach is somewhat different from the usual books on the subject. In the first two parts of the book, the author covers the conceptual framework and the impact of internal environment on national security. It describes the various dimensions of the paradigm in the context of India's internal security environment. In the third part, there is an overview of the geo-political environment and author's comments and recommendations on India's security management and foreign policies.

The author, Brigadier Deepak Sethi, has had a distinguished career in the Indian Army. In 1997, he took pre-mature retirement and then built a second distinguished career as an academician in the USA. As he states, "Living in the United States for past 20 years has provided me deep insights into the society, institutions and the security milieu in USA. This has helped me to gain a wider perspective about national security issues. However, it could be said that I am *out of touch* with ground realities in India in my analysis of the paradigm in the Indian context. That is not necessarily true. I closely follow all events in India and am in constant touch with my *matrbhoomi.*"

The author has put in commendable labour and research to ensure that he has the latest facts and figures relevant to the subject. Having been associated with Indian army for 30 years, and continuing to take deep interest even after retirement; he has covered India's military and its management candidly and in detail.

It is apparent that the author has more faith in India's citizens and soldiers than in its political leaders to correct the fault lines that exist in India's national security and strategy. Hence the title: *'Citizens and Soldiers Keeping India's Tryst with Destiny'.*

It is an informative and useful book, which should be read by all citizens and soldiers.

(V. P. Malik)

General (Retired)

September 2018　　　　　Former Chief of the Army Staff, India

ACKNOWLEDGMENTS

To write a book in this genre of National Security, when for the past twenty years I have published only papers in academic journals, has indeed been a tall order. More so, since it involved analysis of the proposed *National Security Paradigm* in India's context, despite my being away from *home* for over two decades.

I am therefore truly indebted to the eminent strategic thinkers and authors who did not let me stray too far from the ground realities of India; my annual trips back *home* notwithstanding.

Foremost I acknowledge with deep gratitude the candid comments and guidance from Brig Kuldip Chhokar, who painstakingly read the manuscript several times and gave me his invaluable insights.

Equally invaluable, helpful, and encouraging have been the advice and perceptive comments of Maj Gen Pushpendra Singh, Maj Gen Abdo Sandhu, Lt Gen Kamal Davar, Lt Gen Gurdeep Singh, Lt Gen Prakash Katoch, Lt Gen Ashok Kapur, Maj Gen Partho Sen and Brig Bimbo Verma.

Last, but certainly not the least, I am very grateful and do feel extremely privileged to have received a Foreword for my book from the doyen among strategic thinkers, General V.P. Malik, former Chief of the Army Staff, Indian Army.

PART ONE

THE CONCEPTUAL FRAMEWORK

1

The Nation-state and its Security

Security is the most basic instinct, not just of human beings but also of fauna and flora. Organisms have survived over millions of years through mutation and *natural selection,* but humans seem hell-bent upon pursuing a path of self-destruction.

So, are we truly secure – as individuals, as society, and as a Nation? How does the Nation guarantee the security of its citizens? And, what about security of the Nation-state itself?

Type of threats and security measures against them vary according to the entity involved. Thus, connotation of *security* is different for individuals from that of the larger collectives. It is therefore essential to establish the *level of analysis* first.

While in Social sciences the three levels of analysis are *micro* (individual, family), *meso* (clan, community) and *macro* (society, Nation, International), in Political science they are *Individual; State* (Nation) and *International* (systemic level). However, due to relatively new phenomena such as globalization, global warming and non-state actors, International Relations (IR) scholars consider *Global* as another level of analysis[1].

In this book the level, and the unit of analysis is the *State* - to be more precise the *Westphalia*[2] *Nation-state.* The *Westphalia* doctrine purports to guarantee the sovereignty of countries, and forms the basis of International law and World Order.

The fact that *National security* has different dimensions is also now well accepted. The earlier view was *absence of military threat* to the Nation's land and sea frontiers, and after the advent of airpower also to its airspace. Another simple definition was *freedom from military threat and from political coercion.*

Even the discourse on security strategies has seen a paradigm shift. They vary from the *Classic,* which pertains to the Nation-state, to other dimensions such as *Human security, International security, Global security, Environmental security* (damage to

---

[1] Rourke, John T. (2005). "Levels of Analysis," from *International Politics on the World Stage,* 10th Edition.

[2] The "Peace of Westphalia" signed in 1648 ended 'The Thirty Years War' between European states. It is the basis of the Westphalia doctrine of *Sovereignty of Nation-states,* which is now the centrepiece of International law and World Order.

environment from wars, pesticides and chemicals), *Ecological security* (of land and water resources in ecologically fragile regions), *and Cyber security.* However to keep it simple, this book will focus only on the *Classic* – i.e. the Nation-state; and not discuss other esoteric notions.

While the unit of analysis is the Nation-state, it has geopolitical, diplomatic and economic linkages with other countries, as also with the United Nations and multilateral institutions. The quality of interactions with its *external environment* has a critical bearing on the Nation's security.

Likewise, while analyzing security we also need to factor in political stability, social cohesion, economic equity and institutional integrity within the Nation-state. In fact, a stable internal security environment is the most vital for enhancing the Nation's security in its external environment.

Security of the Nation-state therefore has multiple dimensions, which are not discrete or unrelated. They are intertwined and interdependent; best described as *complex interdependence.* Consequently, as the *complexity theory*[3] suggests, a holistic top-down approach is essential to obtain a correct overall perspective. Otherwise, we could end up *missing the woods for the trees.*

There is also a need to adopt a multi-disciplinary approach. All through history, Nations have gone to war to plunder and exploit riches of annexed territories. In the Colonial era, objectives were the same, but attained through trade to begin with and then by subjugation. National security and economic interests thus have a symbiotic relationship, and must be analyzed together.

Post-World War 2 era has seen more subtle politico-economic power play. While military force and hegemony are decreasing (but remain important), tariff wars, economic sanctions and other forms of economic exploitation through unjust trade practices are increasing in numbers and complexity[4].

---

[3] *Complexity theory* is an interdisciplinary theory that grew out of *systems theory* in the 1960s. It has been used in fields of strategic management and organizational studies to study how organizations adapt to environments and how they cope with conditions of uncertainty. Complex structures are dynamic networks of interactions that are adaptive, which mutate and self-organize according to a change-initiating micro-event or collection of events.

[4] Keohane, R. & Nye, J. 1989, *Power and Interdependence: World Politics in Transition* 2nd Ed. Boston: Little-Brown.

Over past several months however, they are no longer subtle. Because of Trump's *America First* policy, there is lot of acrimony even among traditional trading partners.

The *International Political Economy* literature shows linkages also between conflict and economic interdependence. The *liberal* school of thought argues that increased economic interactions foster cooperation and inhibit hostilities[5]. However, *realists* argue that unfair gains of trade and investment adversely affect inter-state relationships, which could even trigger military conflicts.

As an illustration, despite avowed US policy against totalitarian regimes, US MNCs have invested heavily into Communist China. Keeping China *engaged* serves US geopolitically, despite it having a huge adverse trade balance. Remarkably, even when China shot down a US military aircraft in 2000, US business interests did not let that explosive situation to escalate.

MODERN STATE SYSTEM AND THE WORLD ORDER

Modern state system enshrines principle of *state sovereignty* that grants a Nation-state exclusive sovereignty over its territories without interference from any external power. Notion of the *Westphalia Nation-state* subsumes cultural and linguistic traits of a *Nation*, together with the political nature of a *State*.

Its basis is *Peace of Westphalia,* signed in 1648 that ended *The Thirty Years' War* among European nations that left eight million dead. It started as a war between Protestants and Catholics but became a wider political conflict among major European powers[6].

Many signatories of the treaty continued as monarchies and empires, e.g. the Prussian and Russian empires, until they attained their current form of democratic countries. The treaty was only among European states, but they did not apply its tenets to their colonies in Asia, Africa and Latin America.

Obligations under International Treaties

Along with the right to *sovereignty*, Nation-states are obligated to comply with various International treaties. In late 19th century, international protocols evolved codes of conduct during war, rules of engagement, and prohibited weapons. *Geneva Conventions,* formulated in 1949, promulgated international law on humane

---

[5] Russett, B. & Oneal, J.J. 2001. *Triangulating Peace, Democracy, Interdependence and International organizations.* New York: Norton.
[6] Peter H. Wilson, *Europe's Tragedy: A New History of the Thirty Years War* (London: Penguin, 2010), pp.787.

treatment of wartime prisoners and non-combatants. These comprised four treaties; two of which updated terms of the 1929 treaties while other two were new[7].

The Hague Conventions of 1899 and 1907, and *Bio-chemical warfare Geneva Protocol* of 1925, prohibited the use of chemical and biological weapons.

Nuremberg and Tokyo trials had investigated cases of wartime excesses and crimes against humanity, and sentenced some top commanders of Nazi Germany and Japan. Nation-states are now accountable for the conduct of their soldiers and militias, even for atrocities committed during undeclared conflicts, civil wars, counter-terrorism operations and insurgencies.

UN-mandated International tribunals have investigated crimes against humanity in Serbia, Cambodia, Rwanda and Sierra Leone. The *International Criminal Court* set up in July 2002 is currently investigating 11 cases of mass killings and rapes in Uganda, Congo, Darfur, Libya, Georgia, and Central African Republic. It has opened *Preliminary examination* of incidents in Iraq, Guinea, Afghanistan, Colombia, Nigeria, Palestine, and Ukraine[8].

The United Nations

League of Nations founded in 1920 was the first organization designed to prevent war. It however had no Forces of its own to enforce its writ. United States did not even join it. The League's permanent members, France, UK, Italy and Japan often showed bias in enforcing its resolutions, and hence it proved to be a dismal failure in preventing World War II.

Established in 1945, the *United Nations* was expected to be more effective than the League in maintaining peace. However, the five permanent members of the UN Security Council (UNSC), USA, UK, France, Russia and China, who alone have the veto power, virtually preside over the fortunes of the rest of the world.

Geopolitical interests of the *permanent five* dictate UNSC's response to crises. They brazenly support their proxies, or just refrain from intervening when it does not suit them. In the Iran-Iraq war (1980-1988), USA initially supported Iraq due to the Iranian revolution. Later, they let the two countries keep fighting

---

[7] Yingling, Raymund (1952). *"The Geneva Conventions of 1949"*. The American Journal of International Law. 46: 393–427.

[8] Cases under investigation by the International Criminal Court. https://www.icc-cpi.int/Pages/Main.aspx#

in a mutually destructive conflict. It mattered little to them that the war caused the deaths of one million soldiers and civilians[9].

Big Powers deem themselves above the same International law, which they enforce on others. USA got the UNSC to *rubber-stamp* its invasion of Iraq in 2003, based on dubious evidence about its weapons of mass destruction. Real intent was ouster of Saddam Hussein, and the world is still reeling from that *regime change*.

Russia's ruthless anti-terror operation in Chechnya and foisting a pro-Russian regime despite US protests is a *fait accompli*[10]. Although UN General Assembly has condemned Russia annexing Crimea, but that is no remedy for *de facto* violation of Ukraine's right to sovereignty[11].

Big Powers condemn crushing of separatist movements in other nations, but remain mute against similar acts by *one of their own*. Thus, China's ruthless actions in the Tiananmen Square student uprising in 1989, which left thousands dead and wounded, did not elicit anything beyond token protests.

Likewise, China's brutal actions against Uyghur in Xinjiang and against the Tibetans, systematic destruction of their cultural heritage, and forcibly altering demographics in these provinces have been ignored. China is flexing its military muscle with impunity in South China Sea, Southeast Asia and Bhutan.

Even lackeys of Big Powers get away with gross violations of International law. After Pakistan Army's crackdown in East Pakistan 10 million refugees poured into India, imposing a huge logistical and economic burden. Whole world was aghast when details emerged about the horrendous genocide, which left over three million dead and 400,000 women raped.

Pakistan Army even confined Bengali women in their camps for use as sex-slaves. It systematically massacred leading professors, doctors and authors in its plan to eliminate Bengali intellectuals[12].

USA turned a blind eye to such atrocities, as Pakistan was a CENTO and SEATO alliance partner, and facilitating its detente with China at that time. USA even routed arms to Pakistan via Jordan and Iran. PM Indira Gandhi had to visit all major world

---

[9] Karsh, Efraim (2002). *Iran–Iraq War, 1980–1988*. Oxford: Osprey Publishing.

[10] Andrew Meier (2005) *Chechnya: To the Heart of a Conflict*. New York: W.W. Norton.

[11] Fred Dews (19 March 2014). "NATO Secretary-General: Russia's Annexation of Crimea Is Illegal and Illegitimate". Brookings. Retrieved 8 March 2018.

[12] Sisson, Richard, Leo E. Rose. *War and Secession: Pakistan, India, and the Creation of Bangladesh*. University of California Press, 1992.

capitals to highlight the crisis and plead for help, but the Western bloc and the UNSC remained mute spectators.

Only when India entered the war did USA call for an urgent ceasefire. It tried to threaten us by sending in the nuclear-powered USS Enterprise. Later, USA shielded Pakistan by preventing the UNSC from ordering probes into the genocide. In exchange for its formal recognition by Pakistan, Bangladesh returned 195 soldiers and 5 Generals held guilty by them for the massacre[13].

Record of USA itself is not exemplary. In the infamous *My Lai massacre* of 1968 in S. Vietnam, US soldiers shot 400 unarmed men, women and children, gang-raped women, and mutilated bodies. They tried to cover it up, but after worldwide outrage, 26 soldiers were charged, but only one, a Lieutenant was convicted and awarded a life sentence. However, he served only three and half years under house arrest[14]. Treatment of detainees in the *Abu-Ghraib*[15] and Guantanamo Bay prisons too was most shocking.

Geopolitical considerations invariably skew UNSC-authorized economic sanctions, interventions against human rights abuses, and even genuine humanitarian assistance, even when there is broad consensus in the UN General Assembly.

Capability of the current World Order to cope with new forms of warfare is even more suspect. *New War Theory* describes them as *wars waged by mercenaries and militias with transnational ethnicities, who indulge in ethnic cleansing through population expulsion and murders.* Non-state actors get arms from the global arms market, financed by drugs trade and Diaspora fund-raising[16].

Remarkably, this theory pre-dates the horror of 9/11. Thus, it foresaw the rise of terrorism by non-state actors, terror outfits like Al Qaeda, LeT *etc,* and the hydra-headed ISIS. USA and the Western bloc later tried to forge a new post-Westphalia order, to justify intervention due to human rights violations. However, Russian and Chinese veto thwarted them in the UNSC[17].

---

[13] S. Linton, 'Completing the circle: accountability for the crimes of the 1971 Bangladesh war of liberation', Criminal Law Forum (2010) 21:191–311, p. 203.

[14] Greiner, Bernd. *War without Fronts: The USA in Vietnam*. New Haven, Connecticut: Yale University Press, 2009.

[15] Seymour Hersh *Chain of Command: Road from 9/11 to Abu Ghraib*. New York: Harper Collins. 2004

[16] Mary Kaldor. 1999. *New and Old Wars: Organized Violence in a Global Era*. Polity, Cambridge.

[17] Charbonneau, Louis (8 Feb 2012). "Russia U.N. veto on Syria aimed at crushing West's crusade". Reuters.

Neo-imperialism

Neo-colonialism, coined by Kwame Nkrumah of Ghana, refers to using capitalism, globalization and cultural imperialism against a developing country, instead of military control (*imperialism*) or indirect political control (*hegemony*)[18]. Used interchangeably with neo-imperialism, it highlights the unease of Third World countries about economic and political exploitation by old colonial powers.

Colonial mindset persists, but means of attaining those goals are subtle and couched in trade policies. Globalization might seem mutually beneficial but MNCs exploit them in Third World nations by exploiting corrupt regimes to secure windfall profits.

Trade however, is not the villain. David Ricardo's *Comparative Advantage* theory (built on Adam Smith's *Theory of Absolute Advantage*) laid the framework for boosting world trade, instead of *zero-sum* protectionist policies that most countries followed.

He argued that countries must produce and export only items where they have a *comparative advantage*, and import those where indigenous capability was not cost-effective. It was thus an *efficiency-based* argument and a *win-win* solution, which would ultimately benefit consumers in all countries[19].

However, exploitative propensity of MNCs in nations with weak regimes is a harsh reality. MNC practices, especially before WTO came into being, were scandalous. They spawned books such as Vernon's *Sovereignty at Bay*, which described how MNCs undermined sovereignty of vulnerable Third World countries[20].

Wal-Mart, which ranked first in the Global 500 list in 2017, had annual revenue of $ 485.9 billion. This was more than the GDP of 167 countries in the world in the same period. With its *deep pockets*, it can virtually drive to bankruptcy any number of indigenous competitors in those countries.

Banana republic refers to countries where there is collusion of the State with monopolies, to benefit the ruling oligarchy. In early 20th century, US firms monopolized the export of bananas from countries like Honduras and Guatemala. By colluding with the corrupt regimes, they ended up owning millions of acres and controlled the economy, virtually the country itself. Since then it has become a pejorative term to describe corrupt puppet regimes.

---

[18] Sartre, Jean-Paul (2001). *Colonialism and Neocolonialism*. Psychology Press.

[19] Steven M Suranovic (2010). *"International Trade Theory and Policy"*.

[20] Raymond Vernon (1971) *Sovereignty at bay: The multinational spread of U. S. Enterprises,* Longman.

These are not isolated incidents. How can we forget our brutal occupation by East India Company and the British Empire? Sadly, despite end of colonialism, MNCs use predatory policies to exploit Third World countries in Africa, Latin America and Asia.

Hence, can Nation-states feel assured about security and non-interference in their internal affairs? Will principles of *Westphalia* doctrine apply equitably, regardless of the State's size, strength and stature in the comity of Nations?

It is a travesty that the UNSC disdainfully dismisses resolutions passed unanimously by UN General Assembly quite often. Hence, there are persistent demands for reforms of UNO to make it more just, and less vulnerable to authoritarian diktats of the Big Powers.

Foremost priority is reconstitution of the UNSC. Proposal to increase permanent members to ten has wide support. Germany, Japan, India and Brazil are leading contenders, with one more seat going to an African nation. India meets all objective criteria as it represents one-sixth of humanity, is third largest economy (GDP in PPP terms), and has fourth largest military. It is a nuclear-weapon state and contributes most to UN peacekeeping missions.

Some mid-rung powers led by Italy, are however stymieing the situation. The current *permanent five* are quite content with this impasse. Their ostensible support for expansion is likely nothing but *diplomatic doublespeak*. Who would want new entrants into an exclusive club that would cause dilution of their own power?

In sum, *Westphalia doctrine* notwithstanding, Nations have to be vigilant themselves. Current World Order does not guarantee absolute protection and total non-interference, nor justice and fair play. All Nations have to fend for themselves and devise their own strategies to ensure their security against multifarious threats.

Only when a Nation-state is internally stable and strong, will it face its external challenges effectively. Then alone it would *stand tall* in the comity of Nations. Central idea of the following Urdu couplet, which exhorts *individuals* to strengthen themselves, is relevant to *Nation-states* too.

> *"Khudi ko kar buland itna ke har taqdeer se pehle*
> *Khuda bande se khud pooche bata teri raza kya hai."*

> (Develop the self so that before every decree
> God will ascertain from you: "What is your wish?")

Once India is internally stable and united, economically and militarily strong, Big Powers will have to provide us a seat on the *Global High Table,* howsoever grudgingly.

2

Brief Overview of our Security Environment

Although the *Westphalia* doctrine ostensibly guarantees the sovereignty of a Nation-state it has serious limitations as highlighted in the previous chapter. In the extant World Order, the geopolitical interests of the permanent five of the UNSC circumscribe the degree to which Nations are unfettered by foreign interference. Nations therefore have no other option except to be fully prepared to safeguard their own security.

Nations have to build their military power, not necessarily for aggressive designs, but to ensure their territorial integrity. Even Sweden and Switzerland, which have not fought a war since 1814 and 1815 respectively and remained neutral ever since, maintain credible military strength.

However, do the Armed Forces alone guarantee security and stability of a nation? External aggression did not threaten China as much as the political and social turmoil caused by Mao's *Cultural Revolution,* or the Tiananmen Square student uprising. Likewise, the *Arab Spring* caused severe disruption and instability despite those regimes having formidable military forces at their disposal.

Nations have varying perceptions about threats to their security, and these are not only about their external environment. It will be instructive to see how other Nations conceptualize National security. In the United States President Obama widened the scope of the existing US National Security Strategy to include four intertwined and enduring *National interests*[21]:

- *Security:* Security of the United States, its citizens and US allies and partners.
- *Prosperity:* A strong, innovative and growing US economy in an open international economic system that promotes opportunity and prosperity.
- *Values:* Respect for universal values at home and around the world.
- *International Order:* An international order advanced by US leadership to promote peace, security and opportunity through stronger cooperation to meet global challenges.

---

[21] Obama, Barack. *National Security Strategy, May 2010.* Office of the President of the United States, White House, p 17. Accessed 11 March 2018.

Russia defines its National Security Strategy as *"situation in which the individual, the society and the state enjoy protection from foreign and domestic threats to the degree that ensures constitutional rights and freedoms, decent quality of life for citizens, as well as sovereignty, territorial integrity and stable development of the Russian Federation, the defence and security of the state."*

China's Ministry of State Security includes *"the security of the state through effective measures against enemy agents, spies, and counterrevolutionary activities designed to sabotage or overthrow China's socialist system,"*[22] among other elements.

Remarkably, the US doctrine does not speak of any internal threat, while the Russian document does include *domestic threats* in its concerns. China is even more fearful about internal threats from *'spies and counter-revolutionaries to its socialist system'*.

Nations are threatened more often by social strife, insurgencies, ethnic divisions, secessionist movements, political and economic instability than they are by outright external aggression. China's security doctrine amply highlights that concern.

So, what is India's conceptualization of National Security? *Your guess is as good as mine.* Perhaps, only the National Security Advisor knows about it. It is astonishing that 71 years after Independence we still do not have a *National Security Doctrine.* Next only to a country's Constitution, it is perhaps the most important document that defines the Nation's permanent interests and how those are to be safeguarded.

In its absence, we have lurched from one crisis to another, and countered them only with *ad hoc* reactions. Have we not wondered often, why despite having valiant security forces, the situation in J&K has been worsening? Why deaths from ceasefire violations and terror strikes have increased alarmingly, while stone-throwing incidents in the interior have now attained the scale and character of the Palestinian *intifada*? Why is it that various Govt agencies often seem to be working at cross-purposes in matters relating to National security?

A comprehensive review of India's internal and external security environments will follow in Parts 2 and 3 respectively. However, the following brief overviews are only *illustrations.* They seek to highlight the dire need for an integrated and comprehensive *National Security Doctrine.*

---

[22] Ministry of State Security, *Intelligence Resource Program,* Federation of American Scientists.

Snapshot of the External Environment

Pakistan has been our perpetual problem. It has an unlimited supply of highly radicalized youth for terror strikes, not just in India but worldwide too. Whatever comfort may we draw from the USA designating LeT and other outfits as *terror organizations*, and we may feel vindicated that it is a failing, pariah state, the fact remains that it is succeeding in its avowed strategy of *bleeding us by a thousand cuts*. Unfazed by US sanctions and buoyed by Chinese support it is nowhere close to mending its ways.

Both, the impromptu *stopover diplomacy* as well as *surgical strikes* having failed, we seem to have run out of options. Kashmir remains on the boil. With flag-draped coffins of service personnel and civilian casualties now a daily occurrence, the entire country is crying out for concrete actions rather than routine *dire warnings*.

Sadly, there was neither coherence nor rationality even in internal policies, when the BJP and PDP were jointly in power. Therefore, we have the inexplicable spectacle of their Govt filing cases against the Army and Central Armed Police Forces (CAPFs) for so-called excesses, even while their comrades were being killed brutally On the other hand, their Govt withdrew cases against stone-pelters and terror abettors.

China is becoming increasingly intransigent, having completed its massive infrastructure and military build-up in Tibet. Defusing of Doklam standoff does not mark the end of strident actions to keep us unhinged. Along the *Line of Actual Control* (LAC), it has improved all-weather connectivity and augmented troop levels.

Increased incidence of provocative *nibbling* attempts clearly indicates that the border dispute is not getting resolved any time soon. Its stance has also hardened due to our firm and justifiable opposition to its ambitious *China Pakistan Economic Corridor* (CPEC) project.

Interactions with China are multi-dimensional - geopolitical, diplomatic, military, economic and cultural. This calls for a holistic approach towards a coherent response. As per the adage that there are no permanent friends, only permanent interests, we must not constrain ourselves with limited options due to historical baggage.

China's *string of pearls* policy has enabled it to make deep inroads into our backyard. Thus, whether it is Gwadar port in Pakistan, obtaining Hambantota port on 99-year lease from Sri Lanka, and getting island facilities in Maldives; all such events these have vital strategic implications for us.

For years, China has assiduously cultivated warm relations with Nepal, Bangladesh and Myanmar, while our own policy has been inconsistent. We have often caused resentment among neighbours due to *big brother* attitude and ham-handed interference.

It is no surprise then that Maldives and Nepal often seem to be *cocking a snook* at our diplomatic establishment. Our relations with neighbours apparently depend more upon a particular party or leader coming to power in those countries, rather than based on intrinsic strengths and shared interests.

Snapshot of the Internal Environment

Sadly, our internal environment has seen a marked increase in religious and caste polarization in recent times. Politicians of all hues have been recklessly accentuating the fault-lines for electoral gains, with utter disregard for the scars they leave on our psyche.

Religious and caste riots have become rampant, and miscreants have brazenly committed horrendous atrocities. Law and order has become hostage to the Ruling dispensation of respective states. On one hand, criminals go scot-free or are even get official pardon, while on the other there are innumerable cases of police excesses. All of these hinge entirely upon political patronage.

Political morality and probity in public life seem to be at the lowest ebb. Many in our political class, irrespective of their parties, have brazenly acted in self-serving manner that is creating endemic corruption. Various high-profile businessmen escaping abroad after defrauding banks of astronomical sums have shaken the faith of the common man in the Govt and its agencies.

All this when coupled with very high unemployment rates, agrarian distress, and numerous farmer suicides, is leading to an alarming increase in anger among youth. Even among the general populace there is growing unease about the sharp downslide in all walks of life, and near-absence of the rule of law.

The economy had been growing at a decent pace until an ill-conceived demonetization and a shoddily implemented GST regime dealt it sever blows. Apart from reducing the GDP and the growth rate, both measures caused collateral damage to small and medium enterprises (SMEs), traders, and artisans. Many SMEs had to shut down, which aggravated the unemployment situation.

In any case, GDP and growth rates are not a true barometer of a nation's economy. What matters more is how equitably fruits of economic development are percolating down to the poorer sections of society. In that respect, our Human Development Index (HDI) figures are dismal. On several parameters, those are lower than the figures for our neighbours, Pakistan, Bangladesh, Bhutan and Sri Lanka.

Credibility of some of our reputed institutions too has taken a beating. Even Supreme Court Justices have publicly questioned alleged partisan and unethical practices on the Bench. The lower judiciary never did enjoy a high reputation for probity.

Need for a Comprehensive Analytical Framework

It is very evident from the foregoing snapshots that there are many issues of serious concern in our external and internal environments. These require in-depth deliberation in order to evolve a holistic *National Security Doctrine*. Based on that broad doctrine, the Govt can then formulate a comprehensive National Security Strategy.

Both terms, the *National Security Doctrine* and National Security Strategy are used interchangeably sometimes. However, there are subtle differences between the two. The *National Security Doctrine* must foremost determine how we envision ourselves as a Nation. Have we been a Nation that covets other lands, or do we believe in peaceful coexistence? From that vision, should emerge our *strategic intent* and a broad enunciation of our vital *National interests*.

This broad analysis of National security issues will help us to evolve strategies that are more specific and detailed. Thus, the National Security Strategy is a more elaborate formulation that specifies security norms and actions required by various agencies to safeguard and enhance national security in all its dimensions.

The Executive at highest level is responsible for both, the Prime Minister in our case. He would be advised by members of the National Security Council, comprising the Defence, Foreign, Home and Finance ministers, the National Security Adviser and the Chief of Defence Staff, with other experts being co-opted as required.

National Security Paradigm presented in this book is different from both, the *National Security Doctrine* as well as the National Security Strategy. It is primarily an analytical framework. It seeks to holistically identify, and thereafter systematically analyze all the factors that have a bearing on National security, both in the internal and external environments.

It thus provides the means of undertaking a comprehensive analysis of all aspects of National security. The clarity attained through such a thorough analysis would eventually facilitate the formulation of a sound *National Security Doctrine* and an effective National Security Strategy.

Security concerns of nations are quite diverse and vary according to each nation's situation. Hence, there cannot be a *one size fits all* mechanism for analyzing National security. *National Security Paradigm* proposed herein is a generic analytical tool. It is possible to add to it dimensions and factors that are relevant to each nation's specific context.

For this book, I have tailored the paradigm to India's context. It addresses India's geopolitical, diplomatic, economic, and military challenges in the external environment, as well as her various internal security concerns and challenges.

3

National Security Paradigm

Numerous factors have a bearing on a Nation's security. Those that relate to external security are different from factors that affect the internal environment, and therefore it is necessary to analyze both separately. Given the multiplicity of factors, it is best to group them into *dimensions* based on their affinity, so that they enable more focused analyses. Thus, there will be distinct *dimensions,* separate for the internal and external environments.

Principal component analysis is a useful statistical technique for affinity-based grouping of factors. Using that methodology, I have delineated factors relating to *Internal security* under five dimensions: *National will and ethos; Political morality and stability; Social cohesion; Robust economy and inclusive growth;* and *Integrity of institutions.* A graphic depiction is in Figure 1.

Dimensions relating to *external security* are *Military power; Foreign policy; Economic strength,* and *Soft Power.* Figure 2 depicts those dimensions.

The list of factors is not comprehensive. I have selected limited number of factors merely to illustrate the paradigm. It is possible to add more security-related factors if identified, to enhance and update the framework and make it more contemporary. This either can be to an existing group or kept as a separate dimension.

Quantitative analysis is the ideal tool for a systematic analysis of all dimensions. This is because the inputs will be of quantifiable data, and thus results would be more objective and easy to apply.

For instance, to analyze *Economic strength,* expert groups could select factors such as GDP per capita; growth rate; rate of investment, savings rate, FDI, balance of trade and similar indices. They could also assign *weights* to these indices according to their relative importance. To assess *Inclusive growth* the indices could be worker wages, income disparities, poverty-line figures, and HDI figures etc.

While the foregoing illustration is of easily quantifiable factors, it is also possible to develop indices even for dimensions that are abstract or judgement-based. To analyze *institutional integrity* of the judicial system, experts could devise indices that capture the efficacy and speed of delivery of justice. They could use data on number of pending cases; average time from filing to final disposal; appeals; vigilance cases against judicial officials etc.

Utility of *quantitative analysis* is that it provides an objective picture of the dimensions. They are useful to compare trends, identify areas for improvement, and policy changes. Of course, all this is contingent upon the cardinal rule *do not move goalposts*, and no political party upon coming to power alters the parameters to *colour* its performance *vis. a vis.* its predecessor.

The framework can also be analyzed using *Qualitative analysis* tools. This might seem less objective than *Quantitative analysis,* but it is possible to reduce subjectivity by using think tanks, opinions of experts of various disciplines, and scientific surveys to evaluate the dimensions.

Next section provides a brief description of the dimensions, separately for the internal and external environments. Chapters in Parts 2 and 3 of the book respectively, will comprehensively analyze these dimensions.

Internal Environment

The Core. Innermost core represents the demographic essence of the Nation. Given India's huge diversity there are inbuilt religious, ethnic, social, lingual, caste, and class fault-lines. These fault-lines could either worsen, or remain in harmony. The core thus represents extent of cohesiveness in our society at any given time.

Dotted lines used to bind the core, denote that it is not finite. It is in constant flux and sputters like molten lava. If all societal factors (social, economic, institutional, political, and morale) were optimal, the core would be dormant and stable. There would be internal harmony, in spite of the fault-lines. However, if there were problems within any dimension, it would accentuate related fault-lines and send the core into turmoil, which will create unrest.

Political Morality and Stability. It is unarguably the most important dimension that contributes to internal stability since it influences all other elements. Foremost, it involves upholding the Constitution in letter and spirit, ensuring free and fair elections, and providing an effective and responsive Government.

In the present context, *political morality* might sound like an oxymoron, but it is the most critical element that influences the *health* and probity of all other institutions. A self-serving political class, focused only upon winning elections, can become a fountainhead of polarization and corruption. A strong and effective Opposition is essential to act as the watchdog, and prevent unilateral authoritarianism by the Ruling party.

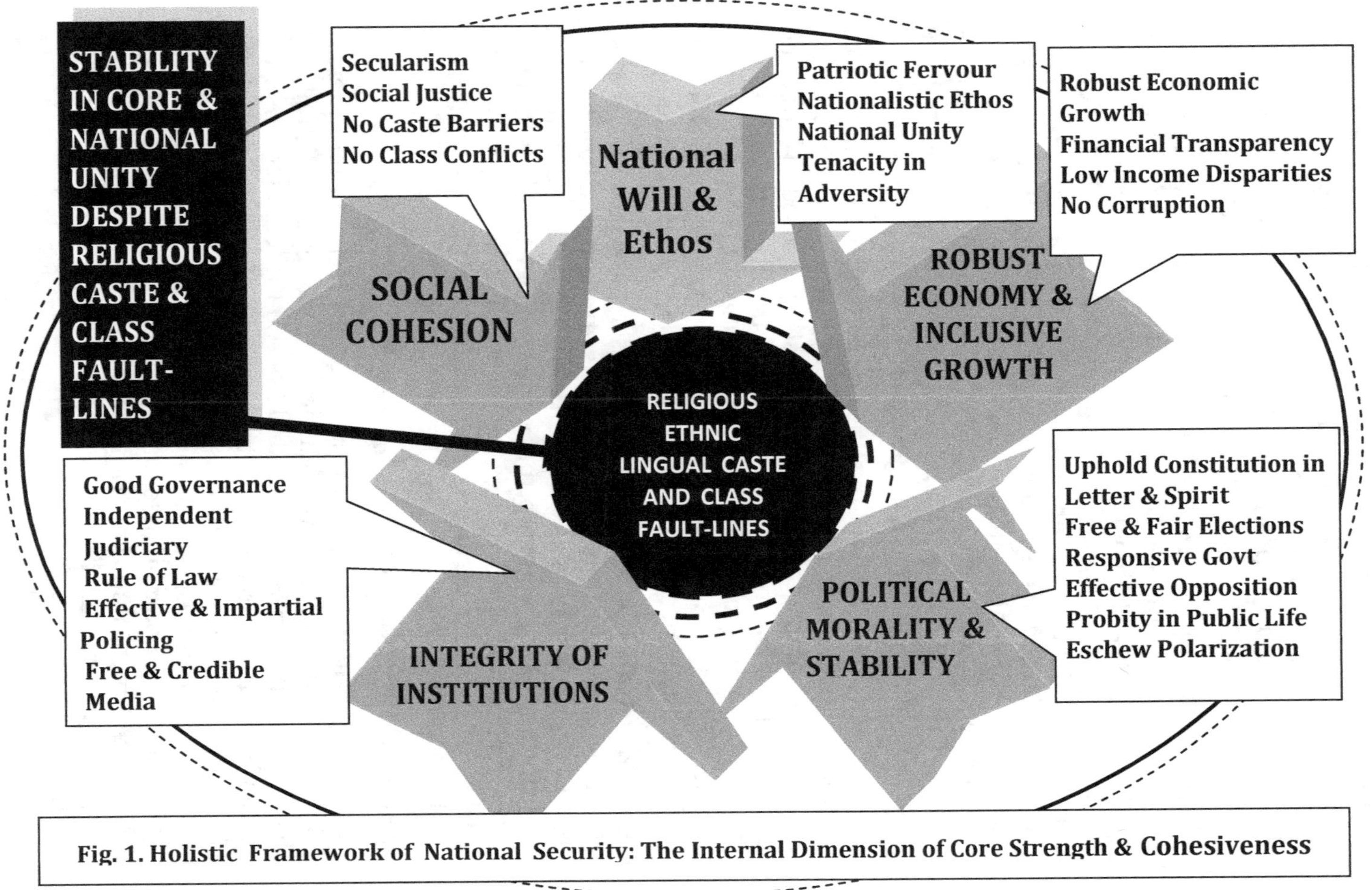

Fig. 1. Holistic Framework of National Security: The Internal Dimension of Core Strength & Cohesiveness

Integrity of Institutions. It includes independent judiciary, effective policing, and impartial investigative agencies, to ensure the *Rule of law*. Transparent and effective governance and bipartisan legislative processes are essential. Free and credible media too is among the important pillars of democracy.

Robust Economy and Inclusive Growth. A stable economy with steady growth is a key component of National strength. It provides the wherewithal for the Nation's development and for the well-being of its people. It is also provides for strong defence capability. Regulatory institutions must transparently plug revenue leaks and stamp out corruption. Growth must be inclusive to ensure distributive justice, and fruits of development must benefit the poor. There should be no large income disparities between the rich and poor, different sectors of the economy and geographical regions, as that would breed social unrest

Social Cohesion. Our Constitution guarantees equality to all citizens regardless of religion, ethnicity, caste, as also cultural, social or economic differences. This must be ensured in letter and spirit as it is most critical for our National unity and ethos. Absence of social justice and religious, caste and class polarization for electoral gains can spur extreme social turmoil, which will have serious consequences for the economy and all other institutions.

National Will and Ethos. This represents the patriotic fervour, spirit, and morale of the Nation, and its strength of character and resilience in the face of adversity. It needs to be nurtured through transformational leadership that eschews petty considerations of electoral politics, and which is genuinely pluralistic. We all must zealously guard this because once damaged, it will leave deep scars on the Nation's psyche.

External Environment

Military Power. It is the most important factor in the external dimension. It includes the numerical strength and military hardware of the Armed Forces, and how do those match up to the nation's external threats. The structure, ethos and morale of the Armed Forces are vital too, as is the technological vintage of their weapon systems. Does the nation have a military-industrial complex to support indigenous production, or is it heavily dependent upon imports? How efficient is the Research and Development organization in keeping the Forces abreast with the latest technology?

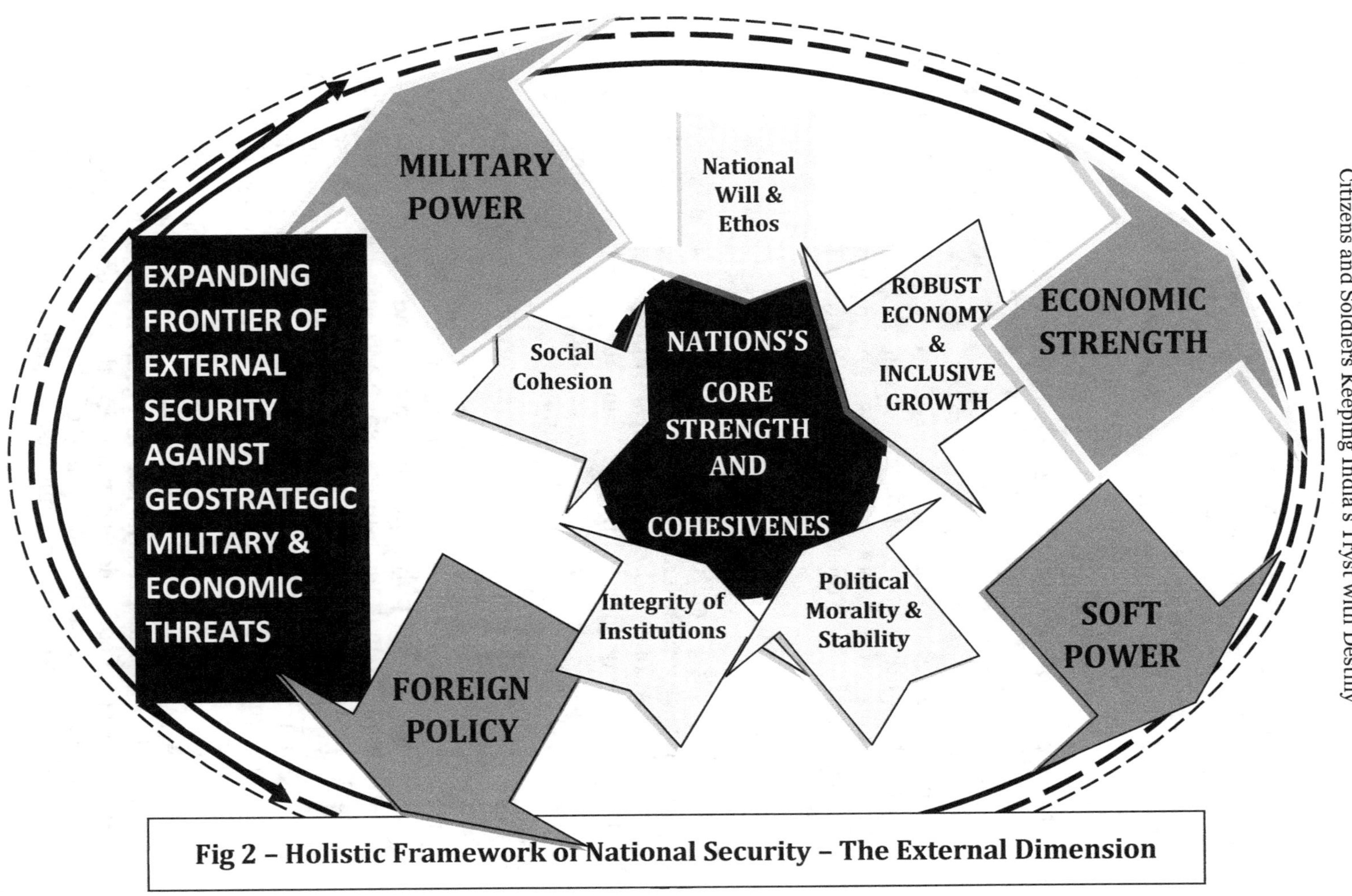

Fig 2 – Holistic Framework of National Security – The External Dimension

Economic Strength. Factors to be included would be GDP, growth rate, foreign exchange reserves, balance of payments, trade balance, savings and investment rates, IMF loans, FDI, FPI etc. Does the nation have an influential presence in multilateral organizations such as WTO, World Bank, G20 and regional trade blocs? Is the nation facing economic sanctions or does it have serious trade disputes?

Foreign Policy. In this dimension, important factors would be membership of alliances and bilateral treaties. Does the Nation have an independent foreign policy? Is it free to exercise its best options? Is it hamstrung by historical baggage and geopolitical constraints? How influential and active is it in the UNO, and regional political and economic groupings? How are its relations with major world powers, Afro-Asian countries, ASEAN and neighbours? Are there any serious territorial or maritime disputes?

Soft Power. This is an important dimension of a nation's stature and influence. It depends upon the extent to which it can project its rich heritage, culture and accomplishments in a positive and non-obtrusive manner. Promotion of cultural exchanges, tourism, organization of world events, sports, film and music festivals etc go a long way in creating a favourable impression. Diaspora's achievements, their law-abiding conduct and contributions to their host countries, are very helpful too.

Co-relation of the Internal and External Environments

It is also possible to visualize the dynamic interaction of internal and external environment from the model. Human body is in good health only when all organs and systems function in harmony. Any malfunctioning organ can cause the whole body to be unwell. Similarly, all internal dimensions too must be in harmony in order to keep the core, with all its fissiparous fault-lines, dormant and stable. Turbulence in the core caused by any factor reduces the capacity of the four external dimensions to fight off foreign threats.

The model can also statistically validate such positive co-relation. A stable internal environment boosts economic strength, which in turn enhances the nation's geopolitical influence, and its soft power. Economic strength in the internal environment improves the standard of living of the people, while inclusive growth helps contain economic distress and reduces social unrest.

Economic strength provides the required resources to boost our military power in the external environment. It increases our geopolitical and diplomatic manoeuvrability. It can help the Nation to provide economic assistance to neighbours and Third World countries, and thus enhance our influence.

For ease of comprehension by the target audience, I have not opted for *Quantitative analysis* of the model, as that would very heavily depend upon complex statistical techniques. Hence, I have analyzed all dimensions of the internal and external environments in the model through *Qualitative analysis*.

PART 2

IMPACT OF THE INTERNAL ENVIRONMENT ON NATIONAL SECURITY

4

Scope and Intent

Chapters in Part 2 seek to analyze the impact of the Internal Environment on National Security. The central premise of the *National Security Paradigm* is that various dimensions of internal security are critical for ensuring the Nation's security from external threats. Internal stability and cohesion provides the strong foundation, which enhances the Nation's strength in the external dimension. For this reason, I am undertaking the analysis of the internal environment first.

To recap, in Chapter 3 by using *Principal Component Analysis* I had grouped various factors of the internal environment that affect National Security under five orthogonal dimensions. These were *National will and ethos; Political morality and stability; Social cohesion; Economic strength and equitable distribution* and *Integrity of institutions*. I will now discuss each of these dimensions in succeeding chapters.

Foremost, however, it is necessary to clarify the scope and intent of these chapters. Several factors in the internal dimensions can trigger diverse, often contrary opinions, as regards their historical background, underlying causes, and their denouement. There could also be different views as regards apportioning the responsibility for various ills that are afflicting our society.

However, it is neither within the scope of the book nor the intent to examine the merits and demerits of various viewpoints, and to sit in judgement thereupon. This is because the book does not purport to have readymade solutions for those infirmities, especially relating to the internal environment.

The aim of these chapters is to discuss how weaknesses and disorder in the internal dimensions can cause unrest and turbulence inside the Core. How the resulting imbalances and upheavals will affect the Nation's intrinsic strength, and in turn reduce its capabilities to counter external challenges.

These chapters will therefore trace the origin, contributory conditions, and historical progression of all these factors since Independence. Based thereupon, I will discuss their effect on internal cohesion and stability.

While doing so, I have made a conscious effort to avoid subjective conclusions about individuals or the political parties responsible, since that is not germane given the aim of this book.

Consequently, to maintain total objectivity, for analyses of all factors I have depended extensively on data and statistics from reputed Global and internal sources. I have also provided authentic citations of individual experts and agencies to support the analyses.

5

National Will and Ethos

National will and ethos are the most formidable strengths of a nation. Throughout history, even tiny nations have vanquished larger and more powerful opponents through sheer tenacity and strength of character.

Despite Britain's small size, there was a time when *the sun never set on the British Empire.* Israel not only beat back all hostile Arab nations many times, but also gave them a bloody nose and captured their territories. Tiny and beleaguered Vietnam defeated the mighty US Army and beat back the Chinese invasion.

How have we fared as a Nation? How do we see ourselves? Are we a Nation of conquerors? Or, are we *peaceniks,* who believe in *Vasudhaiva Kutumbakam*[23] - the world is one big family?

Even though India won her independence 71 years back, our National ethos has evolved over 3500 years. Numerous migrations and invasions, and colonization took place, which contributed to our composite culture. It is therefore essential to review salient events and eras that left both, positive as well as negative imprints on our National psyche.

INSPIRATION FROM OUR HERITAGE

Even in our mythology, *Bharat* comprised only independent kingdoms that often fought with each other. Powerful kingdoms established suzerainty over others through *Ashvamedh Yagya.*

Indus Valley Civilization (3300-1300 BCE) extended into parts of Punjab, Rajasthan and Gujarat. It flourished around urban centres of Mohenjo-Daro and Harappa in Pakistan, and Ropar and Lothal in India. On its decline, Aryan migrations ushered the *Vedic Civilization* (1500-500 BCE), the base of our culture[24].

By 520 BCE, the Achaemenid Empire under Darius had annexed areas around River Indus. For two centuries, thereafter Persian and Vedic cultures coexisted in Takshashila, both of which by most accounts were the offshoots of the same Aryan migration from Central Asia.

---

[23] S Shah and V Ramamoorthy (2014), *Soulful Corporations*, Springer Science, page 449. The phrase appears in several ancient Hindu texts such as the *Maha Upanishad,* which basically implies that the world is one family.

[24] Thapar, Romila (1977), *A History of India. Volume One,* Penguin Books.

After capturing Persia, Alexander defeated Porus across the Jhelum. Sadly, no kingdom came to his help even though it was clear that Alexander's ambition was to conquer whole of India. Valour of Porus however, unnerved Alexander's Army and caused a revolt, which forced him to return. He died en route to Greece.

Mauryan Empire under Asoka came closest to fulfilling Chanakya's vision of a pan-India identity. However, after his victory over Kalinga he embraced Buddhism, as he was too distraught over the deaths and destruction in that war[25].

Migrations kept taking place from the northwestern gateway over centuries. They established kingdoms in Afghanistan, which left Greek, Scythian Parthian and Sassanid influences on Indian culture. Kushans from northwest China established their empire in Gandhara in 1st century BCE, with Kabul as capital. They had extensive trade, both sea-borne and along the *Silk route*. Their empire was at its zenith under Kanishka who extended it into the Gangetic plain. On its decline, Hindu *Kabul Shahis* ruled Kabul Valley and Gandhara from the 3rd to early 8th century[26].

For over 12 centuries, several empires and dynasties gained power and fell apart, mainly due to constant internecine wars. The more prominent among them were Mauryan, Shunga, Satyavahan, Pala and Gupta empires in the North, and Chola, Chera, Pandiyan, Chalukya, Rashtrakuta and Vijayanagar empires in the South.

Gupta Empire (320–550 CE) has been called the *Golden Age of India*. To its credit, it had magnificent achievements in science, architecture, engineering, mathematics, philosophy and art. It was also the largest economy in the world in that era[27].

After Islam's advent, Muhammad bin Qasim conquered Indus valley in 712 CE for the Umayyad Caliphate. Upon its break-up, Rajputs set up kingdoms in Sindh, Afghanistan and Rajasthan. They fought off numerous Turkic invasions, but never as a united force. In early 11th century, Mahmud of Ghazni invaded Northwest India 17 times to plunder, and not to set up a dominion.

After holding out for several centuries, Rajputs under Prithviraj Chauhan lost the second battle of Tarain to Muhammad Ghori. The Turkic Mamluk slave dynasty then established the Delhi

---

[25] Raychaudhuri, H. C.; Mukherjee, B. N. 1996. *Political History of Ancient India: From the Accession of Parikshit to the Extinction of the Gupta Dynasty*. Oxford University Press, pp. 204-9, pp. 270-71.

[26] Dr D B. Pandey, *The Shahi Afghanistan and Punjab*, 1973, pp 1, 45–46, 48, 80.

[27] *"The World Economy: Historical Statistics by Professor Maddison"* World Economy. Retrieved 16 Jan 2018

Sultanate, which ruled most of North and Central India up to the early 16th century[28]. The Sultanate successfully repelled numerous Mongol invasions, except that of Timur, who wantonly killed, plundered and ravaged Delhi in 1398.

Timur's descendent Babur established the Mughal Empire in 1526, which at its peak was the second largest empire to have existed in India. The Mughal era is considered India's *last golden age*. It had surpassed China to become the world's largest economy with a 24.4% share, and had 25% of global industrial output[29]. Agrarian reforms and industrial manufacturing had led the economic surge.

Aurangzeb reversed most of the tolerant traditions of his predecessors, which led to deep resentment, palace intrigues and revolts. The Mughal Empire started declining after his death, and finally ended when the British defeated the Indian uprising of 1857. India then came under the British Crown.

The British annexed Indian kingdoms by invasion or stratagem. For the first time in our history, India was united as one country, albeit under the British flag. Only the Portuguese retained their colony in Goa, and the enclaves of Daman, Diu, Dadra and Nagar Haveli, while the French had theirs in Pondicherry.

Assimilation

India thus experienced numerous migrations over centuries. Just as the Aryan and Dravidian cultures had comingled earlier, the language, customs, and traditions of other migrants too were assimilated, to form a rich composite culture. It was thus a melting pot, wherein different cultures imbibed the best from each other.

The Delhi Sultanate had promoted a fusion of Indo-Muslim cultures, and made lasting contributions to architecture, music, literature, clothing and food, as well as religious harmony. Urdu, an important addition, became the spoken language of most people as *Hindustani*. Amir Khusrow and Sant Kabir epitomize the syncretism of religious beliefs, language, and cultures during that period.

Likewise, unlike the plundering hordes of Mahmud of Ghazni and Timur, the Mughal invaders settled down here. The Mughal era saw rich contributions to our heritage in arts, literature, music, commerce and architecture - Taj Mahal being a prized possession.

---

[28] Ramananda Chatterjee (1961). *Modern Review*, 109. Indiana University, p.84

[29] John F. Richards (1995), *The Mughal Empire*, page 190, Cambridge University Press

The British on the other hand exploited and impoverished us. They ruined our indigenous crafts and industry to boost exports from England. Nonetheless, they did contribute by creating railways, infrastructure, telegraph, and the administrative system. However, this was not entirely with altruistic intentions. It was rather to facilitate their rule over the colony.

British Influence on our Military Heritage

Perhaps the most important contribution of the British was to mould Indian soldiers into a potent fighting machine. Competence professionalism and ethos of our Armed Forces is attributable to the *baptism of fire* in the conduct of modern warfare, received under them. The value of the command and control structure, organization of HQ and staff, and modern weapons and equipment, has been tremendous. Likewise, first-rate officers trained in Sandhurst and other Service academies; all tried and tested in two World Wars were invaluable too.

They set up top-class training institutions like the Indian Military Academy, Schools for different Arms, Staff College, and regimental centres. From them germinated our skills and capabilities, which allowed us to hit the ground running soon after independence, when we had to face Pakistani invasion of Kashmir.

Equally priceless were attributes like military discipline, rich traditions and soldiers' ethos. Field Marshal Chetwode's motto[30] etched in the psyche of officers passing through the portals of the Indian Military Academy, has been their beacon. We inherited the ideal of *an officer and a gentleman,* which even today is the bedrock of honourable and ethical conduct of our officers.

Secular ethos of our military has been another precious asset. The British shed their *'divide and rule'* policy and moulded our secular outlook in order to get a unified force to fight their wars. They respected and participated in the religious festivals of the troops, and that rich secular tradition remains embedded to this day. It is a shining example for the country, which sadly is plagued with growing divisive tendencies.

---

[30] Field Marshal Philip Chetwode was the Commander in Chief of the Indian Army and was instrumental in the Indianization of the Indian forces, and setting up the Indian Military Academy in 1932. His motto: *"The safety, honour and welfare of your country come first, always and every time; the honour, welfare and comfort of the men you command come next; your own ease, comfort and safety come last, always and every time"* has been immortalized in letters of gold in the Chetwode Hall of the Academy.

Indian Heroes through History

Our martial traditions are a vital part of our ancient heritage and heroic tales of our warriors are immensely inspirational for our youth. It is imperative that we keep these alive not only in our folklore, but also through grand memorials so that they may inspire future generations of soldiers.

Mahabharata,[31] with the *Bhagavad Gita* embedded therein, has been a shining beacon. It exhorts warriors to overcome moral dilemmas and fulfil their obligation for *dharma yudh* – righteous war against tyranny and oppression. Thus, while the world enacted the Geneva conventions only 75 years back, our warriors have adhered to far more profound rules of engagement and moral code of conduct during war, for over three millennia.

Tales of the valour and chivalry of legendary warriors such as Bhishma, Arjun and Karan have inspired generations. Our youth have also been eulogizing bravery and grit of great Indian warriors such as Porus, Asoka, Prithviraj Chauhan, Maharana Pratap, Banda Bahadur, Shivaji, Tipu Sultan, Ranjit Singh, Hari Singh Nalwa, Zorawar Singh, to name just a few. Our folklore has immortalized their exploits, and youth aspire to emulate them.

Heroes also emerged from the 1857 war for independence. Valour of Rani Laxmibai, Tatya Tope, Nana Sahib, Mangal Pandey, Begum Hazrat Mahal and many others, too became a part of Indian consciousness. Later, revolutionaries like Bhagat Singh, Sukhdev, Rajguru, Chandrashekhar Azad, Ashfaqullah Khan, Ramprasad Bismil and Jatin Das, struck an emotive chord in Indians, who still venerate their martyrdom.

Over 1.5 million Indian soldiers fought during the First World War and saw action in Western Europe, Middle East and Africa. At the end of the war, 74,746 were dead or missing. Their gallantry won them 13,000 medals, including 12 Victoria Crosses[32]. The British built Delhi's India Gate in 1931 to commemorate our soldiers who died in that war.

During World War II, over 2.5 million Indian soldiers fought in Africa, Europe and Asia. In this war 87,000 died, 34,354 were wounded, and 67,340 became POWs. They won 4,000 gallantry medals including 18 Victoria Crosses or George Crosses[33]. Among

---

[31] C. Rajagopalachari, *Mahabharata.* Abridged English translation of Rishi Vyasa's original epic. It was first published by Bharatiya Vidya Bhavan in 1958.

[32] *"Participants from India in the First World War",* Memorial Gates Trust.

[33] Sumner, Ian (2001). *The Indian Army 1914-1947.* Osprey Publishing

them were Lt Gen PS Bhagat, VC, Gen KS Thimayya, DSO, Gen PP Kumaramangalam, DSO, MBE, Marshal of the Air Force Arjan Singh, DFC, Field Marshal SHFJ Manekshaw, MC; four of whom rose to become Service Chiefs.

Tales of valour of our heroes throughout our ancient history, the 1857 uprising, and the two World Wars, inspired our soldiers to perform even more gallantly in all wars and counter-insurgency operations since Independence. The chapter on Military power in Part 3 of the book will cover them.

FEUDAL MINDSET AND FISSIPAROUS TENDENCIES

Unlike many ancient civilizations that prospered and declined, our Vedic heritage retains many good traditions and spirituality. However, our rulers perpetually fought amongst themselves and their lust for power, intrigue and treachery did not let any pan-India political consolidation to take place.

Thus, Porus had to fight Alexander without help from other kings. This was so, also with Lodi against Babur and various rulers against Robert Clive. Shamefully, on many occasions they even colluded with foreigners to settle scores with rivals. Inherited fissiparous tendencies and amoral traits, which kept us subjugated for centuries, continue to permeate our consciousness even today.

Causes of Disunity

What were the reasons for such lack of unity? Was it cultural and lingual differences? Not likely, as those were not too radical, and besides they had coalesced into a composite culture. Religion too could not be a major factor as Hindus, Buddhists and Jains have lived in harmony since the pre-Christian era. After Islam's arrival, barring the killings and plunder by Mongol invaders, there was religious and cultural syncretism under the Delhi Sultanate. In the Moghul era too, except during Aurangzeb's reign and sporadic persecution in between, wars were not on religious lines.

On the contrary, Hindu kings fought fellow Hindus throughout our history, and Muslim rulers fought Turko-Mongol invaders and the Sultanates of Deccan and Bengal. Elsewhere, if religion were the cause, why would there be wars between Christian nations in Europe, or between Muslim Iran and Iraq? Why did Bangladesh separate from Pakistan? Hindu Nepal and India should be one, as also Southeast Asia should be a Buddhist nation.

Wars were primarily due to the egos, jealousies and selfishness of rulers, and driven solely by lust for power and wealth. They ignored larger National interests, and foreign powers readily exploited their myopic selfishness. While ideal of *Bharat* is even in our scriptures, yet there was no emotive devotion towards it.

Pomp and splendour of rulers contrasted sharply with abject poverty of their subjects. Their tyrannical and greedy ways trickled down even to the nobility, who created own *fiefdoms* to exploit the masses. Such *feudal mindsets*, flaunting of power, and amassing wealth by means fair or foul, still pervade our consciousness.

Among core tenets of Indian culture are *dharam* and *karam* (moral and ethical conduct, duties, spirituality). Our scriptures cite sins such as *kaam, krodh, lobh, moh, ahankar, irshya* (lust, anger, greed, arrogance, jealousy) as the root causes of evil. Whole world, which is reeling with violence and materialism, is slowly veering towards *spirituality*. Ironically, we are drifting away from our own culture, which embodies *spirituality*.

Contemporary Manifestations of such Traits

The following academic concept provides a clear understanding of manifestations of such mindsets in today's context. Hofstede in his seminal study had delineated culture along four dimensions, one of which – *Power distance,* is relevant here. Later in his research, he had added two more dimensions[34].

Power distance refers to the extent to which people accept a hierarchical structure and are deferential to people in power. It varies along a continuum; e.g., Asian cultures accept *power distance* more than in the west, and seldom question hierarchy.

Indian culture scores high on the *Power distance* continuum. Feudal mindsets still prevail, especially in rural areas, where people seek to wield power or assume pre-eminence by virtue of their birth (caste, lineage, affluence). Hierarchy is highly regarded in Govt and private jobs, institutions and organizations.

People try to create own *fiefdoms* to lord over others. Factions that fail to get prominence in any organization often splinter and start parallel outfits. Bureaucracy's *feudal mindset* impels it to guard its domain zealously. It is averse to economizing or restructuring for fear of losing their status. Instead, the effort is to add layers of subordinate staff to boost their eminence. It matters

---

[34] Hofstede, Geert (2001). *Culture's Consequences: comparing values, behaviors, institutions, and organizations across nations* (2nd ed.). Thousand Oaks, CA. The original dimensions were: *Power distance; Individualism vs Collectivism; Masculinity vs Femininity;* and *Uncertainty avoidance.* Later he added the dimensions of *Long-term orientation vs Short-term orientation* and *Indulgence vs Restraint.*

little to them that this increases inefficiency and creates more opportunities for corruption, while diffusing accountability.

By far the biggest manifestation is evident in politics, where anyone *elected* assumes *divinity,* and the right to unbridled power. This is most visible in the *Lal batti* culture, which no one is willing to give up. Even those who pass orders against the practice are averse to foregoing it themselves. If this persists, we may soon have the ludicrous spectacle of *elected* office bearers of Trader or Resident Welfare associations claiming the same privilege.

Corruption in all walks is now endemic. Not just politicians, bureaucrats, bankers and *wheeling-dealing* businesspersons are mired in corruption; shockingly some of our hallowed institutions too are no longer immune. People no more feel *shocked* by such incidents, whereas during childhood I had often seen how society used to ostracize anyone facing just an inquiry. Sadly, the *threshold of shame* has got lowered alarmingly.

The term *jugad* actually should mean innovation and initiative, but in our context, it is synonymous with circumventing rules through patronage, greasing palms, dishonesty and cunning.

Our politicians suffer from bloated egos, and flaunt their status through crass trappings of power and unwarranted privileges. Even top leaders, who ought to be setting examples of rectitude, are guilty of egregious conduct, as the following episode will illustrate.

On 6 December 1992, riots broke following demolition of *Babri Masjid.* I had just joined as Col Q (Operational Logistics) at HQ Southern Command, and got orders to arrange five special trains to move troops from Rajasthan for deployment within 72 hours at many locations in Southern India. Direct liaison with the Railway Board helped, and all troops reached their assigned locations in time, except for those in the special train headed to Kerala.

The train was halted upon entering Tamil Nadu, on orders of its Chief Minister. Whether local railway officials allowed parochial allegiance to triumph over duty, or they did not dare incur the CM's wrath, is a moot point. But, it shows her immaturity and arrogance that she ignored National interest just because the PM or RM had not spoken to her before sending troops through her State. They still did not do so, but asked Army Commander to fly to Chennai to placate her. Only then the train resumed its journey.

IMPACT ON NATIONAL WILL AND ETHOS

Given the foregoing inspirational as well as negative influences of our heritage, how do we perceive our national ethos? Do we see ourselves as *Indians* first, or do we identify ourselves more with our religion, caste, province or vocation?

Regrettably, the latter seems to be the overwhelming case. It is natural and quite acceptable to be proud of one's roots, provided the overarching identity is that of a proud *Indian,* and National interests come ahead of parochial considerations.

However, this was not so in the early years after Independence. The elation of achieving freedom and fervour of Nation-building was the predominant emotion. Even those of us, who had lost our homes and hearth due to partition, did not nurse either religious animosity or despair.

Only later, electoral politics, with all the power, pelf, privileges and patronage that go with it, corrupted the entire system. Winning elections by fair or foul means became the politicians' credo. Barring many exceptions, the number of unprincipled and corrupt *netas* kept increasing. They exacerbated religious, caste, ethnic and lingual fault-lines merely to garner votes.

Once set into motion, this trend gathered momentum, making it a sure-fire method for winning an election. Politicians seem least bothered whether their self-seeking actions could lead to riots, and leave permanent scars on the communities. From their perspective greater the polarization, more electoral dividends would they reap.

Closely linked to this malaise is the blight of corruption, which has struck deep roots in our ethos. It is a vicious circle involving poll financing by corporate houses, which in return get licenses, contracts and loans, while bureaucratic malfeasance eases the process. With the *Neta-Babu* combine indulging in brazen corruption, lower level functionaries too have no qualms about fleecing the common man in their respective domains.

In this mad race, everyone seems hell-bent on cheating others only to enrich themselves. Hence, it is traders adulterating and overcharging, inspectors, with palms greased looking the other way, or the rapacious police and judiciary; *all have their hand in the till.*

As highlighted earlier, the *threshold of shame* has hit a new low. It is now passé for high-flying businessmen to abscond after defrauding banks, or for *Netas and Babus* to be jailed for serious crimes and corruption (after exhausting all legal tricks). No institution or vocation seems immune, media, medical profession, education, bankers, and even the higher judiciary and the Armed Forces. It is a murky swamp all around.

In such an environment, do we still have a National will and character? It certainly exists, though it is lying dormant. It gets aroused whenever there is a crisis; be it war, natural calamity, or a grave international or domestic challenge. It is also very much in evidence when we rejoice at our national achievements; in sports, space launches, international awards, and honours to Indians.

The moot question is, why does it take a war or crisis, or alternatively sports and other achievements to rekindle our patriotic fervour and National will? It boils down to the absence of enlightened, transformational leadership at the highest level. Such visionary leadership alone can galvanize masses to rise above parochial mindsets, eschew self-serving and corrupt ways, and contribute their mite enthusiastically for the nation's benefit.

It certainly has happened before. Gandhiji is the best example, who inspired millions without holding any political office, just by virtue of his moral authority. Other examples are Nehru's building the infrastructure of a modern India and its institutions; Shastri's *Jai Jawan Jai Kisan* rousing call at a very difficult time; Indira Gandhi's astute leadership and steely resolve that got us the 1971 victory; or Vajpayee's calm and bold handling of the Kargil crisis.

However, it has to be genuinely motivating leadership that goes beyond just catchy slogans and enticing promises. Sincere actions and personal example must back it. The common man has grown tired of empty rhetoric, platitudes, and unfulfilled promises, and is now too cynical to be swayed by mere gimmickry.

Top National leadership has to rise above electoral politics, promote plurality, and be fair and transparent in dealing with States, people, and issues. There is nothing more disillusioning than to see actions not matching words. How can the common man feel reassured when even abhorrent and dastardly acts of inhumanity are reacted to, either with sharp castigation or inexplicable silence, all this contingent upon political factors such as the religion and community of the victims and the oppressors?

In sum therefore, National will stand strengthened only when there is social and economic justice, level playing field irrespective of religion, caste, class and ethnicity, rule of law, and responsive good governance.

Our Nation has a very rich ancient heritage. We have borne numerous trials and tribulations with fortitude and resilience. We have also borne the consequences of disunity, parochial considerations and internecine conflicts. Having waited over 3000 years to get a united Nation, we must not allow fritter it away. Enlightened and motivating leadership can help strengthen National will and ethos, and help us attain all our aspirations.

6

Political Stability and Morality

The hallmark of a vibrant democracy is a stable political system that is a true reflection of the peoples' *will*. It has a direct and profound impact on all dimensions of the nation's internal and external environments. Its sound *health* is vital, since if it lacks credibility or is unresponsive to peoples' aspirations they would lose faith in democracy and plunge the nation into anarchy.

Howsoever political stability may be essential, political morality is even more critical. While in the present context morality in politics may seem a pipedream, but it is imperative for us to shun a corrupt political system like the plague.

Like a virulent virus, it spreads rapidly and spawns corruption in all spheres. Even worse, once it has seeped into the nation's psyche, it causes lasting damage to National character and esteem. There can be nothing more galling for a nation's honour than to be perpetually rated low on the worldwide index of corruption.

The country's Constitution is the soul of its political system. We are truly fortunate to have an excellent Constitution, arguably the best in the world, which eminent intellectuals, legal luminaries and wise Statesmen had crafted. It has stood the test of time and has not failed the country. Actually, the political class has failed it, by not adhering to the principles enshrined in our Constitution.

Despite the country's traumatic partition on the pernicious two-nation theory, India has more Muslims than even Pakistan or Bangladesh. We also have large populations of all the religions in the world, and therefore India could not have been anything except a secular nation. Our *Founding fathers* wisely did not adopt the theocratic state model of Pakistan even though we had a vast Hindu majority.

Although we now have a composite culture that has blended over centuries, it is not homogenous either. There is still vast diversity in customs, attire, food and festivals. With 122 major languages and 1599 dialects according to the 2001 census, we have far more diversity than whole of Europe.

Our pluralist and inclusive Constitution therefore guarantees freedom of thought, speech and action, without making any distinction of religion, caste, colour, creed or ethnicity. We also adopted a Federal structure, which further promotes plurality by fulfilling all regional aspirations.

Track Record since Independence

How has our political system fared since Independence? It is essential to take stock, or else history could repeat itself apropos those episodes where we have faltered.

In the early years after Independence, our political system functioned quite well. Countries in our neighbourhood, as well as many newly independent Third world countries saw breakdown of their Constitution, which resulted in intense political turmoil. Many of them had their duly elected Governments overthrown by military coups. However, in those geopolitically turbulent times Indian democracy stood out as a shining exception.

Parliament used to function without disruption and it enacted several landmark legislations. Parliamentary norms were adhered to in letter and spirit, and there was high mutual regard between legislators on either side of the aisle. Politicians of that era deserve all credit as they behaved responsibly and maintained decorum

Nehru, especially, was a stickler for adherence to parliamentary norms. He did not let Congress party's brute majority smother the Opposition. The Opposition too reciprocated admirably and did not create unruly scenes. It was a delight, and indeed an education to listen to debates between eminent and erudite parliamentarians such as Ambedkar, Maulana Azad, SP Mukherjee, AK Gopalan, Asoka Mehta, Gopalaswamy Ayyangar, Frank Anthony and Vajpayee among many others.

Nehru's towering persona and Congress party's majority in the parliament ensured ample political stability. However, his failing health after the 1962 India-China war debacle triggered questions such as *after Nehru who* and party seniors began jockeying for power. However, Nehru had anointed Lal Bahadur Shastri as his successor and hence the transition was smooth.

Shastri's tragic death in 1966 however threw the succession question wide open, which essentially ushered in the era of turmoil in Indian politics. Stalwarts like Morarji Desai, Jagjivan Ram, SK Patil and YB Chavan, all of whom nursed Prime Ministerial ambitions, set off a power struggle within the party. Our historical heritage of palace intrigues and selfish ambitions once again came to the fore in full force.

Indira Gandhi with some deft political and populist moves split the party and consolidated her position. Her crowning glory came in 1971 when she led the Nation to an epoch-making victory over Pakistan, and which led to the creation of Bangladesh. During this period, the Opposition was in complete disarray. There were numerous splits and realignments among various parties, such as Congress (O), Swatantra party, Jan Singh, PSP, CPM, CPI, Lok Dal, Janata party. Janata Dal, Samajwadi Janata Party etc.

This era saw a sharp decline in standards of probity, political wheeling-dealing and brazen corporate malfeasance through political patronage. Legislators shamelessly switched parties after being *purchased,* and the term *Aya Ram – Gaya Ram* entered the Indian political lexicon. Political stability remained elusive.

By 1975, the JP movement that fanned resentment against the Indira Gandhi Govt, and the All India railway strike had already vitiated the atmosphere. After her election was aside by Allahabad High Court, the political system and indeed the entire Nation was plunged into acute turmoil. Her Govt declared Emergency, stifled the media, and imprisoned opposition leaders. Anger also built up among the people due to sterilization and slum clearance drives.

Congress suffered a resounding defeat, but even the Janata Govt failed due to its obsession for vendetta politics, ambition-driven intrigues of its leaders, and abject non-performance. Indira Gandhi came back to power in 1980, but her second innings was fraught with immense chaos due to the Khalistan movement and Op Blue Star, which ended with her tragic assassination in 1984 followed by the ghastly anti-Sikh riots.

Rajiv Gandhi was sworn in as PM, and in the elections that followed Congress received a strong mandate. Although he was not cut out for the skulduggery of Indian politics, he did bring a fair measure of stability. While he ushered the computer revolution, and took decisive action in Maldives, he was also responsible for the ill-fated military intervention in Sri Lanka.

However, the same old scourge of ambition and intrigue engineered his downfall, when his own minister VP Singh raised the Bofors scandal. Vote-bank considerations, which have been the bane of the Indian political system, led VP Singh to unleash the Mandal Commission *genie* to garner OBC votes. This triggered massive protests among students; even resulting in a horrifying, much-publicized self-immolation by a student.

To counter the caste card, Advani along with BJP, RSS and Hindutva cadres took out a *Rath Yatra* on the Mandir issue. This caused intense religious polarization and there were widespread communal riots all over India. This time the communal *genie* was unleashed, which inflicted incalculable harm upon the Nation. It created deep fissures in our society from which we are reeling to this day. Fall of VP Singh Govt led to further political instability and in the process of realignments Chandra Shekhar became PM for a brief tenure. Table 1 shows the tenures of all Prime Ministers since Independence.

Table 1

Tenures of Indian Prime Ministers

No	Prime Minister	Party	Tenure	Period
1	Jawaharlal Nehru	Congress	15 Aug 1947-27 May 1964	16 years 286 days
2	Gulzarilal Nanda (Interim PM)	Congress	27 May 1964 – 9 Jun 1964	13 days
3	Lal Bahadur Shastri	Congress	9 Jun 1964 – 11 Jan 1966	1 year 216 days
4	Gulzarilal Nanda (Interim PM)	Congress	11 Jan 1966 – 24 Jan 1966	13 days
5	Indira Gandhi	Congress	24 Jan 1966 – 24 Mar 1977	11 years 59 days
6	Morarji Desai	Janata Party	24 Mar 1977 - 28 July 1979	2 years 166 days
7	Charan Singh	Janata Party (secular)	28 July 1979 – 14 Jan 1980	170 days
8	Indira Gandhi	Congress	14 Jan 1980 – 31 Oct 1984	4 years 291 days
9	Rajiv Gandhi	Congress	31 Oct 1984 – 2 Jan 1989	5 years 32 days
10	V.P. Singh	Janata Dal	2 Jan 1989 – 10 Nov 1990	343 days
11	Chandra Shekhar	Samajwadi Janata Party	10 Nov 1990 – 21 Jun 1991	223 days
12	P.V. Narasimha Rao	Congress	21 Jun 1991 - 16 May 1996	4 years 330 days
13	Atal Bihari Vajpayee	BJP	16 May 1996 – 1 Jun 1996	16 days
14	H.D. Deve Gowda	Janata Dal	1 Jun 1996 – 21 Apr 1997	324 days
15	I.K. Gujral	Janata Dal	21 Apr 1997 – 19 Mar 1998	332 days
16	Atal Bihari Vajpayee	BJP	19 Mar 1998 - 22 May 2004	6 years 64 days
17	Manmohan Singh	Congress	22 May 2004 - 26 May 2014	10 years 4 days
18	Narendra Modi	BJP	26 May 2014 - till date	

Just when the Congress appeared to be making a comeback, the LTTE assassinated Rajiv Gandhi. Narasimha Rao became the PM, and with Manmohan Singh as Finance Minister, he initiated far-reaching economic reforms. As a result, there was a dramatic increase in foreign exchange reserves, which earlier had fallen so low that India had to seek an IMF loan, and even sell her gold reserves to pay for imports.

Communal harmony however was still in a very bad state. In that volatile environment, fanatic Hindutva forces created a far more explosive situation by demolishing the *Babri Masjid* on 6 December 1992. Resulting riots drove a deeper wedge between communities and set off a chain reaction of tragic events. The Mumbai bomb blasts in March 1993 were the immediate fallout.

Except for the blot of *Babri Masjid* demolition on his watch and despite leading a minority Govt, Narsimha Rao not only completed his tenure but also turned the economy around to a high growth path. However, the next elections returned a fractured mandate and there was a succession of three PMs in less than two years.

Vajpayee Govt in 1998 brought back a modicum of stability. It lasted its full tenure, although it had to face several crises such as hijacking of an Indian Airlines plane, Kargil War of 1999, terrorist attack on Parliament in 2001, and going on the verge of a full-blown war with Pakistan in 2002. Godhra train tragedy, and the killings and devastation in Gujarat exacerbated communal tension even further, and the Nation is feeling its repercussions even now.

Manmohan Singh was the PM in Congress-led coalition Govts, UPA1 and UPA2 during 2004-14. On 1 October 2008, US Congress granted India a waiver under the landmark Indo-US Nuclear Deal. While the entire country applauded, it almost brought down the UPA1 Govt when the CPM withdrew its support. Despite great uncertainty due to their minority status, both Govts lasted their full terms, and provided a fair amount of political stability and economic progress.

The Modi Govt came to power in 2014 with a massive majority. Given its assured stability there were very high expectations that it will initiate the next phase of crucial economic reforms, undertake restructuring of the defence sector, and provide all-round good governance. However, hopes did not fructify due to the disruptive, ill-conceived demonetization, and the shoddily implemented GST. While there is still ample political stability, there has also been a substantial increase in religious and caste polarization. Agrarian distress, high unemployment, and a deteriorating situation in J&K are also a cause for serious dissatisfaction.

Table 2

National Vote Share of Top Three Parties in General Elections

Year	Party	Vote %	Seats Won	Prime Minister
2014	BJP	31.0	282	Narendra Modi
	Congress	19.3	44	
	ADMK	3.3	37	
2009	Congress	28.6	206	Manmohan Singh
	BJP	18.8	116	
	BSP	6.2	21	
2004	Congress	26.7	145	Manmohan Singh
	BJP	22.2	138	
	RJD	2.2	21	
1999	BJP	23.7	182	AB Vajpayee
	Congress	28.3	114	
	CPM	5.4	33	
1998	BJP	25.6	182	IK Gujral
	Congress	25.8	141	(United Front)
	CPM	5.2	32	
1996	BJP	20.3	161	HD Deve Gowda
	Congress	28.8	140	(Janata Dal)
	CPM	6.1	32	
1991	Congress	36.3	232	Narasimha Rao
	BJP	20.1	120	
	Janata Dal	11.8	59	
1989	Congress	39.5	197	VP Singh
	Janata Dal	17.8	143	(Janata Dal)
	BJP	11.4	85	
1984	Congress	49.1	404	Rajiv Gandhi
	CPM	5.9	22	
	Janata Party	6.9	10	
1980	Congress	42.7	353	Indira Gandhi
	Janata Party(S)	9.4	41	
	CPM	6.2	37	
1977	Janata Party	41.3	295	Morarji Desai
	Congress	34.5	154	
	CPM	4.3	22	
1971	Congress	43.7	352	Indira Gandhi
	CPM	5.1	25	
	CPI	4.7	23	
1967	Congress	40.8	283	Indira Gandhi
	Swantantra Party	8.7	44	
	Jan Sangh	9.3	35	
1962	Congress	44.7	361	Jawaharlal Nehru
	CPI	9.9	29	
	Swantantra Party	7.9	18	
1957	Congress	47.8	371	Jawaharlal Nehru
	Independents	19.3	42	
	CPI	8.9	27	
1951	Congress	45	364	Jawaharlal Nehru
	Independents	15.9	37	
	CPI	3.3	16	

Source: Election Commission of India

What Ails the System?

Table 1 lists Indian Prime Ministers along with the duration for which their Govts lasted. It is very evident that there have been several prolonged spells of political instability since Independence. These were due to fractured mandates, party splits, realignments and defections. All of them were due to the ambitions of power-hungry politicians.

***'First past the post'* System.** Unrepresentative voting is generally due to it, since often the winning candidate and party poll only one-third of the votes cast. Table 2 shows the vote share of the top three parties and the number of seats won by them in the general elections. No party has ever received more than 50% votes. Even for the highest number of 404 Lok Sabha seats won by Rajiv Gandhi in the 1984 elections, Congress polled only 49.1% votes. Similarly, Prime Minister Modi's vote share was just 31%, but it got him 282 seats in 2014.

While Govts have come to power with just one-third of vote share, often parties getting a higher share do not get to form the Govt. For example, in the 1999 general elections BJP polled only 23.7% votes, against Congress's vote share of 28.3%. Yet, despite a lower vote share, BJP won more seats than the Congress and Vajpayee became the PM. This was not an isolated instance, and similar anomalies were in the 1996 and 1998 elections too, as can be seen in Table 2.

This clearly highlights that the extant *first past the post* system does not necessarily represent the *will* of the majority. More infirmities and electoral malpractices have crept in because of this. Overall vote share is no longer relevant. What matters is to select a winning candidate as per religious and caste demographics of that constituency. This has spawned an industry where demographic data of each constituency, voting profile and inclination of voters, and lists of influential opinion-makers, are in great demand. Often this is collected furtively, as in the recent Face book data leak.

This does not end there. Once voter-blocks are identified based on religious and caste equations, focused canvassing, booth-level coaxing, and *persuasion* target them. Such *persuasion* involves a mix of intimidation, impersonation, monetary inducements, liquor and several other forms of voter fraud.

Use of Electronic Voting Machines (EVMs) has significantly reduced the enormous logistical burden of paper ballots. However, parties have raised doubts about their reliability, which the EC has stoutly refuted. Nonetheless, given that, no electronic system is immune to hacking; many advanced countries have stopped using them. They could afford to do so due to smaller number of voters involved. With our huge electorate, EVMs alone can be a manageable and relatively inexpensive option.

Using the analogy of *trust but verify,* a more satisfactory via media would be to use EVMs with a paper trail. This would be very useful wherever EVMs malfunction or in case of doubts about any electoral malpractice. In addition, it is imperative to take stringent deterrent action against the election officials involved, to maintain sanctity of the electoral process. The beneficiary candidate and political party should also face penal actions to send out a strong signal against voter fraud.

Multiplicity of Political Parties. Our feudal heritage, which fuels proclivity to create own *fiefdoms*, gives rise to multiplicity of political parties. Factions keep jockeying for power, which lead to frequent defections and splits in parties that increase political uncertainty. The Anti-defection law had attempted to remedy the instability caused by defections.

However, one can always trust wily politicians and scheming parties to find devious ways to defeat the intent of any law. Therefore, defectors below the threshold set by law to recognize a split enter the House through the backdoor via Rajya Sabha or Legislative Councils. Others receive *compensation* through offices of profit, such as Directorship of PSUs, Chairmanship of Rural Banks and sundry Boards, and through a host of similar subterfuges.

During the sixties and seventies there were debates about a switch to a Presidential form of Govt. Options were, either the US model where the President directly exercises Executive authority, or the French model where the elected President appoints a PM to run the Govt, and who is answerable to the President.

Such a major change would have required another Constituent Assembly, and this was never pursued. Perhaps rightly so, given the popular saying, *"If it ain't broke, don't fix it."* No system is perfect and whether the system will deliver or not depends upon the rectitude and morality of the political class. The evil genius of self-serving politicians will always find ways to outwit any system.

In any other democracy, it would be well nigh impossible for any convicted politician to stand for election on moral-ethical grounds alone. Not so in India, where politicians convicted even for serious criminal offences such as rape and murder are given party tickets. Despite their grandstanding and claims to the *high moral ground*, no party is an exception in this shameful practice. All that matters is which candidate will win them that seat.

Given the feudal mindset prevailing especially in rural areas, convicts taking refuge in politics and becoming *bahubali netas* are their best bet. With intimidation, they not only win their own seat but also ensure victory of other party candidates in that region.

With the local police and administration doing their bidding, they increase their clout by providing patronage to henchmen and shielding them from law. With an eye on the next elections, party bosses have no option but to ignore such high-handedness.

No wonder then that such *bahubali netas* bring shame to the entire political class with their crass and irresponsible behaviour. Yet, in spite of all the public outrage, not a single political party has denied tickets to such tainted *netas*. Table 3 lists the number of sitting MPs and MLAs from political parties holding the top three positions in the dubious *Dishonour Roll*. It also shows the number of tickets given to tainted *Netas* by the top three parties.

Table 3
Criminal Record of Crimes against Women

Sitting MPs and MLAs – Top Three Positions						
Total	**BJP**		**Shiv Sena**		**Trinamool Cong**	
51	14	27.5%	7	13.7%	6	11.8%
Tickets Given by Parties in Last Five Years Top Three Positions						
Total	**BJP**		**BSP**		**Congress**	
327	47	14.4%	35	10.7%	24	7.3%

Source: Association for Democratic Reforms

Poll Finance. It is another area of serious concern, since it spawns corruption not just in our political system but also in the society itself. When corporate houses finance political parties, there is always a *quid pro quo* by way of licenses, contracts, and *sweetheart deals*. This nexus has bred crony-capitalism, which has now attained alarming proportions. High-flying corporate honchos, after defrauding banks of billions of Rupees of public money, have simply fled the country; all this obviously with political and bureaucratic connivance.

Even those that have stayed back, recover their *investment* manifold through profiteering, illegal practices, favouritism and patronage. Their *Neta-Babu* patrons keep tweaking rules in their benefit, and shield them from regulatory agencies. In turn, they keep receiving their *cutbacks*. It has become one big, well-oiled nexus, all at the expense of the poor, helpless common man.

Every party has stonewalled attempts to bring transparency into the poll finance system. No political party is willing to bring their party funds within the ambit of the RTI. Shockingly, the Govt has enacted a law against disclosure of foreign funding, instead of bringing transparency.

Even public financing of polls does not find favour with political parties since that would shut down sources of *personal* benefit. Moreover, the larger parties, which have greater access to corporate funds due to better prospects of coming to power and extending patronage, do not favour it. Reforms that would help clean this morass do not suit any of the *predators in the swamp.*

After a lot of public outrage, all parties had acquiesced, though grudgingly, to the appointment of Lokpal and Lok Ayukts. It is sad and ironic that the BJP, which came to power on the plank of fighting corruption, has still neither fulfilled its major poll promise at the Centre nor in the States governed by it.

These systemic flaws have crept in over the years and have totally corrupted the environment. While the entire political class certainly is to blame, all of us too are responsible. We – the voters - elect them, and put them in that position of power from which they wreak havoc with the system. If we do not go out and vote, or if we vote a candidate not on the basis of merit, but based on religion, caste and other parochial reasons, then we have no right to complain.

A corrupt and dysfunctional political system is the wellspring of corruption in the entire polity, institutions, and in society itself. It breeds crass materialism, and scant regard for ethics, values and norms. It exacerbates the class divide between the haves and have-nots, breeds the *get rich quick through shortcuts* mindset, which invariably boosts crime.

If the silent majority – the common man – does not speak up against such loathsome practices, and does not vote for only upright and secular candidates, we would perpetuate the rot. All through history, many a civilization, kingdom and Nation have decayed and disintegrated when its body politic got corrupted. We owe it to our future generations to STEM THE ROT NOW.

7

The Dimension of Social Cohesion

Social harmony and cohesion is the most significant contributor to a Nation's intrinsic strength. While it is imperative that people coexist peacefully, it should not be merely due to fear of law. For genuine national unity, this has to be natural and spontaneous. If discord and conflict are rife for any reason, the Nation can never be strong enough to fight off external threats.

For a country of such vast diversity as India, inherent religious, cultural, ethnic and economic fault-lines are ever-present. Due to inherited historical baggage, these have left a deep imprint on our National psyche. To ensure social harmony they must remain dormant. We must not allow any individual, group, or political party to exacerbate and exploit them.

For centuries, our people have lived together in peace despite all the diversity and fault-lines. This has been due to our interwoven social fabric in which kinship, commerce, and societal interdependencies link people. Disruptions were mainly due to wars, imposed by foreign invaders or when own rulers engaged in internecine conflicts. Such conflicts invariably affected livelihoods, indeed their very existence.

The section on *Feudal Mindset and Fissiparous Tendencies* in Chapter 4 had highlighted how throughout history we never nurtured a *Nationalist* ethos of *united India*. This was primarily because all Rulers consciously promoted *sub-Nationalism*. By convincing their subjects about their distinct identity, they invoked their loyalty to the *motherland*, in effect to themselves. Notion of *motherland* narrowly meant only that kingdom.

Sub-nationalist mindsets took root not due to significant cultural differences, but because of the ambition of Rulers and Chieftains to carve out their own fiefdoms. Thus, they imposed taxes and raised armies to fight internal wars in furtherance of such feudal mindsets. There was never a notion of pan-India unity therefore even in the face of foreign invasions.

Rulers of yesteryears are present-day politicians who nurse similar ambitions of power and pelf. In their quest for personal influence, they exploit religious, caste, and cultural differences among people, who otherwise would want to live peacefully.

A brief overview of the nature and intricacies of the fault-lines is necessary to appreciate how they are accentuated.

FAULT-LINES

Religious

Fig 3 shows the percentage of followers of different religions in India as per the 2011 census.

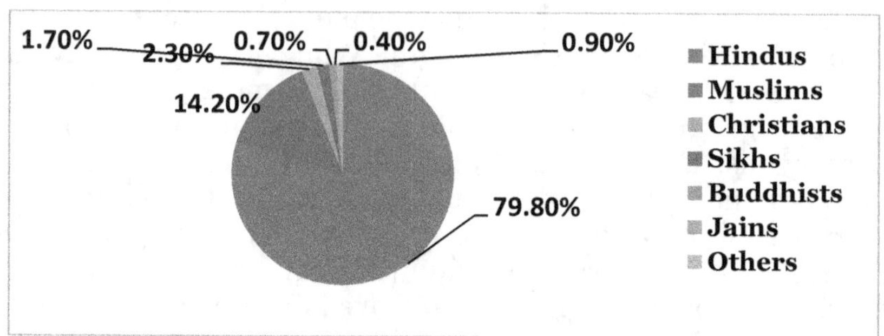

Fig. 3 - Religious composition of India's population

Religion is a very emotive issue in human relations. It is very ironical that even though all religions propound humanity, compassion and peace, mankind has a long history of committing inhuman violence on its account. Communal harmony is particularly vital in our country to ensure social cohesion, as it is home to all the religions of the world.

Hinduism, which has 1.15 billion followers worldwide, is practiced by 80% of our population. It is essentially *dharma,* or a way of life. It is a synthesis of several Indian cultures and traditions, has diverse roots, and no founder[35]. It spans many ideas of spirituality but has no ecclesiastical order, no supreme religious authority, no governing body, no prophet(s) nor any binding holy book[36]. A Hindu can choose to be polytheistic, pantheistic, monotheistic, monistic, agnostic, humanist, or even atheistic, and still be called a Hindu[37].

Buddhism and Jainism, both of which originated in India 3000 years ago, share many spiritual tenets with Hinduism. In a way, they were a reformist movement against Brahmanical orthodoxy. Both faiths espouse non-violence and their adherents have lived here in total peace and harmony for three millennia.

---

[35] *Narayanan, Vasudha (2009), Hinduism, The Rosen Publishing Group*

[36] Julius J. Lipner (2009), *Hindus: Their Religious Beliefs and Practices*, 2nd Edition, Routledge

[37] MK Gandhi, *The Essence of Hinduism,* Editor: VB Kher, Navajivan Publishing, see page 3; According to Gandhi, "a man may not believe in God and still call himself a Hindu."

After the advent of Islam in India in early 8th Century, relations between Muslims and Hindus have had a mixed record. Mongol invaders such as Mahmud of Ghazni and Timur had inflicted wanton killings during their campaigns of loot and plunder. On the other hand, Turkic-Mamluk slave dynasties that settled down here were relatively less violent, and there was a fair degree of religious synthesis and cultural blending during their reign.

The Mughals, although of Mongol descent, came to India not to plunder but to settle down here after the conquest. Except for the extreme religious persecution by Aurangzeb, conflicts were not on religious lines but were mainly to annex kingdoms, Hindu and Muslim alike. Despite some unease due to their following different religions, the common folks lived in relative peace, bound as they were by social and commercial links.

Steadfast Hindu-Muslim unity during the 1857 uprising, had alarmed the British, who then employed their *divide and rule* stratagem to sow dissensions. Deplorably, as has often happened all through our history, personal ambitions of politicians fanned and intensified religious polarization for their selfish ends. This culminated in the tragic partition of the country, which caused over a million deaths and uprooted several million.

Sikh religion was born around the end of 15th Century, it spread all over northwest, and north India. It ultimately emerged as the *sword-arm* of Hindus to fight persecution by Muslim rulers, especially Aurangzeb. There was a long-standing practice in Punjabi families for the eldest son to embrace Sikhism, and join the fight against tyrannical Muslim rulers and chieftains.

So, what has been the state of our communal relations since Independence? Hindus, Buddhists, Christians, Jains, Parsis and Jews; all have lived in complete harmony. Some Hindu groups have however targeted Christian charities for alleged proselytizing.

Hindus and Sikhs bore the brunt of communal massacres and traumatic relocation from undivided Punjab during partition. Their common pain and the age-old bonds of kinship and business links ensured that they live in perfect accord. They share a common language and culture, celebrate the same festivals, and visit each other's shrines with utmost devotion.

However, the bane of ugly, self-serving and divisive politics struck again. During the early eighties Punjab witnessed a spate of extremist violence and insurgency by Khalistani militants, who were supported by Pakistan. This culminated in Op Blue Star, Indira Gandhi's assassination by her Sikh bodyguards, and tragic large-scale killings of innocent Sikhs in its aftermath.

Mercifully, wiser counsels prevailed and people realized the futility of such strife. Punjab pulled back from the brink and the traditional harmony between all communities was restored.

Relations between Muslims and Hindus however have been more tenuous. It is quite a paradox that there is more distrust and antagonism between the two communities now – 71 years after Independence, than there was in the immediate aftermath of the partition when communal frenzy was at its worst.

It is also a paradox that communities that bore the brunt of the killings and losses during partition are largely less prone to communal hatred. Having borne the sheer trauma and horror, no one wants to go through it again. Though my parents moved to Delhi as refugees from Pakistan, I never heard even one word of anger against Muslims. All they said was that total madness had taken over everyone, and partition was due to political reasons.

During the early decades, communities were not as polarized as they are now. Communal riots were sporadic, and often triggered by minor incidents such as an accident, eve teasing or a petty dispute. However, some of these did escalate into major conflagrations, and caused a large number of casualties.

Authentic statistics on communal riots and casualty figures are hard to come by. Whatever data is available in the public domain reflects mostly on local reports, which are often subjective. The graphic below on people killed in communal riots shows data from a Case Study from the Lal Bahadur Shastri Police Academy.

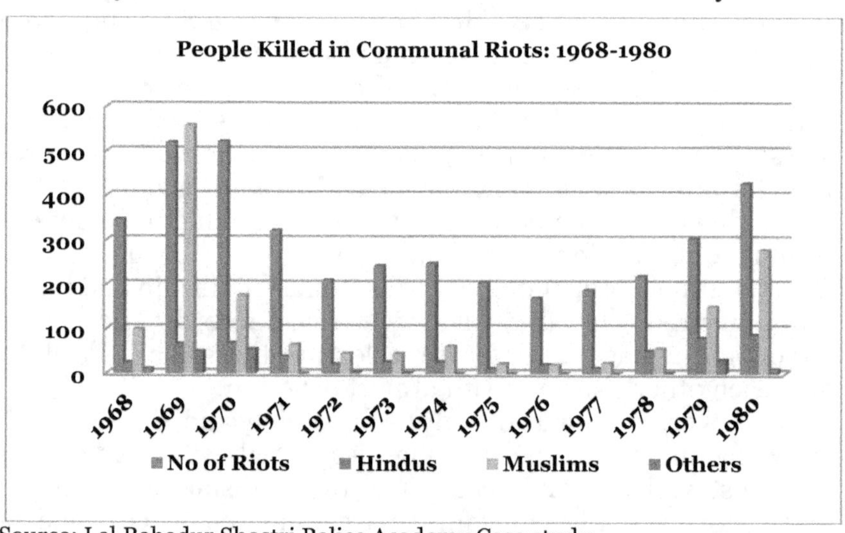

Source: Lal Bahadur Shastri Police Academy Case study

Fig. 4 – People killed in communal riots: 1968-1980

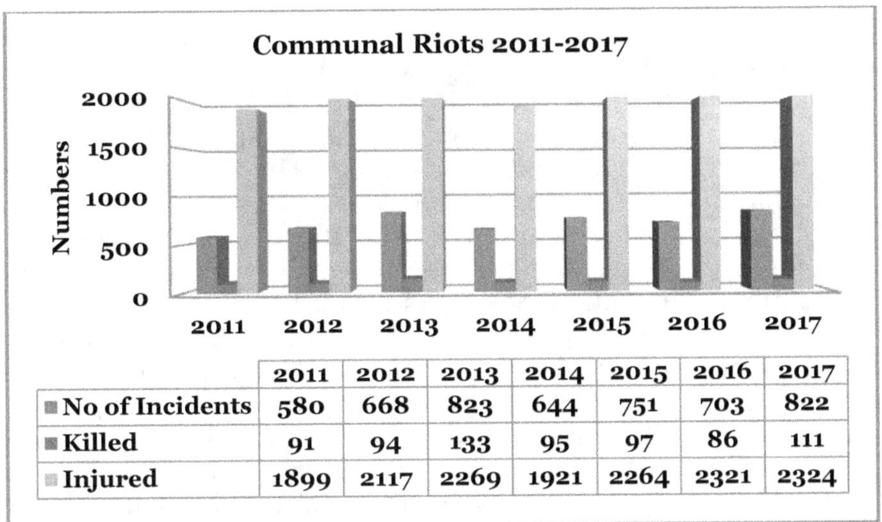

	2011	2012	2013	2014	2015	2016	2017
No of Incidents	580	668	823	644	751	703	822
Killed	91	94	133	95	97	86	111
Injured	1899	2117	2269	1921	2264	2321	2324

Source: NCRB, Ministry of Home Affairs

Fig. 5 – Casualties in communal violence 2011 - 2017

Data in the graphic at Fig. 5 are from NCRB, and these were given out in replies to Lok Sabha questions.

Large-scale communal flare-ups became more rampant when political parties began polarizing communities for electoral gains. The series of inflammatory incidents started with the Rath Yatra, which reached a crescendo with Babri Masjid demolition. The Mumbai bomb lasts, Gujarat carnage of 2002, and the recent Muzzafarnagar riots, have created a deeper chasm.

As per data from the National Crime Records Bureau (NCRB), communal incidents increased 41% during the three years 2014 to 2016. The top three states were UP, Maharashtra and Madhya Pradesh, closely followed by Rajasthan, Karnataka and Gujarat[38].

Constructing a temple in Ayodhya at the site of the demolished Babri Masjid is plaguing Hindu-Muslim relations. The case is *sub judice*. Although both sides affirm abiding by the court's verdict, politicians of all hues will exploit it for electoral gains. As before every election, political parties will intensify religious and caste polarization in the run-up to the crucial assembly elections later this year, and the 2019 Lok Sabha polls.

The already simmering communal cauldron had a more disturbing dimension added to it. There were a several attacks and bomb blasts that apparently targeted Muslims specifically, such as

---

[38] Mukesh Ranjan, Tribune News Service, Jul 26 2017. Accessed Apr 28, 2018.

the Malegaon bombings (8 Sept 2006), Samjhauta Express attack (18 Feb 2007), Mecca Masjid blasts (18 May 2007), Ajmer Dargah blasts (11 Oct 2007) and the Malegaon blast (28 Sept 2008).

These blasts had a sinister overtone, as in apparent retaliation of attacks by Islamist terrorists, militant Hindutva groups were blamed for them. Many cases are in courts, but many people nurse doubts due to the series of flip-flops by the investigative agencies, allegedly at the behest of ruling parties, which were then in power.

Politics has muddied the waters again. Public is now sceptical since the Agencies have lost credibility; with even the Supreme Court castigating the CBI as a *caged parrot*. How can people have confidence when some investigators and prosecutors have publicly protested Govt interference, and even the Govt has removed many others, including Judges, midway from their cases?

I will discuss the aspect of Institutional credibility in another chapter. I must also clarify that it is not within the scope of this book to discuss the merits of these cases. The focus here is only on the consequences of political and politico-religious manipulations on communal harmony and our social cohesion.

Graphic at Fig. 6 shows communal riots that had the highest number of deaths. However, all three graphics are only disjointed snapshots, which do not provide a realistic picture of the scale and trends of communal violence. The death tolls too are as per official figures, whereas the unofficial estimates are much more.

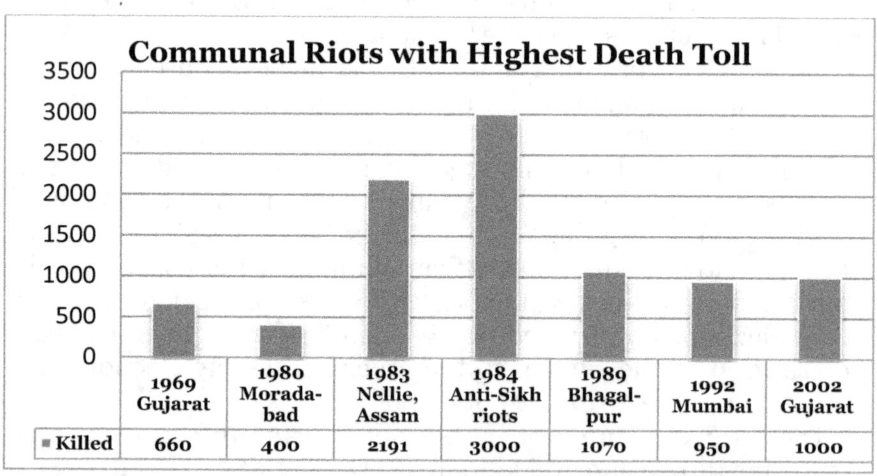

	1969 Gujarat	1980 Morada-bad	1983 Nellie, Assam	1984 Anti-Sikh riots	1989 Bhagal-pur	1992 Mumbai	2002 Gujarat
Killed	660	400	2191	3000	1070	950	1000

Fig 6 - Post-Independence communal riots with highest deaths

No meaningful analysis of communal violence is possible unless the data are collated on specified parameters. There is neither a set procedure for reporting casualties, nor uniformity in State wise collection and collation. Official figures on casualties seldom give breakdown by communities; perhaps rightly, as political parties could misuse them to inflame passions further. Even the reports of various Commissions inquiring into major massacres are not in the public domain for same reason.

Inaccuracy of data apart, it is clear that communal violence since Independence killed more people than soldiers martyred in all conflicts. That is a sad and sordid commentary on the state of cohesion and harmonious relations in our society. How can we aspire for a seat at the *Global high table,* when our societal turbulence and violence resembles that of a *Banana Republic?*

Yet, the irony is that left to themselves all people wish to live in peace and harmony. Communities fully realize that there is just no other option for their mutual well-being. Communal strife harms everyone's livelihood since all communities are interdependent. Trade, vocations and businesses are interlinked, upstream as well as downstream in the value chain.

It is always political parties, radical groups of all communities, and *outsiders,* who pounce on petty local issues, or even *engineer* new ones to fan communal passions. Once they have triggered mayhem, the *action-reaction dynamic* sets in, while they quietly sneak away leaving the hapless people to suffer.

The Pew Research Centre in its 2017 report released a ranking that hardly does credit to an avowedly secular country like India. It ranked India at fourth position among countries that saw an increase in communal violence in the preceding three years. Only Syria, Nigeria and Iraq saw more violence than India. Surely, we hate to be bracketed with such dubious company[39].

Communal strife is not inherent in our society, in the sense that while religious fault-lines are ever-present just *below the surface,* they do not flare up unless stoked. Such provocation could be either inadvertent like a petty squabble, or deliberately *engineered* to trigger a communal riot. Latter is the case most of the times, especially in recent years. This is the stark reality behind almost every single riot in our country.

Communal riots and the immense disruption caused by them have cost the Nation very heavily also in economic terms, which I will highlight in the next chapter. It is even more unfortunate that

---

[39] Pew Research Centre Report http://www.pewforum.org/2017/04/11/global-restrictions-on-religion-rise-modestly-in-2015-reversing-downward-trend. Accessed April 28, 2018.

the hapless common man, the people who actually suffer still fall prey to the machinations of cunning politicians and self-styled custodians of different religions.

Have we paused to consider if there is any other option except to live in peace and harmony? Muslims that stayed back after partition had made a conscious decision to adopt India as their country. A vast majority of them have served the Nation with distinction in all occupations. We have had Muslim Presidents, Chief Justices, industrialists, scientists, military commanders, entrepreneurs, educationists, administrators, sportsmen and artists. Even the ordinary folk have contributed to the Nation in their own way in respective fields.

The 175 million Muslims of India are an incontrovertible fact, which we cannot wish away. They are as worthy citizens of India as any other community, and are the second largest segment of our population. They do not need to be appeased, nor should we distrust and marginalize them.

The global scourge of terrorism fanned by highly radicalized Islamic groups, which jolted the world with the 9/11 attacks, has polarized the entire world. There is wide-ranging backlash against the Muslim community that borders on *Islamophobia,* with even the innocent having to face the brunt of suspicion and ostracizing. This often fuels a counter reaction and both feed on each other.

Ultra-right and Christian groups in Europe are spearheading the campaign against the large-scale immigration of Muslims from the Middle East and North Africa. Such growing animosity among communities is making the spectre of Samuel Huntington's *Clash of Civilizations* hypothesis getting entrenched worldwide[40].

It is pertinent to note that despite the widespread radicalization elsewhere, the number of reported cases of radicalized youth in India as a proportion of the large Muslim population is miniscule. This could well change if political and religious leaders start fanning growing resentment due to provocations and hounding.

Even the most extremist zealots of both communities know that the 175 million Muslims in India are here to stay. So, if no other fanciful solutions such as mass deportation, *ghar wapsi* or even pogroms are feasible, then why create polarization and mayhem just for short-term electoral gains? Do we really want to jeopardize our freedom, for which we had to wait thousands of years? Better sense must prevail.

---

[40] Huntington, Samuel P., *The Clash of Civilizations and the Remaking of World Order*, New York, Simon & Schuster, 1996.

Caste

Caste system is the bane of Indian society and is responsible for many ills plaguing India it. However, caste in essence is merely an age-old division of labour, but it still provokes derision. It is often misunderstood as much within the country, as it is abroad.

In the early Vedic period of *Rigveda* (1500-1000 BCE), there were only two *varnas*, or tribal distinctions. The *Aryas* were from Vedic tribes and were deemed noble, while *Dasa* or *Dasyu* were from rival tribes and considered inferior.

Towards the end of *Atharvaveda* period, two new distinctions emerged. *Dasas* were renamed *shudras* and *aryas* as *vaishyas*. Two elite classes - *Brahmins* (priests) and *Kshatriyas* (warriors) were new *varnas*. Vedic society also assimilated aboriginal tribes as *shudras*. However, Vedic society did not segregate *shudras*, nor treated them as untouchables[41].

Over the centuries, different castes and sub-castes were added under the above-cited four *varnas*. These stratified society based on different vocations to facilitate management and taxation. Skills and knowledge passed down through generations, which ossified and institutionalized the castes. Given the varying nature of vocations and the earnings therein, castes eventually also came to be associated with socio-economic status within society.

However, rigid caste system evolved only after decline of the Mughal era. In late 18th Century, elite groups emerged and as per anthropologist Susan Bayly, they *"associated themselves with kings, priests and ascetics and deployed symbols of caste and kinship to divide the populace and consolidate their power"*[42]. This was the typical *feudal mindset,* which prevails even today.

British rulers promoted *caste* rigidity as it conformed to their own rigid *class* system. Importantly, it enabled *divide and rule* policy by using the elite to help them govern the poor masses. From 1860 to 1920, they segregated Indians by caste, and gave jobs and senior appointments only to upper castes. After protests, they adopted the policy of affirmative action under which some Govt jobs were reserved for the lower castes[43].

---

[41] Sharma, R. S. (1958), *Śūdras in Ancient India, Delhi*: Motilal Banarasi Dass (published 1990) pp. 29–38

[42] Bayly, Susan (2001), *Caste, Society and Politics in India from the Eighteenth Century to the Modern Age*, Cambridge University Press,

[43] Burguière, André; Grew, Raymond (2001), *Construction of Minorities: Cases for Comparison Across Time and Around the World*, Univ of Michigan Press.

In absence of authentic data, there are about 3000 major castes and 25000 sub-castes. Predominantly, Hindus follow the caste system but other religions too have some measure of caste differentiation, even though they are more egalitarian[44].

Just like religion, caste fault-lines are present in our society. They too simmer below the surface, but are more prone to eruption since they affect larger sections of society. Instances of discrimination and atrocities against scheduled castes (SCs) and scheduled tribes (STs) still occur, especially in rural areas, where medieval, feudal prejudices are widespread.

Despite stringent laws, such incidents take place due to socio-political power of the oppressors. In most cases, law-enforcement agencies look the other way, and even connive at them. In the few cases that are publicized, justice is rarely delivered due to botched investigation, witness intimidation, and judicial apathy.

Like religious polarization, exploiting caste also suits political parties, being more dependable vote bank. Parties on both sides of the caste divide get electoral benefits from the cleavage between the under-privileged and upper castes. Parties supported by the upper castes exacerbate the divide by citing *reverse discrimination,* and ill effects of *affirmative action* on quality.

Table 4 below shows the caste categories by religion.

Table 4

Distribution of Population of each Religion by Caste

Religion/Caste	SCs	STs	OBCs	General class/ Others
Hinduism	22.2%	9%	42.8%	26%
Islam	0.8%	0.5%	39.2%	59.5%
Christianity	9.0%	32.8%	24.8%	33.3%
Sikhism	30.7%	0.9%	22.4%	46.1%
Jainism	0.0%	2.6%	3.0%	94.3%
Buddhism	89.5%	7.4%	0.4%	2.7%
Zoroastrianism	0.0%	15.9%	13.7%	70.4%
Others	2.6%	82.5%	6.25	8.7%
Total	**19.7%**	**8.5%**	**41.1%**	**30.8%**

---

[44] Facts and Details, *Different Hindu Castes*. Accessed May 01, 2018 http://factsanddetails.com/india/Religion_Caste_Folk_Beliefs_Death/sub7_2b/

Table 5 shows the breakdown of people below poverty line. These data are from National Sample Survey Organization (NSSO 55th & 61st Rounds). Justice Sachar Committee, set up in 2005 to analyze socio-economic status of Muslims, used these data[45].

Table 5

Breakdown of People below Poverty Line

Caste & Community Groups	Rural	Urban
Scheduled Tribes	45.8	35.6
Scheduled Castes	35.9	38.3
Other Backward Castes	27.0	29.5
Muslim Upper Castes	26.8	34.2
Hindu Upper Castes	11.7	09.9
Christian Upper Castes	09.6	05.4
Upper Caste Sikhs	00.0	04.9
Other Upper Castes	16.0	02.7
All Group	27.0	23.4

Source: National Sample Survey Organization.

Socio Economic and Caste Census (SECC) conducted in 2011, aimed at determining the socio economic status of rural and urban households, and rank them on various parameters. While several errors and overlaps were resolved between the States and Centre, there is limited compatibility between Census 2011 and SECC 2011 data. This is because their objectives, data collection modes, agencies involved, and confidentiality norms were different.

It clearly emerges that significant socio-economic differences and levels of deprivation across different religions and castes exist. Such factors can contribute to social discrimination and class conflict by themselves, even in the absence of politicization. Given the growing income inequalities, rising aspirations, acute agrarian distress and high unemployment, many issues can mar social cohesion and cause the discontent to boil over.

However, when political parties enter the fray, it is rarely for altruistic motives of ameliorating the lot of the poor and the discriminated. It is primarily to seize upon these issues to garner support of their vote banks, and in the process further deepen the fissures between castes and communities.

---

[45] Sachar, Rajinder (2006). *"Sachar Committee Report (2004–2005)"* (PDF). Government of India. p. 6. Retrieved May 01, 2018.

Among the most contentious issues is, *reservations*. In the heat and dust of politics, legitimate measures to address the genuine problem of inequality are obscured. Passions run high and rational discourse becomes impossible.

Many countries, including advanced economies such as USA practice *affirmative action* to help marginalized communities. Similarly, our Constitution too provides reservation of 15% to SCs and 7.2% to STs in Govt jobs and institutions of higher learning.

Janata Party govt under PM Morarji Desai set up the *Socially Backward Classes Commission* (SEBC) in 1979. The SEBC, better known as *Mandal Commission,* recommended *Other Backward Classes* (OBCs) be granted 27% reservations in addition to the 22.5% reservations already available to SCs and STs. This changed the entire socio-political dynamic. When the case reached the Supreme Court, it upheld OBC reservations, but ruled that the total percentage should not exceed 50%.

There was intense resentment among Upper castes, especially students, who saw it as *reverse discrimination,* and patently unfair to them. The intelligentsia too saw it as discouraging meritocracy. This set the trend of large number of students going abroad for higher studies. However, this did not deter Tamil Nadu, given the tempting electoral dividends, from enacting legislation to increase reservations to 69%.

Caste fault-lines are thus quite deep and affect social cohesion. Emotions are surcharged easily, especially in rural areas, where caste prejudices are still rampant. Caste violence invariably precedes every Local body, State or Lok Sabha poll.

Culture

Although culture is a comprehensive term that embraces all aspects of social customs, traditions and beliefs, I have discussed religion and caste separately because those two have the greatest impact on social cohesion. India is a vast sub-continent that has significant diversity in other cultural aspects too, such as language, apparel, food, ethnicity festivals etc.

While the Official Languages Act of 1963 accords official status to 22 languages, as per Census 2001 there are 122 major and 1599 other languages, along with numerous dialects. Indo-Aryan languages are spoken by 65% of the people, and Dravidian languages by 25%. Remaining 10% are minor languages.

The Madras Presidency launched the first agitation to oppose Hindi in 1937. Although Article 343 of the Indian Constitution provides for Hindi as the official National language, Southern

States opposed its introduction. Major riots broke out in Tamil Nadu in 1965, which subsided only after Prime Minister Shastri assured English continuing as official language until non-Hindi States wanted.

Politics and chauvinism have needlessly complicated the issue. The entire country communicates very well despite the multiplicity of languages, using the easy-to-understand *Hindustani* - a hybrid of common usage Hindi, Urdu and other dialects. However, the propensity of Hindi chauvinists to introduce grandiose terms, and equally stubborn refusal of politicians from the South to accept Hindi, still makes this a politically sensitive issue.

The common man couldn't care less; he is happy savouring Bollywood films, which are a melting pot of Indian culture. Sadly, there is politics here too, with some community or other raising objections to films on the ground that sentiments of their religion or community have been hurt. In many cases, riots and arson have taken place. Fortunately, the Supreme Court has refused to intervene if the Censor Board has cleared those films.

Ironically, numerous vocalists from the South have enthralled people with their rendition of Hindi songs, including *ghazals*. The public has bridged the cultural divide in music, arts, language, cuisine, apparel and festivals. Only politicians and self-anointed community leaders rake up such issues, generally close to polls.

Sub-Nationalism impedes social cohesion, as it flaunts its distinct identity, which militates against adopting a National perspective. However, when it creates extra-territorial affiliations at expense of National interests then it is the fraught with danger.

It was quite justifiable for Tamils to be upset over the plight of Tamil minority in Sri Lanka. However, pursuant to the launch of IPKF operations, for some of them to berate Indian soldiers who were merely acting on orders, cannot be justified. Perhaps the most deplorable manifestation of sub-Nationalism was elements in Tamil Nadu helping LTTE to assassinate Rajiv Gandhi.

There is inadequate emotional integration between people of Northeastern states and rest of India. Although most erstwhile insurgencies stand settled, proactive measures are required to remedy their sense of alienation. People of India, especially in the Hindi heartland, must be more sensitive towards their culture and help assimilate them into the mainstream.

Alienation among some people in J&K, though confined only to Muslims in Kashmir valley, is actively conspired and abetted by Pakistan. Hindu population in Jammu region, Shia Muslims in

Kargil and Zanskar valley, and the Buddhists in Ladakh however do not feel alienated from the rest of the country.

Geopolitical factors confound this issue, which has a long history, and it can only be resolved politically. Presently cross-border terrorism, street turbulence amid stone pelting by youth, and a volatile situation on the LoC are a cause for deep concern.

Naxalite violence affects large areas of the Indian heartland in Jharkhand, Chhattisgarh, Andhra Pradesh, Maharashtra and Orissa. Their alienation is due to socio-economic factors, exploitation of traditional tribal lands, and ongoing indoctrination of the local populace by interested parties.

To sum up therefore, for a country of 1.3 billion people having such extraordinary diversity in religion, caste, culture and ethnicity, having absolute social cohesion is indeed a tall order. Yet, in the past 71 years we have done very well as compared to many other Nations having much less diversity, but which are still gripped by serious unrest and disorder.

The foregoing review and analysis however highlights that had it not been for political machinations of polarizing people for electoral gains, we would be an even more cohesive society.

8

Robust Economy and Inclusive Growth

National security interests of countries and their economic interests have a symbiotic relationship. They are inextricably intertwined and mutually reinforcing, and hence should not be considered in isolation. Countries do not merely safeguard their economic interests, but constantly advance them through suitable politico-economic, national security policies. Even military power has been used to increase economic strength, as wars all through the ages amply illustrate.

In the present-day world however, security and/or economic alliances are subtle manoeuvring by countries to increase their economic power. Use of military force for *power balancing* is decreasing, while economic relations are increasing in numbers and complexity[46]. Even in multilateral agencies like the WTO, the writ of powerful nations prevails.

Economic strength provides the resources to maintain a strong military force to ensure defence against foreign aggression. It is also a dependable safeguard against economic exploitation and hegemonic coercion. These aspects pertaining to the Nation's *external environment* will be discussed in Part 3 of the book.

A robust economy is equally relevant in the country's *internal environment,* wherein equitable distribution of economic gains is important. It is also pertinent to examine whether those gains have improved the quality of life of its citizens. This chapter analyzes these aspects.

Data

No worthwhile economic analysis is possible without reliable data. Long-term trend analyses need authentic longitudinal data. Those must be based on defined variables and uniform collection norms across States and their collection and collation agencies.

For a vast country as ours, such data is hard to come by because we have not yet achieved the desired uniformity. Since statistics can be used as much to *conceal* as to *reveal,* Govts often *shift the*

---

[46] Keohane, R. and Nye, J. (1989) *Power and Interdependence: World Politics in Transition.* 2nd edition. Little-Brown, Boston.

goal posts by tinkering with the Base year *etc* in order to colour their performance.

Graphics and analyses in this chapter are based on data from UNCTAD (United Nations Conference on Trade & Development) and World Bank databases that adhere to international standards. These are reliable and have been normalised to constant prices.

It could be argued that these bodies do not themselves collect data and depend only on data collated by various Govts. However, they have panels of reputed experts that sift through the data, reconcile discrepancies, and ensure uniformity.

Industrialization

There was virtually no industrial development or infrastructure at the time of India's independence. Our colonial masters did not create it deliberately, and almost everything was imported. They did construct railway and telephone network but only to help them govern the vast country. They also set up some Ordnance factories to aid their wartime effort.

Independent India therefore started virtually from scratch, and embarked upon industrialization on a huge scale. Resources were very scarce, as the British had drained the economy during the two world wars. However, with astute planning and prioritization large infrastructure projects and industrial plants started coming up.

Tremendous enthusiasm was generated by this epic Nation-building effort. It generated thousands of jobs and the country started saving foreign exchange by reducing imports.

There was tremendous increase in irrigation and hydropower generation from huge dams like the Bhakra-Nangal, Tungabhadra and Hirakud projects. Durgapur, Bhilai, Rourkela and Bokaro steel plants boosted steel production, which is the backbone of any industrialized Nation. Hindustan Machine Tools, Bharat Heavy Electricals, Chittaranjan Locomotives, Integral Coach Factory, Bharat Earth Movers, Vishakhapatnam, and Mazagon Shipyards; these were among scores of projects that were completed within the first couple of decades after Independence.

National Physical and National Chemical laboratories, Indian Institute of Science and several other research and development organizations were established. Indian Institutes of Technology turned out several top scientists and entrepreneurs who went on to make their mark worldwide.

In the defence sector, Hindustan Aeronautics Limited (HAL) produced the HF24 and Gnat fighters (the latter under licence). Heavy Vehicle Factory at Avadi, Gun Carriage Factory at Jabalpur,

DRDO, DRDL, ERDL, ARDE and many other labs helped boost indigenous research, development, and production.

Crown jewels like Bhabha Atomic Research Centre, Tarapur and later series of nuclear reactors, and Indian Space Research Organization (ISRO) have really done the Nation proud. Vision of top political leadership set up these establishments in 1950 itself. Outstanding acumen and leadership of scientists such as Homi Bhabha, Vikram Sarabhai, HN Sethna and Raja Ramanna, who laid the foundation of excellence, gave us our extant advanced nuclear capability.

Vikram Sarabhai was the pioneer who set up ISRO. Later eminent scientists like Satish Dhawan, UR Rao and Kasturirangan nurtured the organization that recorded stunning achievements.

The Public Sector Debate

India consciously adopted the *mixed economy* model when *command economies* of USSR and China had an egalitarian appeal, for countries that wanted to *catch up* with advanced nations. However, virtually every country has a *mixed economy*; degrees vary on *market economy- command economy* continuum.

Our choice was obvious for many reasons, most importantly the need to industrialize rapidly. Besides, the private sector could not raise enormous resources required for huge projects. Govt also had to set up industries in the hinterland to spread development into the interior. Private sector, on the other hand, would have preferred coastal industrial belts that had better infrastructure, for purely economic considerations.

Due to scarce resources, Govt too had to go for financial and technical collaboration with foreign countries. Only inter-Govt agreements could enable this, since in that era there were no means for private sector to raise capital from Global markets.

While the public sector is now synonymous with inefficiency and losses, this was not so in the early years. Only later, trade unions, archaic labour laws, political interference, bureaucratic sloth and corruption started the rot. Even in the public sector there were examples of high productivity wherever there was excellent leadership; e.g. ONGC under Col Wahi's stewardship.

The Agricultural Sector

India is an agrarian economy and over 58% of the rural families depend on agriculture for their livelihood. The agriculture sector, including livestock, forestry and fishery contributed about 20.4%

of the Gross Value Added (GVA) during 2016-17 at current prices[47].

While agriculture dates back to the Indus Valley and later the Vedic civilizations, some accounts indicate South India practiced it even in the earlier eras[48]. Despite this history, post Independence India was not self-sufficient in food and relied heavily on imports.

India faced severe famine when there were droughts in 1965 and 1966. India received food shipments under PL-480 (Public Law 480), which was a US programme to provide food as grants or concessional terms. Touted as a humanitarian gesture, it furthered US foreign policy goals. Thus, even while India was facing a severe famine, President Johnson delayed PL-480 food shipments until India softened her criticism of US Viet Nam policy[49].

In response to this humiliation, Indira Gandhi initiated many agricultural reforms and spurred scientists into ushering in the Green Revolution. Under leadership of the eminent scientist MS Swaminathan, India's food production more than quadrupled and India is now a net exporter of food grains.

Most increases in food production came from the irrigation-fed states such as Punjab and Haryana. Other states, especially in Peninsular India are still dependent on the monsoons. Population growth too is outstripping increasing production. Despite vast improvement in agricultural growth, India still ranks 74 out of 113 major countries in the Global Food Security Index[50].

Floods and droughts hit every year, which belie production estimates. Our agrarian economy and agricultural industry are operating far below actual potential, mainly due to systemic and infrastructural reasons. There is no national-level holistic policy that factors in input costs, remunerative pricing, purchase and distribution mechanism, farm loans, crop insurance, and resolution of inter-state water disputes.

Even basic storage facilities are lacking, causing huge losses. Cold storages, refrigerated transportation, food processing, fisheries, animal husbandry, horticulture and floriculture are areas that could boost food production and reduce agrarian distress.

---

[47] India Brand Equity Foundation. https://www.ibef.org/industry/agriculture-india.aspx. Accessed May 12, 2018.

[48] Fuller; Korisettar, Ravi; Venkatasubbaiah, P.C.; Jones, Martink et al. 2004 "Early plant domestications in southern India: some preliminary archaeo-botanical results". *Vegetation History and Archaeobotany*.13(2),115-29.

[49] Office of the Historian. https://history.state.gov/milestones/1961-1968/pl-480. Retrieved May 12, 2018.

[50] *"India: Global Food Security Index"*. Retrieved May 12, 2018.

GDP Growth Rates

GDP growth rates are a widely accepted metric of the health of a Nations' economy. They are useful to monitor the impact of various policy measures by providing a good annual comparison, provided the measurement parameters remain constant. Charts at Figs. 7 and 8 show the annual GDP growth rates of India's economy during the periods 1961-1990 and 1991-2016.[51]

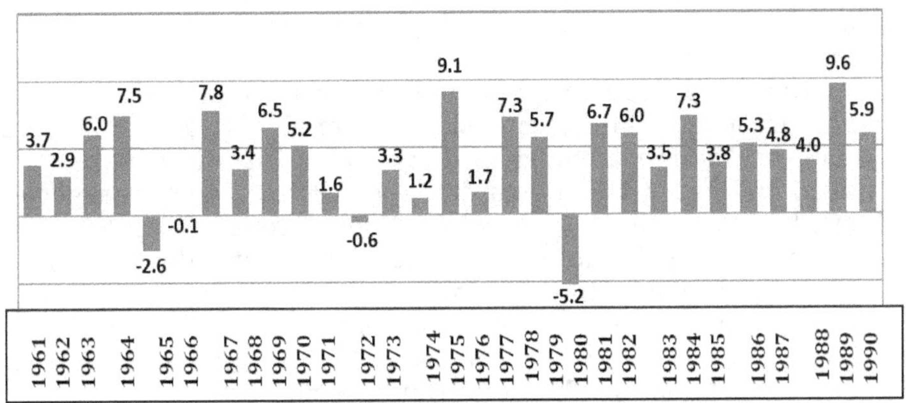

Fig. 7 - Annual GDP Growth Rates: 1961 – 1990

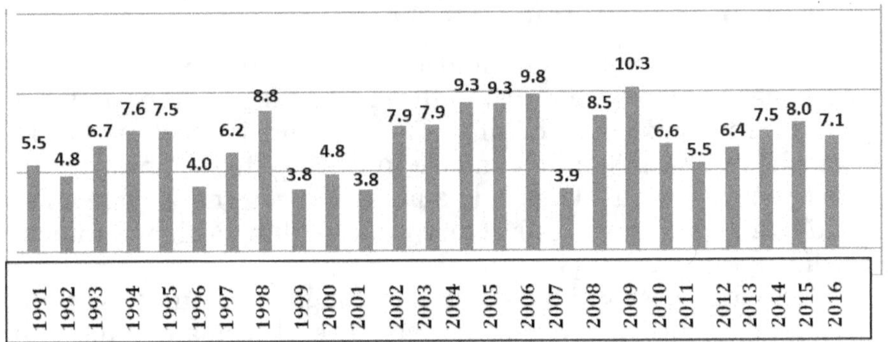

Fig. 8 - Annual GDP Growth Rates: 1991 – 2016

Economic Impact of Social Violence

In the previous chapter, I argued that riots, social unrest and a turbulent internal environment have severe consequences for the economy too. The negative impact on the economy shows up within one to two years. On the other hand, improvements in GDP

---

[51] Source: World Bank national accounts data, and OECD National Accounts data files. GDP growth (annual %). Annual percentage growth rate of GDP at market prices based on constant local currency. Aggregates are based on constant 2010 U.S. dollars.

due to economic reforms and other positive factors take two to three years to manifest themselves.

This can be verified from Fig. 6, when there was negative GDP growth during 1965 and 1966 (1965 War and severe drought), 1971-72 (1971 War) and 1977-78 (JP agitation). Similarly, Fig. 7 shows low GDP growth in 1991 (severe financial crisis); relatively low growth rate in 1992-93 (Babri Masjid riots and Mumbai bomb blasts); 2000-2002 (Gujarat riots, IA plane hijack, Parliament attack, Op Parakaram); 2008 (global financial meltdown, low capital inflows).

The sharp improvements in GDP growth rates during 1994-96 are attributable to the economic reforms initiated by Narasimha Rao and Manmohan Singh during 1991-93. Likewise, 2005-07 and 2010 had high GDP growth due to sound economic management and high capital inflows from FDI, FPI and remittances.

Institute for Economics and Peace, an independent, non-profit think-tank found a more definitive linkage of the negative impact of social unrest and violence on National economy from analysis of 163 countries. According to it, the Indian economy suffered a loss of $1.19 trillion in PPP terms (purchasing power parity) in 2017 due to social violence[52].

Spectacular Economic Turnaround

Indian economy was in doldrums in 1990-91, when its foreign exchange reserves were just sufficient to finance imports for 2-3 weeks. India pleaded for an IMF loan and it received the first tranche of $1.8 billion in January 1991. Despite this, by June 1991 there was a serious danger default on her external payments. We had to sell gold reserves in London, something as ignominious as selling family heirlooms.

Narasimha Rao and Manmohan Singh then initiated radical economic reforms on a war footing. Several regulatory and policy restrictions were removed, a market-denominated exchange rate was adopted, industrial licensing was abolished, and 51% automatic investments were allowed in many sectors[53].

---

[52] *"Economic cost of violence containment"* Report of Institute for Economics and Peace. Reported in The Hindu Business Line, 10 June 2018. https://www.thehindubusinessline.com/economy/violence-cost-indias-gdp-over-1-trn-on-ppp-basis/article24128123.ece

[53] Shankar Acharya, 2002. *India: Crisis, Reforms and Growth in the Nineties.* Center for Research on Economic Development and Policy Reform, Stanford University. Working Paper No.139.

These and many other reforms brought about a spectacular, turnaround in our economy. GDP growth saw a dramatic increase, FDI and FPI poured in, as did remittances from the Diaspora. India not only did not avail the remaining tranches of the IMF loan, but also repaid it before time.

This is in sharp contrast to some other economies. Turkey has been receiving IMF loans virtually every other year. Yet Turkey has never instituted the mandated structural reforms and necessary harsh measures, and has been taking advantage of the *moral hazard* factor of being the only Islamic country in NATO.

EQUITABLE DISTRIBUTION OF ECONOMIC GAINS

A country's economic strength contributes significantly to its overall security, but equitable distribution of economic gains is much more important for internal stability and cohesion. Security experts, economists and social scientists now therefore focus more upon the levels of poverty, Human Development Index (HDI) and income inequality in a country than just upon growth rates.

Poverty Levels

Poverty in India reached abysmal levels during the colonial era. The British did not allow industrialization, and even put curbs on local crafts to boost England's exports. They diverted the artisans for extensive poppy and opium cultivation in the Gangetic belt for export to China and Southeast Asia. Poverty and hunger kept increasing right up to the 1920s due to such crop diversion and many famines, which resulted in the death of millions[54].

Multiplicity of definitions of poverty and models to measure it, defy meaningful comparisons. Even the World Bank has modified its parameters for poverty several times. It now uses the *Modified Mixed Reference Period* (MMRP) method, where the poverty line is drawn at income of $1.90 per person per day at 2011 PPP[55].

In India, both income-based and consumption-based statistics determine poverty levels. Our *Multi-dimensional Poverty Index* also includes some non-economic indices; e.g., *years spent in school* are weighted 33%, and financial condition of a person is weighted 6.25% to determine the poverty level[56]. Different States

---

[54] Maddison, A. 1970, *The historical origins of Indian poverty*, PSL Quarterly Review, 23(92), pp. 31-81

[55] "Poverty & Equity Data" *povertydata.worldbank.org*. Retrieved 14 May 2018.

[56] "Country Briefing: India, Multidimensional Poverty Index (MPI) At a Glance". *Oxford Poverty and Human Development Initiative*. Retrieved 15 May 2018.

have set their own norms and thresholds to determine the number of people subsisting below the poverty line.

Historically India has used *sustenance food standard,* based on the amount spent by each person over a given period for a basket of essential goods. Further, it has set different poverty lines for urban and rural areas.

In 2011, the poverty threshold as per the Tendulkar committee report was ₹ 26 a day ($0.43) for rural areas, and ₹ 32 per day ($0.53) for urban areas[57]. These figures were below World Bank norms of $1.90, but were closer to China's official poverty line of $0.65 per day set in 2008[58]. Following a public outcry in 2014, the Rangarajan committee revised them to ₹ 32 a day ($0.53) for rural areas, and₹ 47 per day ($0.75) for urban areas[59].

Regardless of such variations in parameters, there has been a significant reduction in poverty. Between 2004 and 2011 poverty declined from 38.9% to 21.9% of the population at International poverty line (2011 PPP $1.90 per day). It must be noted that the *absolute* number of people below the poverty line will change if the poverty threshold is altered. Hence, to compare reduction in poverty over time, the poverty line threshold must be set to one standard. Graphic at Fig. 9 shows the reduction in poverty based on the International poverty line of $1.9 PPP.

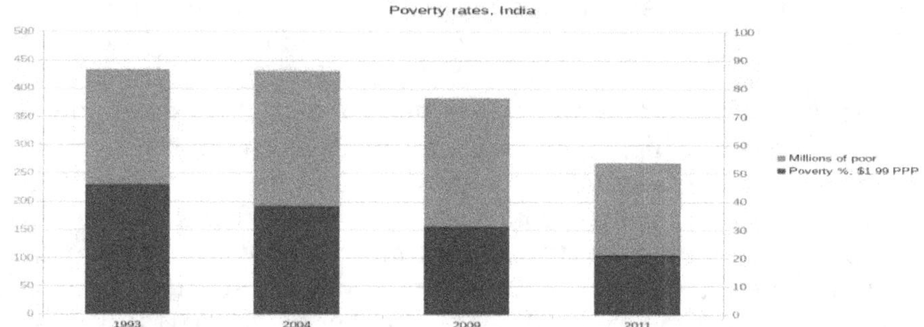

Source: UN's *Millennium Development Goals* programme

Fig. 9 – India's Poverty Rates: 1993 – 2011

---

[57] Panagariya & Mukim (2014), *A comprehensive analysis of poverty in India.* Asian Development Review, 31(1), pp. 1-52.

[58] Chen and Ravallion, *China is Poorer than we Thought, But No Less Successful in the Fight against Poverty.* Policy Research Working Paper 4621, The World Bank (2008), page 9.

[59] "New poverty line: Rs 32 in villages, Rs 47 in cities". *Times of India* 7 July 2014. Retrieved 15 May 2018.

Fig. 10 shows the geographical distribution of poverty levels within India.

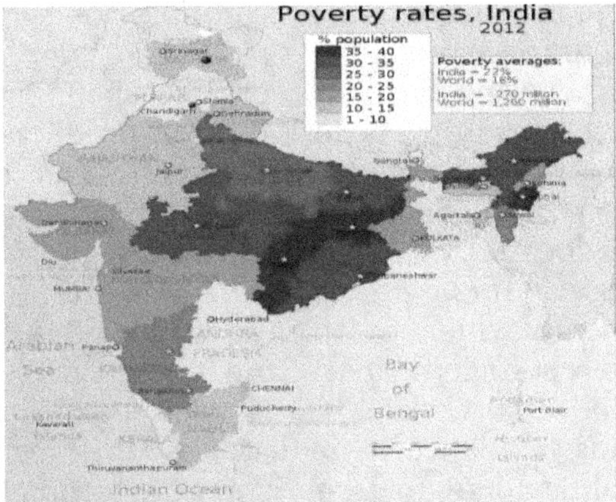

Fig. 10 – Poverty Distribution within India

According to United Nation's *Millennium Development Goals* programme 270 million or 21.9%, Indians were below the poverty line in 2011, based on Tendulkar committee norms. However, as per the Rangarajan Committee's revised norms, 363 million or about 29.5% of the population were below the poverty line.

It is deplorable for Govts to make exaggerated claims of lifting thousands of people out of poverty merely by statistical *jugglery*. We cannot reduce sub-human existence of millions to heartless statistics. Deaths due to hunger are shameful blots on our society, and tall claims to robust economic growth are of no consequence.

Unbridled population growth is a big cause of poverty, and puts pressure on subsistence, all human development parameters, and unemployment. At current growth rates, we will overtake China by 2025, which will have severe socio-economic implications. So-called Demographic dividend could well turn into disaster.

Farmer Suicides

Increasing incidence of farmer suicides is the most distressing element of our rural economy. Inability of farmers to get credit from rural cooperative banks forces them to raise loans at exorbitant rates from loan sharks. When crops are lost or when they are unable to sell even at the *Minimum Support Price,* numerous farmers are driven to suicide.

Due to systemic, policy, and infrastructural issues, suicides in the farm sector have been increasing alarmingly. In 2016, there were 11,370 suicides, which included 6351 farmers and 5019 farm workers[60]. Shamefully, even this humanitarian crisis has seen only crass politicization on either side of the political divide. Ruling party politicians often cite *other motives* for such suicides, like family problems and infidelity.

Many farmers and farm workers are abandoning agriculture. Apart from the resulting in loss of food production, it increases migration to over-saturated cities, and further compounds the unemployment problem.

The Govt does provide some relief through *Mahatma Gandhi National Rural Employment Guarantee Act* (MGNREGA) by giving wage-employment for 100 days in a financial year. This is however barely sufficient, apart from it being unproductive.

State and the Central Govts also occasionally waive off farmers' loans to reduce their distress. However, it has become more of a political ploy to garner votes at election time. Such loan waivers also put great stress on the financial health of banks, which in turn has a cascading effect on the National economy.

Human Development Index

The Human Development Index (HDI) is a composite statistic used to rank countries by the level of *"human development"* based on three dimensions, *life expectancy, education,* and *decent standard of living.* Pakistani economist Mahbub ul Haq and India's Amartya Sen developed it in 1990 for the United Nations Development Programme.

The following graphic shows its dimensions and measures[61].

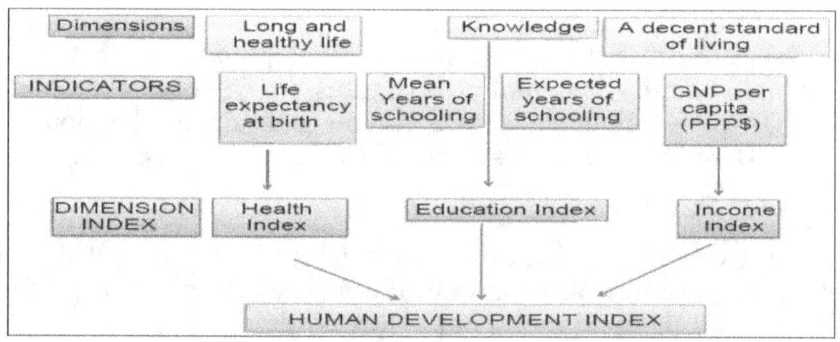

Fig. 11 – Human Development Index

---

[60] The Hindu report based on information provided in Lok Sahba by MOS for Agriculture and Farmers Welfare. Accessed May 12, 2018.

[61] *Sustainability and Equity: A better Future for all.* UNDP. Human development report - New York: Palgrave Macmillan; 2011.

Compared with raw poverty data, HDI is a better measure to rate the quality of life of a country's people since it captures three important aspects of human existence. When combined with other socio-economic parameters it gives a better idea how successful are the country's development programmes, and which aspects and regions require more investment.

While India has indeed done a commendable job in putting its economy on a high-growth trajectory since 1990-91, in terms of the HDI it ranked a dismal 131 out of 185 countries rated in the last report released in March 2017 based on 2015-16 data. Sri Lanka at rank 73 and China at 90 ranked ahead of India. Only Bhutan (132), Bangladesh (139), Nepal (144) and Pakistan (147) were lower than India in South Asia. A large number of developing countries from Asia, Africa and Latin America provide a better quality of life to its citizens than India does.

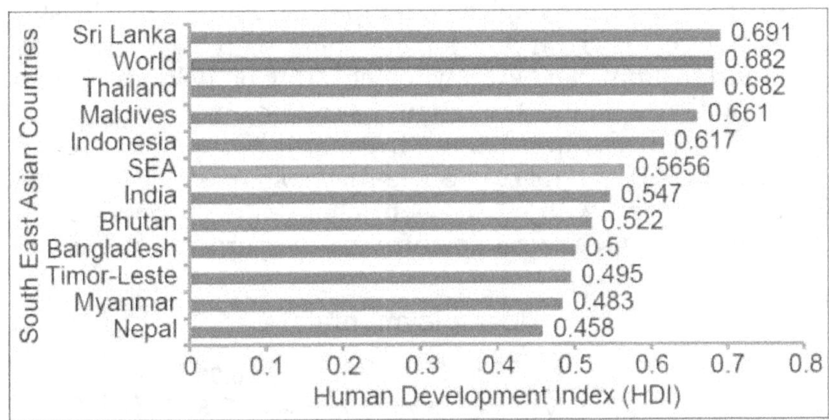

Fig.12 – HDI Scores of South East Asian Countries in 2011

India's 2015 HDI score of 0.624 was an improvement over 2011 score of 0.547. However, this score improved its ranking by just three positions from 134 in 2011, when India stood fifth in South East Asia, behind Sri Lanka, Thailand, Maldives and Indonesia[62].

Unemployment

India has high unemployment rates. Data from the *Centre for Monitoring the Indian Economy* (CMIE) in February 2018 shows 31 million were jobless. The rate rose to 6.1% and was the highest in the preceding 15 months.

---

[62] Kalpa Sharma. 2013. *Human development and South East Asian countries: Special emphasis on India.* Journal of Education and Health Promotion 2:45.

India has a young population and with more youth joining the work force and slower job creation, the problem is getting more acute. Anxiety, despair and angst among the youth can lead to serious problems in society. Unfortunately, Govt has not set clear criteria to define who it considers as being *unemployed*. There is no uniformity in data variables and collation norms, and hence no worthwhile cross-sectional or time series analyses are possible.

Parameters need precise definition, e.g. in the rural sector, farmers and farm labour, seasonal employment, MGNREGA employment, self-employed artisans etc. In urban areas: organized or unorganized sectors, daily-wagers, and self-employment.

Without credible data, there is confusion galore. Here too the political class compounds the problem. While the Ruling party uses dubious statistics, or cherry-picks data to make tall claims and promises, the Opposition projects *gloom and doom*.

All this leaves the hapless unemployed youth more frustrated. When politicians claim that jobless youth with high qualifications are *gainfully employed* even when hawking petty items or working in low-skill jobs, that is tantamount to adding insult to injury.

The following graphic shows the monthly unemployment rates as per the CMIE database[63]. Since they collate data every week on the same criteria without frequent changes, they provide a more contemporary and accurate picture for comparative analysis.

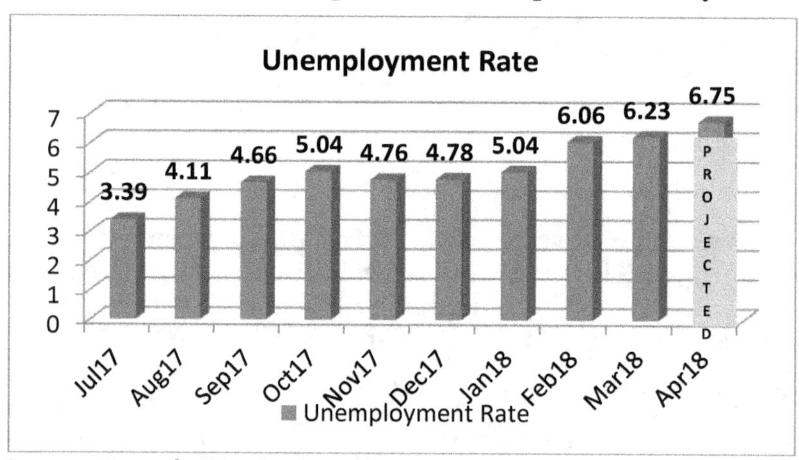

Source: Centre for Monitoring Indian Economy

Fig. 13 – Monthly Unemployment Rate 2017-18

---

[63] Centre for Monitoring Indian Economy.
https://www.cmie.com/kommon/bin/sr.php?kall=warticle&dt=2018-04-17%2009:27:18&msec=093&ver=pf. Retrieved 17 May 2018

Demonetization

It was the most bitterly contested economic measure in recent times; described as *mindless carpet-bombing* of the economy. Its purported intent was to unearth *black money*, stamp out terror financing, and counterfeit currency pumped in by Pakistan.

The Govt when faced with public anger touted other benefits later, as after-thoughts. It is not within the scope to critique Govt policies, since intent is to assess the impact on internal security.

Some basic issues however need clarity to know the cause of economic turbulence. No direct empirical co-relation exists between *cash* inside or outside banking system, and *tax evasion*.

With plethora of sources that generate *black money*, a *one size fits all* solution was infeasible. Several coordinated and coherent measures were necessary. Was demonetization the ideal tool, given its huge cost and terrible logistics?

- Business houses evade corporate taxes through mechanisms such as *transfer pricing, round-tripping,* shell companies in tax havens, etc. The measure did not affect those practices.

- It did not affect personal taxes of corporate honchos, as they do not get salary in cash. Most would have stashed unaccounted wealth in foreign tax havens.

- Many politicians, bureaucrats and professionals too would have deposited their ill-gotten wealth abroad.

- Black money is stashed as real estate, gold and other assets, which required separate detection and punitive measures.

- It affected cash transactions in *satta, hawala,* drugs, weapons, counterfeiting and other illicit activities, but only temporarily.

- The Govt should have anticipated that people would convert *black money* via *Jan Dhan* accounts and third party transactions by keeping them below the announced threshold.

- While tens of thousands toiled long hours in queues to change old notes for new, corrupt bank officials changed astronomical amounts through *the backdoor.*

- *Black money* is the biggest contributor to poll financing of all political parties. There was widespread suspicion that the Govt's intent was to upstage Opposition parties ahead of vital assembly polls. As a bonus, they reaped the propaganda value of dubbing Opposition protests as *pro-black money.*

Reserve Bank of India, in its report released on 29 August 2018, confirmed that 99.3% of cash in circulation upon demonetization, is now back with it. This leaves a tiny amount of unaccounted cash, which begs the question was demonetization worth the pain, expense, and economic disruption it caused. It is obvious the Govt's *stated aims* were not achieved, although its *unstated aims*, as alleged by the Opposition, were certainly achieved.

Demonetization did not yield desired results, but it sucked out 85% of cash and delivered a body blow to the economy. There were huge costs of printing and transportation of new notes to remote corners. Enormous task of replacement, manually and through ATMs - the latter only after re-calibration, took a long time.

By all accounts, there is not even a dent to the scourge of *black money,* in the absence of complementary measures. There is also no reduction in terrorism, terror-finance, or counterfeit currency.

Demonetization severely hit industry, especially small, medium and micro enterprises, which ran out of working capital. Artisans and the unorganized sector suffered most, and many closed down. Lack of cash severely hit the rural economy too, especially since the measure coincided with the sowing season.

It caused a slowdown in GDP growth from 8.1% in 2015-16 to 7.1% in 2016-17 (only for five months of demonetization). It came down to 6.6% in 2017-18, reflecting its full impact. In monetary terms, the country produced $48.01 billion less than its intrinsic potential. As per the erstwhile CAG's notion, India suffered a *notional loss* of that enormous amount.

The long-term impact persists. SMEs and businesses that shut down or incurred huge losses could not have recovered overnight, when money supply resumed. The projected growth rate of 6.9% in 2018-19 thus reflects its cascading effect.

The measure took a deadly toll on the labour market, further aggravating unemployment. Labour participation rate fell from 46.4% in Oct 2016 to 42.8% in Jul 2017. In the organized sector, as against 414 million employed in October 2016, only 407 million had employment by February 2017[64].

Impact was far more severe in the unorganized sector, with daily wagers taking the biggest hit. However, it was not just loss of 19 million jobs overall for eight months, but even more worrisome is the continuing slowdown in the creation of new jobs.

---

[64] Center for Monitoring Indian Economy https://www.cmie.com/kommon/bin/sr.php?kall=warticle&dt=2018-03-13%2009:33:58&msec=963 Retrieved 18 May 2018.

Promise of 20 million new jobs every year in itself was very far from reality. However, with the resultant slowdown aggravating the job market, there is a grave danger that the much-touted *demographic dividend* may not turn into a *demographic disaster*.

Adding to the economic woes was the Goods and Services Tax (GST) regime. It was an overdue measure, but introduced without the planning it warranted. Result was confusion, harassment and protests. Besides, it created more sluggishness in the economy.

Rising Income Inequality

Sections on poverty, HDI and unemployment amply highlight that fruits of high economic growth are yet to reach large sections of our society. Can it be at peace with itself when there are large numbers of farmer suicides and severe hunger and malnutrition? In many dimensions of HDI, our record is worse than even some Afro-Asian and Latin American LCDs (least developed countries).

Growing gap between the rich and poor has serious implication for societal stability. As Fig. 10 showed, vast swathes in the Indian heartland have abysmally high poverty levels. Is it a surprise that those areas have highest social turmoil and even armed rebellion? Fig. 14 shows the rise in income inequality from 2000 to 2016.

As second-most *unequal* country globally, our millionaires control 54% of its wealth. With a total individual wealth of $5,600 billion, India is among the 10 richest countries in the world – and yet the average Indian is very poor[65].

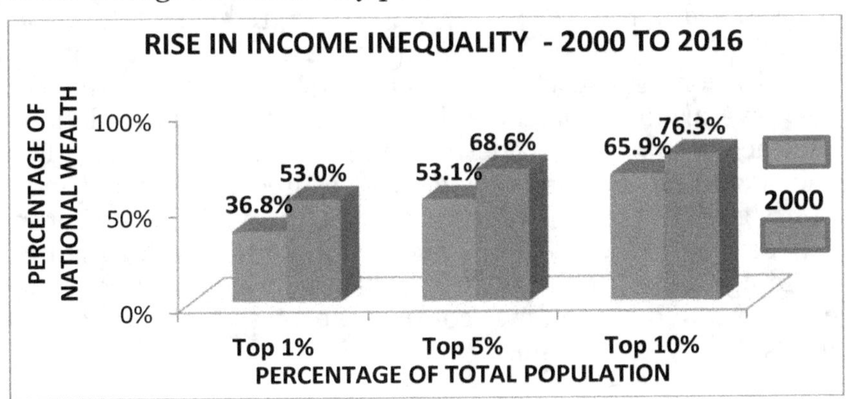

Source: World Economic Forum

Fig. 14 – Rise in income inequality from 2000 to 2016

---

65 World Economic Forum *Inequality in India: what's the real story?* https://www.weforum.org/agenda/2016/10/inequality-in-india-oxfam-explainer. Accessed 18 May 2018.

India's income inequality is the highest even among the BRICS countries, except South Africa. However, South Africa's efforts to close the income gap are better than the measures India has taken. While India spends only 3% of GDP on education, South Africa spends twice as much (6.1%). Similarly, India spends just 1.1% on healthcare, but South Africa spends more than three times (3.7%).

GINI coefficient, a metric used by UNDP, measures income inequality. It is a number between zero and one where zero signifies perfect income *equality,* and one with perfect *inequality.*

India's GINI coefficient as per UNDP is 0.35, which shows that we are just 35% away from perfect income *equality.* China's GINI coefficient is 0.42, signifying greater income inequality than India. This is strange, since the Communist regime claims to be a more egalitarian society[66].

Pertinently, *income* metric does not include income from *black market* economy. *Income distribution* is very different from *wealth distribution. Wealth GINI coefficients* are therefore more revealing, especially for countries that transact large amounts in the *parallel* economy.

India's *Wealth GINI* coefficient is 0.669, while that of China is 0.550. This implies that India has even higher *wealth disparity,* almost double that of *income disparity.* China's *wealth disparity* is also high, but not as high as in India[67].

Correlation with Incidence of Crime

Dire need for poverty alleviation and reduction in income inequality is not just for humanitarian reasons alone. It is obvious that reduction in poverty and income inequality would lower crime rates. Several empirical studies have established that correlation.

In their 2002 study, Lederman and Loayza of the World Bank established that *income inequality,* measured by the GINI index, has a significant and positive effect on the incidence of crime. Their data included homicide and robbery rates in 39 countries (including India) for the period 1965-1995. The statistical results were robust and the findings consistent across all countries, time-periods, and types of crime[68].

---

[66] World Bank GINI index. Accessed, 19 May 2018.

[67] "Global Wealth Databook 2016". *Credit Suisse Research Institute.* Accessed, 19 May 2018.

[68] Pablo Fajnzylber, Daniel Lederman, Norman Loayza, "Inequality and violent crime". *Journal of Law and Economics,* Vol. XLV, April 2002.

Our *National Crime Records Bureau* (NCRB) data for 34 metropolitan cities shows an increase of 13.5% IPC crimes from 2014 to 2016. At first glance, this might seem anomalous, given that in those years India had experienced close to 8% economic growth. However, what is more relevant is the fact that despite the high growth, *income inequality* had increased, thus leading to more anger and increased propensity for resorting to crime[69].

Our polity, society, films and the pervading social milieu too have a major impact in this regard. Our youth are deluged with images of incredible affluence in our movies. Vulgar public display of wealth by business tycoons, politicians, and bureaucrats continually pollute their minds. This contrasts sharply with their own poverty, joblessness, and unfulfilled aspirations.

Their frustration and anger is fanned further since they face corruption and harassment in Govt offices and in almost all their endeavours. On the other hand, politicians and tycoons get away with enormous scams and bank frauds. Law seems to favour only the high and mighty, who conveniently escape abroad.

Unemployment, growing gap between the *haves and have-nots,* an insatiable urge to *get-rich-quick,* together with lax and even complicit law enforcement machinery, is bound to lead to more crime. The increasing incidence of violent as well as white-collar crimes clearly points to the need for more *inclusive growth* and greater economic justice.

In sum, therefore, while India has made impressive gains in overall economic growth, her record in poverty alleviation, economic justice, and employment generation is very poor indeed. These aspects are by far, extremely pertinent for internal stability. If the Govt does not take remedial and ameliorative measures, these are bound to lead to more internal security problems.

---

[69] NCRB Crimes in metropolitan cities http://ncrb.gov.in Accessed 19 May 2018

9

Integrity of Institutions

The principle of *separation of powers* has deep philosophical roots, and is a notion that dates back to ancient Rome. James Madison, who was among the Founding Fathers of the United States and helped draft its Constitution and Bill of Rights had said, *"If men were angels, no government would be necessary."* There is indeed a need for separation of powers of the *Executive, Legislative* and *Judicial* branches of the Government to preclude undue concentration of power or trespass into another's domain[70].

India's Constitution enshrines the same principle in our own system of Parliamentary democracy. Framers of our Constitution had instituted several *checks and balances* to ensure that any attempt by a Branch to usurp excessive power is held in check by other two branches. However, unless the polity follows this dictum in letter and spirit, any despotic propensity of the *Executive* could well turn democracy into a totalitarian autocracy.

Several institutions are instruments of the *checks and balances* regime in a democracy. Our Constitution has vested statutory authority in many of them, and it insulates them from extraneous pressures and influences. Several others function as independent watchdogs based on the professional ethics expected of them and the healthy traditions of a truly vibrant democracy.

Judiciary

Supreme Court (SC) is the *final court of appeal* and the highest constitutional court, with the power of constitutional review. Its rulings are binding on the Central and State Govts and all lower courts. Given its vast powers, including the power to strike down laws passed by Parliament or State legislatures if it deems them *ultra vires* of the Constitution, it has often been in conflict with the Executive.

The Executive in most democracies; more so in India, feels constrained by the limitations imposed by the Constitution in their exercise of power. Just as the Monarchs of yore who believed in the *divine right of kings,* they believe that on being *elected* they

---

[70] *Checks and Balances,* https://www.history.com/topics/checks-and-balances. Accessed 21 May 2018.

are automatically entitled to unbridled power. They view the *checks and balances* mandated by the Constitution as unjustified impositions, and frequently try to circumvent them.

This takes several forms; the least strident of which is the tirade against the SC about *legislating from the Bench*. Fanned through a conniving Media, such assertions are meant to intimidate Judges into exercising self-restraint. There are also the *carrots* of quasi-judicial positions and Chairmanship of various Commissions after their retirement.

Collegium

By far the most brazen way of negating the Constitutional intent is to appoint, *suitable* judges to the SC. Prior to 1993, the President appointed judges on the advice of the Union Cabinet. This allowed the Executive to pack the court with so-called *committed judges.*

All Presidents in the United States seek to appoint *committed judges, conservative* or *liberal,* depending upon their political leanings. However, in USA the Senate Judiciary Committee has to approve the President's judicial nominations, which is a strong and credible check against arbitrary appointments. They also need to get Congressional approval.

In India, there is no such provision and therefore in 1993 after the *Second Judges' Case* the SC ruled that no Minister or even the Union Cabinet could recommend a judge directly to the President. Only the *collegium* of the SC (it comprises: Chief Justice and four senior-most judges of SC, and senior-most judge of the HC of the recommended judge) can send nominations through the cabinet, for approval by the President[71].

Peer-review is a well-established tradition in many institutions, which ensures objectivity in recommendations for appointment or promotion. In academia, all reputed journals accept papers for publication only after a stringent double-blind, *peer-review* process. Tenure and promotions too are granted with the same process. The *collegium* system is therefore fair and objective since senior judges are best suited to appraise the competence of the recommended appointees.

The *collegium* system however needs not only to be fair, but must *appear to be fair* and transparent. Quite often there is

---

[71] Kirpal, Bhupinder N., ed. (2013). *Supreme but not infallible: Essays in honour of the Supreme Court of India* (6th impr. ed.). New Delhi: Oxford University Press. pp. 97–106.

criticism, and in many cases justifiably so, about it being a closed club. Nepotism seems to ensure that a disproportionately large number of relatives get entry into it.

The Govt can return the *collegium's* recommendation only once, and has no option but to accept if the SC reiterates it. However, to thwart this provision the Govt simply *sleeps over* the *collegium's* recommendation. SC vacancies thus increase, and it virtually arm-twists the SC to withdraw its recommendation.

Since Independence, SC has mostly acquitted itself honourably, except during the Emergency. However, of late the tussle between the Executive and the SC has intensified. The fact that all is not well even within the SC was highlighted when four senior judges held a press conference to air misgivings in public. Terms, such as *bench fixing* and *bench shopping,* were hurled by protagonists.

Given the adage *there cannot be smoke without a fire,* the common man can only feel frustrated and disillusioned that even this bastion of our democracy is now under a cloud.

Judicial System and the Common Man

According to a report of *Transparency International,* a NGO based in Berlin, judicial corruption is rampant in India[72]. While in the early years it was confined mainly to the lower courts, later in tandem with the steep decline in public morality in our society, it is now entrenched even in the higher judiciary.

There have been murmurs about corruption even in the highest court of the land. There have been appointments of Judges with a tainted past, not just to the High Court (HC) but also to the SC. One HC judge was impeached and several others have had serious allegations against them.

Besides the concerns raised by prominent members of the Bar, even eminent retired Chief Justices of the SC have voiced their anguish at the increasing levels of corruption[73]. Even former President APJ Abdul Kalam and the usually reticent PM Manmohan Singh had to highlight this menace, which underscores how serious is the malaise[74].

---

[72] "India Corruption Study 2005" (PDF). Transparency International India. Retrieved 22 May 2018.

[73] "Wrong people sometimes elevated to higher judiciary: Ex-CJI Verma". *Times of india*. 27 June 2011. Retrieved 22 May 2018.

[74] Manmohan Singh calls for check on corruption in judiciary, Thaindian News, 19 April 2008. Accessed 22 May 2018

Millions of cases are pending in Indian courts at various stages of the judicial process. This alarming situation is due to many factors, the most important being over 20% of vacancies in judges' appointments. In 2015, there were over 400 vacancies of judges in various HCs. There are vacancies in the SC itself where over 65000 cases are pending[75].

It is a pity that the Govt itself is the biggest litigant. Several courts have adversely commented upon its stubborn propensity to keep going in appeal. Defence personnel and veterans particularly, have faced such harassment at the hands of the MoD, even though courts have passed strictures and even imposed fines on it[76].

Major fallout of the judicial backlog is the huge number of under-trials languishing in prisons for inordinately long periods, which leads to overcrowding of jails. Frequent and unjustified adjournments, no strict enforcement of perjury laws, and litigation of petty issues further compound the problem.

Where does all this leave the common man? Naturally, peoples' faith in the judicial process is at its nadir. They watch with angst how the rich and powerful, assisted by legal luminaries, get away with even serious crimes, or just escape abroad.

Such disillusionment portends dangerous consequences. As highlighted in previous chapter, the poor and the unemployed are increasingly being driven to crime. With lax law enforcement, and the police and the judicial system being prone to corruption, youth are tempted to take this path. Once they enter the world of crime, they can only sink deeper.

Election Commission

Conducting free and fair elections in a vast country, as India, with its huge electorate is an onerous task. Our Constitution provides for an autonomous Election Commission (EC) to conduct elections to both houses of Parliament, State legislatures, and to offices of President and Vice President. Until 1989, it had just the Chief Election Commissioner, but later after an amendment to the Act, it became a three-member body.

Elections in many countries, including advanced Nations are often questioned due to real or alleged electoral malpractices. Even USA is no exception, as the *chad* controversy in the 1999

---

[75] "Report No. 245 (July 2014) – Arrears and Backlog: Creating Additional Judicial (Wo)manpower". Law Commission of India. Accessed 22 May 2018
[76] Seth, Leila (2014). *Talking of Justice: People's Rights in Modern India*. New Delhi: Aleph. p. 115.

election, and the more recent *Russian interference* allegations illustrate.

India can be proud that our ECs have conducted the electoral process diligently, which yielded fair and credible results. This is no mean achievement given the highly politicized and communally polarized environment around election time, and vast swathes of the countryside being prone to electoral violence.

Over the years, the EC has refined and imparted greater credibility with multi-phase elections, adequate deployment of security personnel to preclude booth capturing and use of EVMs. It is now introducing VVPATs to enable a verifiable paper trail.

Occasionally political parties raise issues about EC's fairness, as for instance about the recent the timings of assembly polls, but this institution has largely our democracy well.

Comptroller and Auditor General (CAG)

CAG is an independent statutory body that exercises oversight over the Govt's financial transactions. It audits all receipts and expenditure of Central and State Govt, including those of bodies and authorities significantly financed by the Govt. Its observations carry a lot of weight with the Public Accounts Committee of the Parliament,

However, the CAG does not audit almost 65% of Govt spending. In many cases, Govt departments do not even produce documents demanded by him. An increasing number of high-cost projects are now being financed under the private-public-partnership model, but those too are not under the CAG's purview. Likewise, the Panchayti Raj institutions, which receive a lot of Govt funding, are beyond his scrutiny.

It is hardly a secret that corruption is rampant in these bodies. It is therefore open to question if bringing them within the ambit of CAG does not suit politicians, who have high stakes in them financially and in terms of political patronage.

Although the Constitution intended the CAG to be independent and apolitical, the appointee is selected at the PM's discretion. There has been criticism on both sides of the aisle about the CAG's partisanship, he being a political appointee.

Given his vital role and his stature being that of a SC judge, ex-Deputy PM Advani had recommended that he too should be selected by a *collegium.* Another proposal was to increase it to a three-member body, but the Govt, which would like to retain its leverage, did not accept both.

Does this affect the common man? Not directly. Nonetheless, it adds to the pervading cynicism about the claim of all political parties, that they are strongly committed to transparency and good governance.

Ombudsman

An Ombudsman is an independent official whose role is to investigate complaints of maladministration by public officials and about violation of the rights of the people. The term itself is of Scandinavian origin, where it has been used since the 17th century. However, the concept had been adopted in diverse forms even in ancient China (Qin dynasty 221 BC), Korea[77], India, Japan and Turkey[78].

In the modern era, most countries have such an appointment as a safeguard against corruption and misconduct by high-ranking public servants and politicians. In India, the *Central Vigilance Commission* (CVC) exercises oversight over Chief Vigilance Officers appointed in various organizations, banks and PSUs.

The Administrative Reforms Commission headed by Morarji Desai had recommended setting up of Lokpal at the Centre and Lokayuktas in each state. Though introduced in 1968, the Bill languished since the political class was averse to oversight upon themselves. Reintroduced in 2005, it met the same fate.

After Anna Hazare's nationwide campaign, the UPA2 Govt got the bill passed in 2013. However, despite its poll promise the NDA Govt is yet to appoint a Lokpal at the Centre. Not all states have passed the Lokayukta bill, and many states that have passed it are yet to appoint one.

Numerous frauds keep coming to light routinely, and most involve politicians directly or as beneficiaries. Unsurprisingly therefore, people are angry at the Govt's refusal to appoint a Lokpal in defiance of the Act.

Investigation Agencies

The Criminal Bureau of Investigation (CBI), as the country's premier investigation agency, plays an important role to instil confidence in the rule of law. It investigates complex criminal and economic offences once authorized by the Central Govt. States too

---

[77] Park, S. (2008). "Korean Preaching, Han, and Narrative (American University Studies. Series VII. Theology and Religion)".

[78] Pickl, V. (1987). "Islamic Roots of Ombudsman Systems". *The Ombudsman Journal.*

can recommend a CBI inquiry for important high-profile cases. However, the SC and the HCs can order CBI inquiry without the consent of the Central or State Govts[79].

The public often distrusts local police due to political meddling or incompetence, and hence there are frequent demands for CBI investigations. The CBI therefore has a reputation to maintain, lest its credibility be called to question.

Unfortunately, that has taken a beating. Even the SC called it a *"caged parrot speaking in its master's voice"* due to political interference in its functioning[80]. There have also been cases where the CBI has botched up investigations, due to either incompetence or the agency's internal dynamics.

Given the high political stakes, no Govt has been willing to *free the caged parrot*. Even the appointment of the Director is often a subject of intense political criticism, even though the panel must include the Leader of the Opposition and the Chief Justice or a Judge of the SC, besides the PM. The Govt, in a brazen move, amended the Act in November 2014, to do away with the requirement of a quorum in the selection committee.

The National Investigation Agency (NIA) is a specialized agency set up after the 2008 Mumbai terror attacks. It can investigate cases across all States without taking prior approval of the State Govt. It can set up Special NIA courts to try terror-related cases on a day-to-day basis.

It has notched several successes in seizing high-profile terrorists, and even getting some of them extradited from foreign countries. It has achieved a high conviction rate of 95% since its inception[81]. Although it was criticized for being swayed by political influence in a couple of cases, overall its reputation stays intact.

Police and Law Enforcement

Law and order being a State subject as per India's Constitution, police forces maintained by States are responsible for ensuring that the writ of law runs in their jurisdiction. Since citizens depend on them for the safety and security of their lives and property,

---

[79] *"Supreme Court judgment on power of courts to order CBI probe"*. *indiankanoon.org*. Retrieved 24 May 2018.

[80] Ross Colvin and Satarupa Bhattacharjya. "A *"caged parrot"* - *Supreme Court describes CBI"*. Reuters. Retrieved 24 May 2018.

[81] *"Our conviction rate is 95%: NIA DG YC Modi"*. 2018-01-24. Retrieved 24 May 2018

training, diligence, accessibility and credibility of the police are vital to earn the confidence of the people.

Unfortunately, due to a host of reasons the police have neither attained the standards expected of a modern police force, nor fully earned the people's confidence. Some of them are poor training, antiquated equipment, personnel shortage, long duty hours, low pay, political interference and corruption.

Police reforms that include a complete overhaul of the structure are long overdue. These have not been instituted due to political apathy, lack of resources, and because maintaining the *status quo* apparently suits deeply entrenched interests.

A cosy nexus seems to exist wherein the rich and powerful can get away with any crime through political influence, high-profile lawyers and bribes. The poor and the ordinary law-abiding citizens are often at the receiving end in the current system. This is adding to the growing frustration of the poor and unemployed, and contributing to increase in crime as highlighted earlier.

Media

The *Fourth Estate* is as an important pillar of democracy. It is an institution, which wields significant influence over society, but is not a part of the political system. The term is attributed to Thomas Macaulay, a British historian and politician in early 19th century[82]. Originally, it applied to the *Press*, but now it includes entire *news media,* printed and electronic.

In the context of *separation of powers* principle, it is expected to be a *watchdog* of our democracy, and be independent enough to highlight boldly the shortcomings of other pillars. That is how it is meant to be.

However, is it performing that role in the present times with the required diligence, trustworthiness and integrity? Far from it. Even members of the *fourth estate* will not make that bold claim, although they will cite that *their channel is an exception.*

News and Views

If democracy is all about the *will of the people,* the Media is meant to be a medium for dissemination of information so that people can express their *will* based on facts. Deplorably, large sections of Media have taken upon themselves to *mould* public

---

[82] Macaulay, Thomas (September 1828). "Hallam's constitutional history". *The Edinburgh Review*. London: Longmans. 48: 165.

opinion, based not on facts but on coloured views, *half lies* and even outright fiction.

Moulding public opinion through objective analyses and panel discussions is a legitimate role of the Media. However, very often they blatantly present distorted *news,* and cloak their *views* as *alternative facts.* Peddling such *slanted* and *planted* news to suit agendas of the ruling dispensation, powerful lobbies and interest groups, is the biggest fraud on our democracy.

Inevitably, the Govt of the day has undue influence over the Media, since it is a major source of their advertising revenue. However, when it uses Revenue intelligence and other regulatory agencies for exercising leverage and arm-twisting, only then the Media's claims of fearless and independent brand of journalism will face its true test. Most channels succumb and toe the line.

Given the power of this medium and with high stakes involved in the contemporary state of our democracy, controlling the Media is vital. No wonder, many politicians or political parties have outright ownership of channels. Others try to control it through the usual tools of *power* using political, financial and regulatory intimidation. Independence of the Media thus remains only a faint memory of the distant past.

With the prevailing appalling standards of journalistic morality and ethics, foreign organizations and intelligence agencies have preyed upon many of them. There is a tremendous uproar in many western democracies, especially in USA, about the menace of *Fake news.* The ongoing media war between Trump and News channels has reached a crescendo. Indian Media is far more brazen; now it does not make even make pretence of being *fair and objective.*

The *Press Freedom Index* ranks countries globally, according to the degree of independence enjoyed by the Press. India's ranking in the 2018 index is a dismal 138 out of 180 countries, which was two positions lower than the previous year[83]. More disturbing is the fact that our rank was lower than even a large number of LCDs in Asia, Africa and Latin America, certainly not a good testimonial for a country that aspires to a permanent seat in the UNSC. In South Asia, we were behind Nepal, Sri Lanka and even Myanmar, though just one notch higher than Pakistan.

The *Abuse Score,* within that Index is an indicator of the extent of violence and abuse suffered by journalists and channels. It is a matter of deep concern and utterly shameful for a democracy that

---

[83] Press Freedom Ranking 2018, *Reporters Without Borders,* https://rsf.org/en/ranking_table . Retrieved 26 May 2018.

India's *Abuse Score* was very high at 60.1, almost 11 points higher than Pakistan. Ironically, in popular perception Pakistan is supposed to be dangerous for journalists. Most channels therefore deem it wise to side with establishment. Those who do not side with it, invariably face abuse and coercion.

India's *Abuse Score* has risen in the last few years during which a number of journalists were murdered. In the highly charged and polarized environment, journalists have frequently been assaulted, abused and threatened. Elements from a host of *senas* of political parties and communities, and militant wings of organizations invariably are involved. Due to the patronage provided to such people, the law seldom takes its own course.

Polarization in society and partisanship in Media is not peculiar to India. Even in USA, society and media are polarized on ideological, demographical and party lines, especially after the last Presidential election. Thus one sees CNN and Fox News voicing not just their diametrically opposed opinions, but even flash widely different and subjective descriptions of the same news item.

Social Media

Although it is a relatively new medium, it has become a very potent and dangerous mode for spreading disinformation. With no regulatory oversight, and since the channel providers too shrug away any responsibility, it is now an unbridled menace to society.

The sparks of polarization, lit by wily politicians in pursuance of their electoral games, spread like wildfire through social media. In numerous cases, these have led to disastrous consequences such as lynching, riots and deep alienation. The epidemic of *fake news* too has reached alarming proportions. There is an urgent need to enact and enforce regulations to curb this menace.

NGOs

NGOs in all countries render yeoman service to society by channelizing money and public service of citizens into activities that Govt agencies are unable to perform to the extent required. They receive funds from public-spirited citizens, philanthropic organizations, and Govt grants.

Many such NGOs are doing excellent work in respective fields of social service. However, a large number of NGOs have mushroomed in recent years, not out of altruistic motives, but for a variety of self-serving ends. The most common and least deplorable among them is tax evasion. In many other cases, the motives are far more sinister. Whole Nation cringed with horror and disgust to find that a large number of shelters run by NGOs in Bihar and UP were being used for immoral trafficking of hapless women and children.

Many NGOs run by quasi-religious and social organizations receive funds from abroad. While many of them perform genuine social service, in many cases allegations abound about foreign agencies and elements inimical to Indian interests, promoting nefarious activities through them.

It is imperative that the Govt exercises sufficient oversight over all NGOs. Govt must do so transparently, across the board, lest there are allegations that it is turning a blind eye on the foreign funding and activities of NGOs that have close ideological proximity to the Ruling party.

There are several other institutions such as the Press Council of India, Broadcast Council, Central Board of Film certification, Medical council etc, which ostensibly are independent and ought to function without the Govt's overriding influence. Their role and purpose is defeated if the Govt influences them through political appointees and interference.

Institutions, statutory or otherwise, are an important pillar of democracy. It is imperative that they function with utmost integrity, objectivity, and independence. They are true watchdogs of democracy, which exercise oversight on all three Branches. It is indeed sad that many of our Institutions are functioning neither objectively nor transparently.

Ruling parties, regardless of their political affiliation, are squarely to blame for their decline and for losing the peoples' trust. One can only cringe at the low calibre, unflattering record of public service, and deplorable public demeanour of many of the political appointees. It is high time that the Govt does not treat these vital positions as berths to reward *helpful* retiring bureaucrats, or to placate and accommodate bothersome party men.

10

To Sum up...

So - how have we fared overall as an Independent Nation? What have been our triumphs and failings during this period? What do we reckon as our strengths, and what weaknesses are holding us back?

If we set aside the dimension of politics and politicking, by all accounts we have done very well indeed. For a Nation that had to make up for centuries of colonial exploitation, and ardently wished to *catch up* fast with developed countries to earn our rightful place in the comity of Nations, we have succeeded substantially in our quest. More importantly, we have done it as a democracy, unlike many other newly independent countries of that era that had to endure military rule and violent revolutions.

From a country that produced virtually nothing, we are now an industrialized Nation; thanks to the foundations laid soon after Independence. Not only does our industry produce sophisticated products for domestic consumption, it earns substantial foreign exchange from exports. It is progressively upgrading to cutting-edge technology through foreign collaboration and its own R&D.

Perhaps the most spectacular progress and achievements have been in the areas of nuclear energy and space technology. Credit for this too goes to the vision of the leadership in that era that accorded it the highest priority, as well as to the outstanding professional acumen of the pioneers and successor scientists.

The Indian economy had its share of peaks and troughs like any other economy due to internal as well as global factors. However, as Fig 6 shows even in the early years when our economy grew at, what foreign economists disparagingly called the *Hindu rate of growth,* there were several years of high growth. The dips were because of various factors such as wars, severe droughts, political agitations, communal riots and structural constraints.

The high growth trajectory achieved after liberalization reforms were ushered by Manmohan Singh is indeed laudable. It has forced the world to recognize us as a leading economy. The problem however is that the economy is not creating sufficient jobs to address growing unemployment, which ominously is going to get even worse as our young population enters the workforce.

There is ample empirical and anecdotal evidence globally that there is a negative correlation between increase in economic prosperity and the incidence of crime. However, in India higher economic growth has paradoxically seen an increase in crime. Obviously, the fruits of economic growth are not trickling down to the poor, and the gap between the rich and poor is increasing. In addition to their economic hardship, this is causing increasing frustration and anger among the poor and forcing them into criminal activities.

Attaining food security has been another success story. From a net importer of food grains who virtually had to hold out a begging bowl for PL-480 food assistance, our indigenous *Green Revolution* made us self-sufficient. Dependence on monsoons remains a problem, especially in large tracts of peninsular India. Rural poverty too is a big issue, and the large number of farmer suicides certainly a blot on the Nation.

On institutional integrity, our record has been mixed. The EC has been conducting free and fair elections and it has functioned quite independently as per its Constitutional mandate. However, peoples' confidence in the fairness of the CBI has waned and it is widely perceived to be working at the behest of the Govt in power.

Although there is now unease about *bench fixing, bench shopping,* and even murmurs of corruption, the SC has generally maintained credibility. However, inordinately large number of judicial vacancies overall, and the extremely large backlog of cases is a matter of serious concern. Rampant corruption in the subordinate judiciary, with which the common man has to deal mostly, is also deeply disturbing.

There is an urgent need to initiate comprehensive police reforms and insulate the personnel from political and bureaucratic interference. The large number of vacancies, long duty hours, frequent diversion for VIP duties and *bandobast*, poor training, and obsolete equipment *etc* need attention. However, what concerns the common man most is the deeply entrenched corruption, which is just as endemic as it is in other limbs of our polity.

Independence of the *fourth estate* leaves much to be desired. It is in part due to the paranoia of the Govt in power, which deems it expedient to control the medium in order to mould public opinion for electoral gains. It is also due to the deliberate creation of a climate of fear and intimidation by various *senas*, pressure groups and trolls to pressurize the media.

Social cohesion is the most important contributor to a Nation's core strength. Social conflict can destabilize a Nation and weaken its *will* and capacity to fight external threats. It is even more vital for a Nation of 1.3 billion with its extraordinary diversity, given the inherent religious, caste, class, regional and cultural fault-lines.

Despite these fault-lines, people have lived in relative harmony for centuries. Fissiparous strains have generally remained muted due to societal, commercial and vocational interdependence, until politicians exploit those. Their fanning of communal passions in the twenties and thirties had led to the tragic Partition. What is often forgotten is that such events leave indelible scars that sow the seeds for long-lasting alienation and future conflict.

We have fared reasonably well in this dimension too, although there have been sporadic instances of riots and unrest. Most were triggered only by minor incidents, which later spiralled due to the *action-reaction* dynamic. Not only they resulted in many deaths, injuries and destruction of property, as shown in the graphics in Chapters 7 and 8, they also dealt a severe blow to the economy. Even worse, the anti-Sikh riots of 1984, the deadly communal riots following the *Rath Yatra* and *Babri Masjid* demolition, and the 2002 Gujarat riots left permanent scars on our National psyche.

A more disturbing and dangerous trend has been seen in the last few years when communal incidents have been *engineered* through deliberate provocation, rumours and incendiary speeches. Most incidents have preceded crucial elections and orchestrated to polarize communities for electoral gains.

Proliferation of militant youth wings, *senas* of various parties, castes, and fringe groups is a very dangerous development. They brazenly do *moral policing*, raise inflammatory slogans, enforce *bandhs,* and take the law into their own hands on motley issues and film bans *etc.* This causes social conflict, loss of life and property, and serious economic disruption.

Poverty and unemployment are critical problems that have to be tackled with great urgency. However, when crass politicization downplays farmer suicides and blames them on unrelated causes than on agrarian distress, when qualified youth are constrained to accept low-rung jobs, or subsist only on petty hawking; all this only intensifies peoples' anger.

There is great danger of angst spilling over when people see the vulgar flaunting of ill-gotten wealth by the rich, and the *rags-to-riches* meteoric rise of politicians, who unabashedly voice insensitive platitudes. I hope that the political class will remember the lessons of History, as in the French Revolution and the fate of Marie Antoinette, who mockingly said that *if the people do not have bread, let them eat cakes.*

Despite almost 7% growth rate post-demonetization, ironically the Indian economy is still operating much below its potential. It is possible to alleviate agrarian distress and rural unemployment through well-conceived integrated policies that promote the food and food-product industry in a big way. We already have a very successful *milk revolution* model based on rural cooperatives.

District, State and regional networks for food procurement, processing and packaging, storage, transportation and distribution can effectively ameliorate rural poverty and check rural migration. Consolidation at State and regional levels will also reduce costs due to *economies of scale*[84] and *economies of scope*[85].

Our supply chain between the producer and the consumer is very fragmented, which multiplies costs at each intermediate level. Will the Govt courageously eliminate layers of *middlemen*, which will benefit both, the farmers and consumers? Given that traders and intermediaries form a big part of the vote-bank, politicians have been averse to such consolidation.

Likewise, in manufacturing small and micro enterprises need to be encouraged to help solve the unemployment problem. Such units can be a part of the ancillary networks that inevitably cluster around big industrial hubs. Public sector banks have been over-liberal in giving astronomical sums to Big Business, on which many have defaulted. It is intriguing why the Govt does not encourage banks to advance loans to the much-more deserving entrepreneurs and small start-ups. Importantly, to encourage more enterprising youth the Govt must have facilitation centres to provide guidance and support.

Political Morality

Within the internal environment, among all dimensions of the *National Security Paradigm* the aspect of *political morality* has been the most problematic. Lack of political morality is the root cause of most ills and infirmities that affect our polity.

Politics, especially *politics sans morality*, has become the bane of all democracies in the contemporary world. It has been reduced to a quest for power, for which winning elections by any means – fair or foul – is the key. All lofty claims of *public service* or *serving*

---

[84] Reduction in per unit costs as the scale of production increases since Fixed Costs get distributed over the larger number of units produced.
[85] Cost reduction due to a number of common functions being performed for a family of goods and diversified products.

the Nation are nothing but empty rhetoric meant to seduce the gullible masses.

According to Roger Stone, who gained notoriety as part of the *Dirty Tricks department* of Richard Nixon's campaign, *"politics is not about uniting people. It's about dividing people" and "getting your fifty-one per cent"; "attack, attack, attack—never defend"; and "admit nothing, deny everything, launch counterattack."* Given the high stakes involved, the game has got only dirtier, as the ongoing investigations of Russian collusion are now revealing.

However, as highlighted in Chapter 6, this was not so in the early years of our Republic. There were several reasons; such as euphoria of gaining Independence after centuries of subjugation; enthusiasm about the onerous task of nation building; statesmanship of the top leadership; and patriotic idealism of politicians on both sides of the aisle.

Ambitions, egos, and greed of politicians later caused a sharp decline. These, together with the compulsive desire to carve out personal fiefdoms - a trait reminiscent of our history, increased the propensity of parties to splinter. This has led to multiplicity of parties, which confounds the electoral process and inevitably results in fractured mandates.

The political class is reluctant to reform this system as this serves as a convenient refuge for many a criminal or *bahubali neta* to claim respectability by starting a political party. It also suits major political parties that are in contention for power at the Centre, as it is easy to bargain with smaller parties. Thus, we have the spectacle of single MP/MLA parties being a part of the Ruling or Opposition coalitions.

Many small parties and splinter groups are formed around tainted or *Bahubali netas,* who seek absolution from their pending cases and inquiries by associating with the Ruling combine. All parties have several sitting MPs and MLAs with criminal cases against them, which is indeed a shame on our democracy.

In most countries, there are generally two dominant political parties that provide a credible alternative to the electorate, such as Republicans and Democrats in USA, or the Conservative and Labour parties in UK. However, for a highly diverse country as India, there is also a need to accommodate regional aspirations.

Many countries have *run-off* elections where the top two parties fight again to secure more than 50% votes. With our huge electorate, this is not a viable option both logistically and expense-wise. Nonetheless, there is a need for electoral reforms to restrict the number of parties and banning of tainted candidates.

Power corrupts and absolute power corrupts absolutely; goes the adage. Single party dominance is antithetical to a robust and inclusive democracy since it leads to authoritarian tendencies. Our experience too shows that single party domination has led to dictatorial fiats and subversion of democracy. Ideally, therefore, our polity should evolve around two major pre-poll coalitions, each based on a common minimum programme.

It is inevitable for parties to coalesce around a charismatic, vote-catching personality. However, deifying such personalities, based on dynasty or as a cult figure, soon turns into autocracy. It creates the dangerous hubris of *infallibility* and *invincibility,* as seen in examples, both past and present.

Analyses of all dimensions in the preceding chapters led to the unassailable conclusion that corruption is eating into the entrails of not just our polity, but indeed of all institutions and the society itself. It is impossible to unravel the Gordian knot, and sift the *cause* from *effect*. Power-hungry politicians, corporate greed, complicit bureaucracy, obliging banks, promiscuous regulatory agencies; all are networked into a well-oiled corruption machine.

In the Preface, I had described how earlier it was deemed a big disgrace for an official to face just an Inquiry. Now the *threshold of ignominy* has fallen so low that even high-flying businesspersons and politicians feel no shame in being held guilty. In many cases, they employ all legal tricks to delay the law from catching up with them or simply escape abroad.

Astronomical sums are spent on elections. Corporate houses recover their investments manifold, as do politicians through well-set institutionalized mode of *sweetheart* deals, commissions and fixed shares of the booty up the ladder. In such a predatory environment, everyone extracts his pound of flesh in whatever manner possible.

At the bottom rung of the hierarchy the common man ends up bearing the price tag, as he has no one below him to gouge from. Alas, for him there is no *fortune at the bottom of the pyramid*; a phrase used by C K Prahalad[86] in a different context.

How has our polity reached the nadir of moral and political degeneration? Who is to blame? It is certainly, *we the people* who elect them. When *netas* compound their corrupt and even

---

[86] Prahalad, CK (2004) *"The Fortune at the Bottom of the Pyramid"* Wharton School Publishing. The book makes a case for the fastest growing new markets and entrepreneurial opportunities being found among the billions of poor people 'at the bottom of the [financial] pyramid'.

immoral acts with outrageous conduct and utterances, we wonder how the parties could nominate them. And even if they did, how could we have voted for them? Obviously, we voted not because of the candidate's merit, but were swayed by religious and caste considerations.

In conclusion, therefore, were it not for our corrupted brand of politics, the country would have attained much greater heights. With an eye on electoral politics, politicians are exacerbating religious, caste, class and regional fault-lines recklessly, thus causing lasting damage to our social fabric.

This has to change, and *we the people* have the power to do so through the judicious exercise of our voting rights. There has to be a concerted campaign to demand accountability and rectitude from our politicians. Tainted candidates need to be barred from elections. We need to curtail the privileges they have usurped undeservingly, as also the *laal batti* culture, which gives them a *larger than life* persona and makes them insensitive and arrogant.

Our country has immense untapped potential, and we are quite capable of achieving double-digit growth. Once the dimension of political morality is set right, other dimensions and systems would fall into place. The political leadership will have to create the right conducive, corruption-free environment. It will need to ensure a level playing field where the talent and enterprise of our youth can blossom.

The Gupta Empire and the Mughal Empire were called India's *Golden Ages.* We were then the world's largest economies and had tremendous achievements in arts, science, philosophy, architecture, literature etc. We have the potential and capability to usher in another Golden Age.

If we strengthen our inner core with social harmony, economic strength and equity, institutional integrity, and above all strong National Will and ethos, we will be strong enough to meet all geopolitical, military, economic or diplomatic challenges most effectively. More importantly, we will be able to attain the loftier goal of *National Resurgence* to make up for the lost decades.

We have traversed a long distance on the path of regaining our eminence. Nevertheless, we still have a long way to go. Once we *get our act together,* we will regain our eminence, and rightfully claim a seat on the Global High Table

Finally to paraphrase Robert Frost:

I (we) have miles to go before I (we) sleep...

PART 3

DEVELOPING CAPABILITIES
TO MEET EXTERNAL CHALLENGES

11

Overview of the Geopolitical Environment

No analysis of the geopolitical environment starts without a discussion on polarity; whether the world is *unipolar, bipolar* or *multipolar*. For International Relations scholars, semantics are important since only precise theoretical postulates must anchor their analyses.

Scholars have to identify and analyze patterns among strategies adopted in the past, in order to develop theoretical constructs from them. They then extrapolate it to the future to facilitate more debate and better analyses.

However, is it a critical prerequisite for security strategists for their analyses? Not really, for them it is only an academic typology. A country's external threats would remain the same regardless whether we label the world *unipolar* or *multipolar*.

Strategists use it as a guideline to either formulate an entirely different strategy, or further refine the existing strategy. However, just as in the business world, changes in the extant strategy (*doing things better*) yield only marginal improvements. However, new and unique formulations (*doing different things*) generally lead to greater competitive advantage[87].

As discussed in Chapter 1, the international system is *anarchic* and States have to ensure their own security, in spite of the UNO's existence. *Neorealism,* especially its *defensive neorealism* variant, has been an influential IR theory since the collapse of the Soviet Union[88]. It is essentially a *balance of power* theory in which States do not seek to maximize power, but merely balance it.

During the Cold War, such *balance* was achieved through terror or MAD, *Mutual Assured Destruction*. There was relatively greater predictability as there were only two, notionally *rational* actors. In *multipolarity,* since *balancing* has to be through politico-economic alliances with several *poles,* there is more uncertainty[89].

---

[87] Deepak Sethi and William Judge *"Sustaining Competitive Advantage through Dynamic Adaptation".* Strategic Management Society Conference, San Diego, June 2007.

[88] Kenneth Waltz, 1979 *Theory of International Politics,* McGraw Hill.

[89] Humphreys, Adam (2012) "Another Waltz? Methodological Rhetoric and Practice in Theory of International Politics" *International Relations* 26(4):389–408

Military and Economic Strength of Leading Powers

Multipolar world has now become the favourite buzzword of strategic analysts. However, is it not just a matter of perception? For proponents of *multipolarity* could it not be just an aspiration, where they see a greater role for themselves in the evolving world, where USA is no longer the sole, hegemonic power? They cite declining US domination in world affairs and the concurrent rise of other powers who will increasingly challenge it.

View from US perspective is different, especially given Trump's *'America First'* unilateralism on geopolitical and economic issues. Wedded as USA is to Mahan's doctrine of sea power, its 11 aircraft carrier based strike groups (CSGs) pack far greater punch than do all the contenders combined[90]. While UK and India have two each, Russia, France and China presently have only one. Size, endurance, number and sophistication of onboard aircraft, and the armada of escort ships; all are far more superior too.

USA's strategic airlift capability is also unmatched, giving it a tremendous capacity for *power projection* globally. On the flip side is the growing weariness of American public to various wars abroad. USA's unwillingness to put sufficient boots on ground has been most evident in Afghanistan. Its arsenal of 15,000 lb *Daisy Cutter* bombs and PGMs could not eliminate Osama bin Laden in the Tora Bora Mountains, just as its Predator drones and Hellfire missiles have been unable to neutralize the Taliban.

Neither cajoling nor harsh rhetoric will induce its NATO allies to contribute any more troops and finance, than what they are doing now. The world knows that USA is neither willing nor infinitely capable of playing the *policeman of the world*, and that is why *multipolarity* will become the new normal in geopolitics.

Strategic Arms Reductions Treaties START I and START II, had resulted in fifty percent reduction in nuclear weapons. USA and Russia were limited to 3,000 to 3,500 strategic weapons. While USA ratified START II in 1996, Russia did so in 2000.

Before analyzing current geopolitical hotspots, a brief overview of the military and economic strength, as well as the geostrategic concerns and compulsions of leading contenders in a *multipolar* world would be useful. However, this is not in the order of their power or eminence. China and India are discussed at the end in detail, because of their greater relevance to the theme of this book.

---

[90] Mahan, Alfred Thayer. *Mahan on Naval Strategy: selections from the writings of Rear Admiral Alfred Thayer Mahan* ed by John B. Hattendorf (1991)

In terms of missiles and warheads, Russia comes closest to matching the destructive firepower of the United States. As per the 2018 *Global Fire Power Rankings,* based on a composite index, Russian military is the second most powerful after USA[91]. It too has large investments in R&D and weapon production.

Under Putin, Russia has come a long way from the economic collapse, political and social unrest, and rampant corruption during Boris Yeltsin's Presidency. Its GDP has increased six fold since then[92]. According to the April 2018 Global IMF rankings, its economy is worth $1.7 trillion (Rank 11) in nominal GDP and $4.2 trillion (Rank 6) in PPP terms[93].

Russia has emerged from its geopolitical diminution of the nineties. Hence, it will remain a power to reckon with. Trump himself is promoting it, when he forcefully argued with G7 allies at their Quebec summit, to include Russia in the group.

Russia's quelling of Chechen insurgency and getting Chechnya under its direct control, as well as its brazen annexation of Crimea in 2014, signalled its new assertiveness. It steadfastly backed the Assad regime in Syria against resolute US attempts to topple it.

Leading European countries have a long history of wars and the idea of a European compact, a sort of *United States of Europe*, has been a pipedream. The EU, an *economic union* with its own currency (except UK) and a European Parliament comes closest to a full-fledged *political union*. UK however has always been at odds with other EU nations on many policies, especially immigration, and has now quit the EU with its *Brexit* bill.

UK ranks sixth in military strength and fifth in economy, where its GDP stands at $2.9 trillion in nominal terms. It is also a member of the P5 in the UNSC. Despite that, it is not even a shadow of its halcyon days, when *the sun never set on the British Empire*. It has always sided with USA in global affairs, and was a willing partner in the Iraq war.

UK's exit from the EU will slow down economic growth, and London will likely lose its central position in the global financial markets. Scotland's threat to secede and join the EU and Southern Ireland continuing in the EU; will add to its post-Brexit woes.

---

[91] 2018 Military Strength Ranking.
https://www.globalfirepower.com/countries-listing.asp Accessed 07 June 2018.
[92] GDP of Russia from 1992 to 2007 *International Monetary Fund* Retrieved on 05 June 2018
[93] International Monetary Fund World Economic Outlook Apr 2018. Accessed 7 Jun 2018 http://statisticstimes.com/economy/countries-by-projected-gdp.php

France and Germany are the two most powerful economies of the EU, of which only France is a member of the P5 in UNSC. It is widely expected that Germany too will find a slot as a permanent member in the proposed expansion of UNSC. In military strength France ranks 5th, while Germany is at 10th position. However Germany's economy, with its $4.2 trillion nominal GDP ranks 4th, while the French economy with $2.9 trillion GDP is ranked 6th.

After *Brexit,* influence of the Franco-German core within the EU will increase further[94]. Both are part of NATO, but often at odds with USA on strategic and economic issues. EU and USA have often dragged each other to the WTO for dispute resolution. They are not inclined to get deeply involved in Afghanistan and the Middle East. Both also stoutly contested Trump's diatribes against unfair trade practices and low payment to NATO at the Quebec G7 summit, and are now hitting back at US tariffs.

CHINA

Rising China is the leading challenger to American supremacy. It certainly has the credentials by virtue of its third rank in the military power index. It has achieved credible deterrence against the Big Two, and has a Triad with a second-strike capability.

Its economy ranks second with nominal GDP of $14 trillion. However, its GDP of $25.2 trillion in PPP terms ranks first in the world, far ahead of second placed USA with $20.4 trillion. China's average GDP growth rate has been above 7%, as opposed to just about 2% of the USA.

Chinese civilization dates back to 2100 BC. Several dynasties ruled China until the 1911 Revolution under Chiang Kai-shek. It had many achievements in arts, medicine, commerce and technology, but also underwent disintegration and reunification several times. China has a long history of internecine warfare, as also with Mongolia, Russia, Japan, Korea and the Colonial powers.

The Chinese take pride in their rich heritage, but nurse many grievances about the *'historic wrongs'* done to them by foreign powers. After suffering many defeats in the *Opium wars* and other conflicts in the 19th century the Qing dynasty had to sign, what the Chinese call, *'unequal treaties'* with the Imperial Powers UK, France and Russia. As a result, it had to cede several territories on the Northeastern seaboard and lease Hong Kong to UK.

---

[94] Andrew Moravcsik, 'Preferences and Power in the European Community: A Liberal Inter-governmentalist Approach,' *Journal of Common Market Studies,* December 1993.

After its birth in 1949 as a Communist state, China fought wars with USA in Korea and Vietnam, India (1962 and 1967 skirmish), Russia (1969) and Vietnam (1979). China also experienced political and social turmoil during Mao's *Great Leap Forward* that left millions dead, and later the *Cultural Revolution*.

Only after Deng Xiaoping assumed power in 1978 that China experienced an economic turnaround. Deng embraced capitalism, but not democracy. Using the principle *one country, two systems* he reunified Hong Kong and its capitalist economy, into China.

The Chinese economy grew rapidly on *free market* principles, but he retained tight hold over the polity through the Communist Party. Deng vigorously implemented the *Four Modernizations* (agriculture, industry, national defence, and science & technology) which not only strengthened the industrial base but also forged the Chinese military into a potent fighting machine.

Absence of democracy in a modern state, when the rest of the world enjoys it, is a Chinese anachronism. The regime has invariably jailed or crushed dissenting voices, and the Tiananmen Square uprising in 1989 was the most brutal example.

A major cause for worry is uneven economic development and widespread poverty. Fig. 15 shows the growth rates and economic development in China's 31 provinces. All top seven provinces that have the highest economic development and prosperity are concentrated on the East coast. The next tier of provinces also is adjacent to the coastal provinces, whereas vast areas of the interior have seen relatively much less development[95].

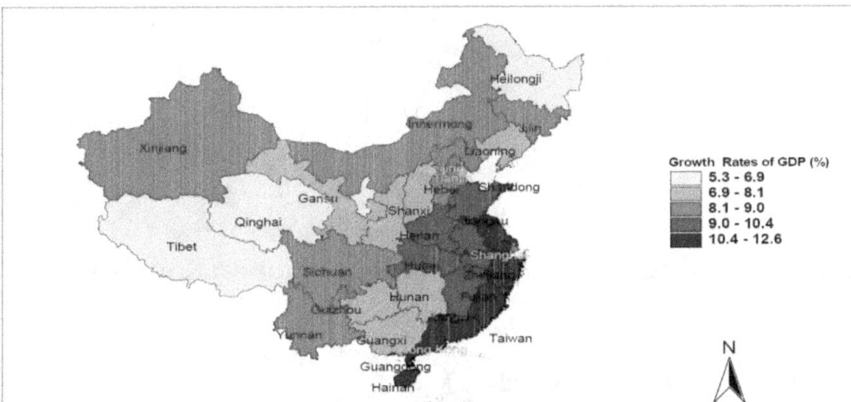

Fig. 15 – Uneven economic growth in China's provinces

[95] Deepak Sethi, William Q. Judge & Qian Sun (2011) "FDI distribution within China: An integrative conceptual framework for analyzing intra-country FDI variations", *Asia Pacific Journal of Management*, 28:325–352.

Given the regime's tight control over media, no news about the restiveness among its poor in the interior gets out. However, the leadership is worried about growing income disparities, which are among the highest in the world, as shown by the GINI Index cited in Chapter 8[96]. China's GDP growth too has slowed down to just 6%, and 500 million Chinese still live in abject poverty.

The strongest evidence came from Xi Jinping himself, who in his address to the 19th Congress of the Party acknowledged it as the *"principal contradiction facing Chinese society"*[97]. He pledged to address the *"unbalanced and inadequate development and the people's ever-growing need for a better life."*

No wonder therefore, that the greatest concern of the Chinese State are disgruntled elements and dissenters *'plotting counter-revolutionary activities designed to sabotage or overthrow China's socialist system'*[98], as was highlighted in Chapter 3.

Foremost among China's strategic constraints is the growing gap between its oil consumption and domestic production. While consumption is galloping, production has been falling of late.

Total Petroleum and Liquid Fuels Production and Consumption, China, 1994 – 2018

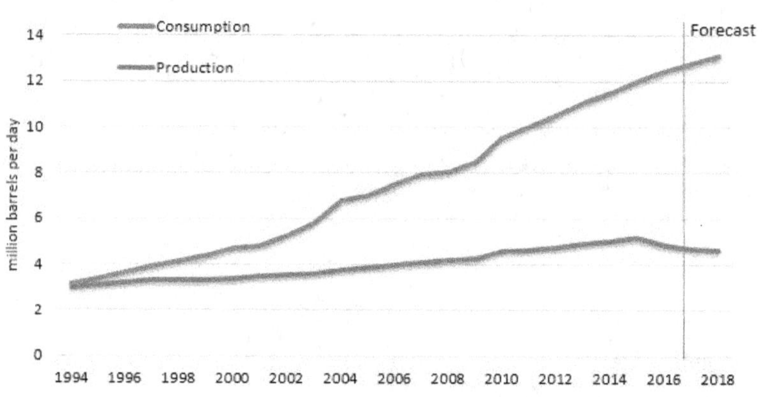

Source: Adapted from U.S. Energy Information Administration data (April, 2017)

Fig. 16- Growing gap in China's oil consumption & production

---

[96] World Bank GINI index. Accessed, 19 May 2018.

[97] Therese Shaheen, *What President Xi Knows about China's Economy,* 25 Oct 2017. https://www.nationalreview.com/2017/10/president-xi-jinping-china-communist-party-congress-speech-economic-challenges. Accessed 8 June 2018

[98] Ministry of State Security, *Intelligence Resource Program,* Federation of American Scientists.

Large oil imports fuel China's booming economy, which is virtually the *factory of the world*. This puts in perspective China's critical strategic imperative; *sea lines of communication (SLOC)*. Except for the Americas, which account for limited oil imports and only 34% exports, its SLOC for the rest of the world pass through the Indian Ocean and the bottleneck of Malacca Straits.

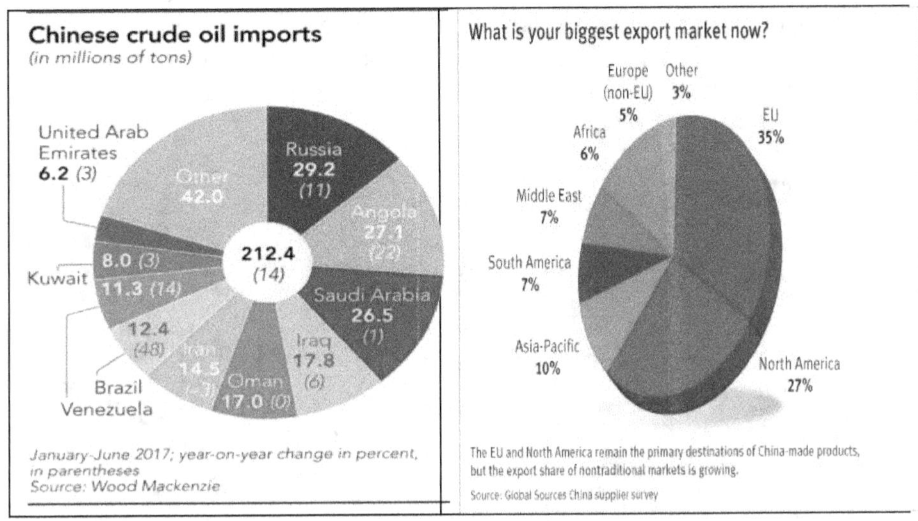

Fig 17 – China's oil import and export destinations

Fig. 18 – China's critical sea lines of communication

Any disruption of China's SLOC, even for a limited period, can be disastrous for its economy. This is the main strategic objective behind its ambitious *Belt and Road Initiative (BRI)*, which aims at establishing connectivity and cooperation with countries in Asia, Europe and Africa[99].

Its main components are the *Silk Road Economic Belt (SREB)*, and the *Maritime Silk Road (MSR)*. The land-based SREB, which roughly corresponds to the ancient *Silk Road*, is for connectivity to the Central Asian Republics and Europe. The sea and land-based MSR is to connect China to Southeast Asia and Africa.

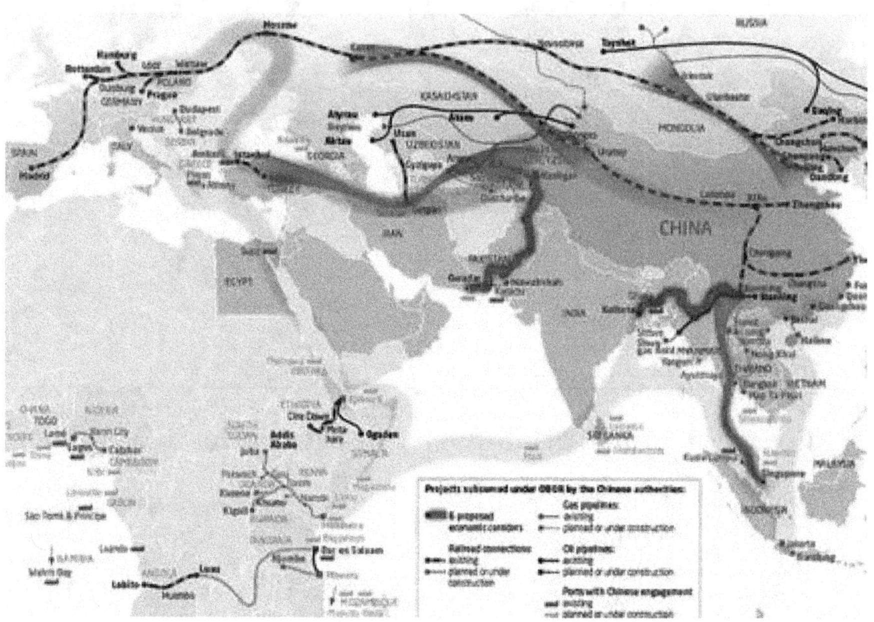

Fig. 19 – China's Belt and Road Initiative (BRI)

Besides connectivity and securing its SLOC, BRI also serves its strategic objectives. For decades, China has forged links with African countries, as a source for oil and as a market for exports. Its investments in many African countries were very small, and meant only to enhance its geopolitical influence.

For instance, out of 42 African nations where China invested, its FDI stock in 13 countries was less than $5 million in 2005; too

---

[99] "BRI Instead of OBOR – China Edits the English Name of its Most Ambitious International Project". *liia.lv*. July 28, 2016. Archived from the original on February 6, 2017. Accessed 09 June, 2018

insignificant to make any economic impact[100]. However, those token investments provided valuable information of future opportunities and gave *first-mover advantages* to Chinese firms, which are now reaping dividends in BRI projects.

MNEs from free-markets do FDI based on economic factors. However, a large number of Chinese firms owned by its military or by provincial oligarchs, made investments only to further the Govt's geopolitical interests. Many analysts believe that now those firms are getting a free hand to recover their investments manifold through BRI projects, often on overpriced terms.

This helped the Chinese regime to satisfy the oligarchs and powerful entities, and to curb dissent, but it has also created serious problems with many host countries. Due to the stringency of financial terms, some countries have cancelled BRI projects.

Due to concerns about its SLOC, China is establishing maritime bases or docking facilities in many littoral states in the Arabian Sea and Indian Ocean. This maritime strategy is called the *string of pearls,* although the Chinese do not refer to it as such[101].

China formally opened its first naval base in Djibouti on 01 August 2017, giving it significant power projection capability in the Horn of Africa and Indian Ocean. It has already constructed a commercial port at Gwadar in Pakistan as part of *China Pakistan Economic Corridor* (CPEC). It is reportedly acquiring a Naval base in Jiwani, 80 Kms west of Gwadar, which already has a Pakistani Naval facility and an airstrip[102].

China has financed a container shipping facility in Chittagong, Bangladesh, and a commercial shipping centre in Hambantota, Sri Lanka. Both have serious security implications for India. They give the Chinese footfall in the Bay of Bengal and Indian Ocean, even though both countries have denied giving permission for docking of naval vessels. However, this could still be the thin edge of the wedge and be militarily exploited later.

Similarly, China is reportedly developing a Naval facility in the Marao Atoll, in the Maldives. China has financed rail link and infrastructure projects in Port Sudan, and is developing port facilities in Bagamoyo, Tanzania.

---

[100] Deepak Sethi, 2009. 'Are Multinational Enterprises from Emerging Economies Global or Regional?' *European Management Journal* 27(5)p.356-365

[101] Revisiting China's 'String of Pearls' Strategy, 2014. CSIS *Issues & Insights* Vol. 14 - No. 7

[102] A New China Military Base in Pakistan?, The Diplomat. Accessed 10 Jun 2018 https://thediplomat.com/2018/02/a-new-china-military-base-in-pakistan/

Its most aggressive activity has been in South China Sea, which it is bent upon controlling. It has disputes with many Southeast Asian countries about ownership of several islands, apart from claims over the 200 nautical mile Exclusive Economic Zone (EEZ).

To buttress its claims China has artificially enlarged several islands and built military infrastructure and airstrips on them[103]. It routinely protests about foreign surveillance ships and aircrafts, though USA and other countries assert right to free passage in international waters. China has a large base on Hainan Island, and is constructing Naval and surveillance facilities on the claimed islands in order to ensure its dominance over South China Sea.

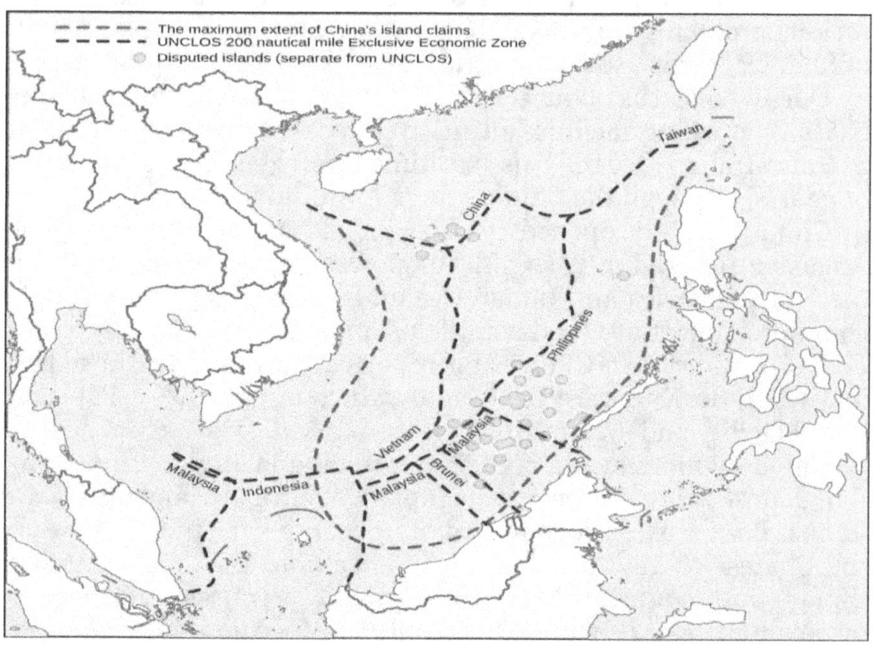

Fig. 20 – Disputes over islands and EEZ in South China Sea

INDIA

India ranks fourth in the 2018 Military Strength Ranking. It is a nuclear power, and even though it has not signed the Nuclear Non-proliferation Treaty (NPT), it is considered a responsible nuclear-weapon state.

---

[103] Tom Phillips, "Photos show Beijing's militarization of South China Sea in new detail", *The Guardian* 06 February 2018. Accessed 11 June 2018.

India has credible deterrence and *second-strike* capability with a Triad of nuclear weapon delivery systems. Although, one leg of the Triad is based on a nuclear submarine leased from Russia, it will soon have the capability to launch SLBMs from its indigenous nuclear submarine.

While her nominal GDP of $2.8 trillion is ranked 7th in the world, as per IMF's *World Economic Forecast* of April 2018 it is ranked 3rd, with $10.4 trillion GDP (PPP). After the dip in GDP due to demonetization, the growth rate has now recovered to 7.3%.

India too is heavily dependent upon oil imports. In 2017-18, its oil production decreased to 32,642 million tons, marking seven years of continuous decline[104]. Its gross petroleum imports in the same period were $92 billion, which was much lower than the 2013 oil import bill of $128 billion. Lower imports despite increasing demand, together with declining domestic production has led to huge increases in consumer prices.

The imposing projection of peninsular India into the Indian Ocean gives it wide reach from the Red Sea and Persian Gulf to the Malacca Straits. Thus, its oil and trade SLOC are unencumbered by choke points unlike those of China. However, China's *string of pearls* strategy and increasing naval activity in our neighbourhood is indeed problematic.

Both China and India have serious concerns about the internal security environment and need to ensure that social discord and violence do not get out of hand. China has already experienced this when the Red Guards perpetrated intense internal turmoil during the Cultural Revolution and later during the reprisals against the *Gang of Four*. It has also seen the disastrous consequences of the Tiananmen Square carnage.

India too is grappling with high levels of poverty and rising unemployment. There is also an inordinate increase in social unrest and violence in the last few years. Naxalite violence that has affected vast stretches of the Indian heartland for decades shows no signs of abating. Magnitude of the internal problem and its economic impact is evident from the fact that the Indian economy suffered a loss of $1.19 trillion (PPP terms) due to it in 2017[105].

A totalitarian state like China can suppress dissent ruthlessly and not let it hamper economic growth. This is not feasible in a

---

[104] "India records lowest crude oil production in seven years", *Energy World* from The Economic Times 06 April 2018. Accessed 11 June 2018.
[105] *"Economic cost of violence containment"* Report of Institute for Economics and Peace. Accessed 11 June 2018

democracy like India. Hence, people can only hope that leadership will rise above electoral considerations, and help calm down social strife rather than exacerbate it.

With its military and economic power and inherent advantages of its geography, India undoubtedly is a significant player in the *multipolar* world. What it lacks is a position at the *Global High Table* as a permanent member of the UNSC. No one doubts India's credentials, but geopolitical wrangling and claims of pretentious candidates is confounding it.

However, is India is willing and ready to play a more assertive role in world affairs? Perceptions of other powers differ in this regard. US strategy think tanks believe India should play a greater role and want it as a regional counterweight to rising China[106].

American career diplomats, however, are more realistic about India's imperative to pursue economic development and retain its strategic autonomy. They are aware of the elitism of its foreign service and characterize Indian diplomacy as *"preachy"* and *"pricklish"*[107]. They know India will not toe the US line always.

Russian strategist Korybko however views the current scenario as India *"shedding multipolarity and recklessly moving closer to USA out of a shared interest in containing China"*. Just like the US *pivot to Asia,* Russia has its own version of *pivot to Asia,* wherein it sees itself as the *ultimate balancing power in Eurasia[108]*.

The cited Korybko article contends that Russia should make overtures to India, Japan, and Vietnam as all three are drawing closer to USA, due to their problems with China. Russia having recovered from its post-Soviet Union political and economic weaknesses therefore must reassert itself in Eurasia much more.

The article calls for deeper economic partnership with India beyond the traditional military-technical cooperation, wherein Russian firms could help modernize its power, railroad and port networks. However, it misreads India's intent. Despite its strategic

---

[106] *"It's Time for India to Take on a Larger Role on the World Stage"* Opinion piece in *Geopolitical Monitor* 29 May 2018. Accessed 13 June 2018.

[107] Teresita C. Schaffer and Howard B. Schaffer. 2016. *India at the Global High Table: The Quest for Regional Primacy and Strategic Autonomy,* Brookings Institution Press.

[108] Andrew Korybko, Article, Retrieved 13 June 2018. https://www.geopolitica.ru/en /en/article/russias-diplomatic-balancing-act-asia-benefit-its-chinese-ally

partnership with USA, India is unlikely to distance itself from its ally Russia, which remains a big supplier of military equipment.

China too is now India's second largest trading partner, despite mutual rivalry and the border dispute. Hence, even with China, as I discuss later in the book, India needs to formulate a more innovative foreign policy based on larger mutuality of interests, the Pakistan factor notwithstanding.

In this context, how does India's *National Security Doctrine* address the extant geopolitical power play? What are our supreme national interests and how do we plan to defend them? However, that answer will have to await formulation of a formal *National Security Doctrine*.

A moot question however is; that intent and aspirations apart, are we even capable of taking on that role at our current level of preparedness? Sure, our military strength ranks fourth in the world, but number of personnel and weapon systems alone do not automatically denote *capability*. Let us take China's example.

China had the world's largest military at Independence, which was battle-hardened after years of war against the Kuomintang. It later fought wars against the USA, India, Russia and Vietnam. However, its performance against fewer and poorly equipped Vietnamese forces showed serious weaknesses. This was evident also against Indian forces during the 1967 skirmishes in Sikkim.

As part of Deng's *Four Modernizations* launched in 1978, the Chinese completely restructured the military, made it leaner and meaner, reequipped it with the latest weaponry, and retrained it in modern combat doctrines. It maintained a low profile during this period of reorganization and intensive drills. It was only after attaining full competence in two decades, did it begin showcasing its new capabilities and announce to the world, *'we have arrived'*.

Indian Armed Forces too were battle-hardened, well trained and well led at Independence. However, for reasons discussed in the next chapter, their neglect led to the 1962 debacle, despite the high valour of our soldiers. Our spectacular victory in the 1971 War was more due to the outstanding political and military leadership, and bravery of our forces, than attributable to any major induction of sophisticated weapon systems.

The Kargil War too was won entirely by the outstanding valour and grit of our troops, despite serious shortcomings in the Higher Defence organization. Sadly, vital recommendations of the Kargil Review Committee remain unimplemented due to the petty feudal mindset of the bureaucracy and political indifference.

Indian Armed Forces are required to fight a two-front war with nuclear-armed adversaries, China and Pakistan. It is a real and potent threat where we are in an eyeball-to-eyeball confrontation along the LAC and LoC. Due to frequent ceasefire violations and an active Pakistan-abetted insurgency; our troops have been suffering far too many casualties even during peacetime.

Our Forces have been facing severe manpower shortages, especially in Young Officers. In addition, there are critical weapon and ammunition shortages and high obsolescence issues. Border roads and infrastructure construction too is way behind schedule.

Our Armed Forces have to *'catch-up'* with China and Pakistan after decades of neglect and backlogs. In such a dire situation, any responsible Govt would allocate more resources and undertake the much-delayed modernization in *mission mode.* So, what has the Govt done to remedy this? Regrettably, it has been downright irresponsible in reducing the Defence budget to a paltry 1.56% of the GDP, which is far less than what our adversaries spend.

India is the world's largest importer of arms, accounting for 14% of the world's imports. That has become inescapable, given years of neglect and our state-owned antiquated defence industry not meeting demands. However, no country that aspires to be an important player on the world stage can attain that status based on imported arms. All others have a strong indigenous military-industrial base to fulfil their aspirations.

National Security Doctrine, Higher Defence structure, budget allocation and the military-industrial complex; aspects that were alluded to in preceding paragraphs, are vital aspects of National security. Succeeding chapters will discuss all these in more detail.

With the broad overview of the military and economic strengths of the leading *players* in the *multipolar* world, let us now briefly review the current state of the geopolitical power play. Among the several current trouble spots in the world, I will cover mainly the Middle East, Far East and South Asia; the latter in more detail.

CURRENT STATE OF GEOPOLITICAL POWER PLAY

In the bipolar era of the Cold War, both USA and Soviet Union had maintained credible deterrence against each other. Their quest for world domination was intensified by their ideological chasm, *capitalist democracy* versus *totalitarian communism.* However, the MAD doctrine prevented a full-fledged war despite the high stakes involved.

The *multipolar* world however is fraught with more uncertainty due to greater number of geopolitical permutations and increased probability of miscalculation among players. Despite this, an all-out war is unlikely according to Thomas Friedman. In his *Golden Arches Theory of Conflict Prevention* Friedman argues that no two adversaries are likely to go to war if both are McDonalds' countries[109].

This odd-sounding *McDonald's*-based theory is attributable to scholars' proclivity for coining catchy phrases for bland academic writings. In effect, what he implies is that countries having large middle classes are unlikely to risk wars on *not-so-critical* issues, which could end up causing serious damage to their economy.

There are several examples to support this argument. After China shot down a US military aircraft in 2000, US business interests did not allow that explosive situation to escalate. Even though China and India fought a war in 1962, China is now India's second largest trade partner after USA. This could be one of the factors behind the mutually agreed de-escalation of the Doklam standoff in 2017.

This does not imply that countries would cease to advance their geopolitical interests merely due to the risk of conflict. In a *multipolar* world, countries would still pursue their vital strategic objectives against another power or its proxies through suitable measured responses. Both parties would try to *push the envelope* to test the intent and resilience of the adversary.

Brinkmanship will stop only when one party *blinks*. When will that happen, will depend upon the assessment of each party as to how critical is its strategic objective, and the *cost-benefit analysis* of pursuing confrontation further, even at the risk of escalation.

Middle East

Middle East has always been a conundrum for security analysts, not just due to its oil wealth and strategic location, but also because of Israel; a key western ally surrounded by hostile Arab countries. As if the Palestine imbroglio, various Arab-Israeli wars, the two Iraq wars, Arab Spring, and orchestrated *regime changes* were not bad enough, the rise of ISIS has confounded the situation further.

---

[109] Thomas L. Friedman, (2000), *The Lexus and The Olive Tree*, Harper Collins Publishers, London. Chapter 12. He argues that '*when a country reached the level of economic development where it had a middle class big enough to support a McDonald's network, it became a McDonald's country. And people in McDonald's countries didn't like to fight wars anymore, they preferred to wait in line for burgers*'.

A long-held, but not explicitly articulated cynical view among Western analysts has been that the world is better off if various Arab nations and factions keep fighting among themselves, rather than being united to fight against Israel and western interests. One would recall how no effective steps were taken to stop the eight-year long Iran-Iraq war, which left more than half a million dead.

Iraq, Libya and Egypt are now considerably weak to be able to threaten Israel. ISIS too has been contained, and most territory under it has been recaptured. However, from the US perspective its biggest failure has been its inability to dislodge Assad in Syria, who has enjoyed the staunch support of Russia and Iran-backed Shiite militias. Likewise, fighting among the Shiite Houthis and Saudi Arabia-led Sunni coalition, the later backed by USA, continues unabated in Yemen. Airstrikes by the Saudis have been taking a heavy toll on civilians and have been widely condemned.

At the heart of all fighting among various regimes, militias and factions in the Middle East is the quest for domination between Sunni Saudi Arabia and Shiite Iran. Iraq's destabilization and regime change had changed the power equation, and Iran has been gaining ascendency. However, with Trump reneging on the Iran nuclear deal and imposing new sanctions, there are uncertainties not only for Iran but also for its trading partners.

India, with 170 million Muslims, mostly Sunnis, but also having a sizable Shiite population, cannot afford to take sides in those conflicts. However, with a very large number of expatriate workers in Saudi Arabia and the Gulf nations, India is in a bind occasionally when there are instances of kidnapping or killing by Al Qaeda and Islamic State fighters.

Far East

North Korea's nuclear weapon and long-range ballistic missile programme has long been a great concern not just to South Korea, Japan and USA, but also to entire volatile region. In the last two years, exchange of vituperative threats and personal insults between Kim and Trump had crossed all bounds of diplomatic niceties and had the world on edge.

China wielded much influence over North Korea's beleaguered regime, which could survive sanctions only through China's aid and trade. It also acted as the interlocutor between the USA and North Korea, but could not get the latter to back off from its pursuit of nuclear weapons.

And just when the situation appeared to be going sharply downhill, the dramatic and unprecedented meeting between Kim and Trump brought it back from the brink. When Kim had made his historic trip to Seoul, it was clear that North Korea had taken a deliberate decision to chart a path-breaking course for détente with South Korea, and eventually with the United States.

The nuclear agreement with USA is indeed a welcome start but many tough negotiations lie ahead. While North Korea might provide credible evidence of its having destroyed all nuclear development and testing facilities, there is no guarantee that it would be as forthcoming about destroying its entire arsenal.

USA has a history of going back on agreements, either by *shifting the goalposts* or by reneging from them outright. Trump with his *America First* brand of unilateralism even with his NATO allies, does not inspire confidence in world leaders. North Korea may therefore well weigh on the side of prudence when it comes to the complete destruction of its nuclear weapons. This could well turn into a *cat and mouse* game involving protracted bargaining about on-site verifications, before any progress on the lifting of sanctions.

Where does this leave China? With direct US-Korean entente, China's advantage stands substantially eroded. Toughening of US stance on trade is already in evidence, with Trump imposing tariffs on $50 billion of Chinese goods. China too has retaliated with $34 billion of US goods. Will the trade war intensify? Not likely, for too long since retaliatory tariffs hit consumers in both countries. There will be gamesmanship and jousting to test out each other, but eventually things will settle down to an acceptable via media.

On geostrategic issues, however USA is likely to be more intractable. For instance, it would show less concern about China's sensitivities in South China Sea and would contest China's island reclamation and infrastructure-building moves more aggressively. US naval ships and aircraft could keep the area under greater surveillance.

Agreement with North Korea does not presage any reduction in US troops stationed in the Far East given Japan's security concerns, as well as USA's own *pivot to Asia,* and concern about China. USA is likely to firmly Southeast Asian countries that have territorial disputes with China, and forcefully seek to enforce the right to free navigation in South China Sea.

How will this emerging situation affect India? With its *Look East* policy, India has increased cultural, economic and strategic relations with ASEAN nations. There is military cooperation with many of these countries and Indian naval ships are increasingly making port calls across the Malacca Straits to them.

India has been somewhat ambivalent about the *Quadrilateral Security dialogue* that includes USA, Japan and Australia. The Malabar series of trilateral naval exercises between the navies of USA, Japan and India is an annual affair. In the 2007 edition, Australian Navy too had participated but later withdrew following China's protests against it. Lately, however it has expressed its willingness to rejoin these exercises.

South Asia

This is a volatile trouble spot where three nuclear-armed states are locked in decades-old confrontation. However, neither India's four wars with Pakistan nor the two with China (including the 1967 clashes) could resolve their disputes over Jammu and Kashmir (J&K) and Indo-Tibet border delineation respectively.

Geneses of these disputes and subsequent history are quite well known and documented in the public domain. Hence, this section will focus mainly on the current geopolitical dynamics and portents for the future.

Pakistan. When two nuclear-weapon states routinely engage in heavy exchanges of fire on the LoC and IB, and suffer casualties almost every day, chances of escalation run very high. This is even more probable since the scourge of global terrorism emanates from the Afghanistan-Pakistan (AfPak) region, where terrorists are still being recruited, indoctrinated and trained. Infiltration and terror strikes, actively abetted by the Pakistani army, are bound to meet with retaliation and could flare-up. These could have serious ramifications, which might not be confined only to the region.

Funding terror groups and infiltrating terrorists into J&K for attacks and triggering *intifada,* is Pakistan's low-cost strategy to make India *bleed from a thousand cuts.* For the Pakistani Army keeping such hostility alive is a dire compulsion, as it is desperate to redeem itself from the humiliation it suffered in 1971.

The Pakistani Army owes its pre-eminent status in the nation's polity to the seven-decade long confrontation with India, and it keeps hyping this to remain relevant. It has ruled the nation for long periods by staging military coups many times, which enabled it to usurp unbridled power and pelf. Pakistani Army's dominance in country's affairs has been institutionalized over many decades.

Even during periods when democracy was restored it was the real power centre. It can still override the elected Govt and even defy the Supreme Court. Having enjoyed unchallenged power all along, it is averse to allowing any meaningful settlement with India as that would strike at the very roots of its *raison d'être.* Its

Army has therefore sabotaged agreements with India, even though its own elected Govts signed those, such as the Simla Agreement, Lahore Declaration and trade liberalization measures.

Pakistan's *deep state,* which includes the powerful ISI, firmly controls the levers of power. Since 2008, when Musharraf had to resign to avoid impeachment, Pakistani Army has finessed the art of wielding the strings of power from *behind the scene.* It even orchestrated the beleaguered former Chief's flight to safety abroad, ostensibly on health grounds, as he was facing treason charges. Wiser after Musharraf's ordeal, it now prefers to call the shots by manipulating democratic institutions away from public glare. Thus, it neither faces accountability issues nor the dangers inherent in staging a *coup d'état.*

Indian Govts have often realized the futility of negotiations or even back-channel discussions with the civilian leadership in Pakistan, since the military can overrule them. Hence, prospects of an enduring settlement have always been bleak unless the Pakistani Army is on board.

However, several recent developments can alter this scenario. USA has long been aware of Pakistan's duplicity in the war against terror and the safe havens it provides to the Afghan Taliban. Most brazen was Pak Army's sheltering of the world's most wanted fugitive, Osama bin Laden. USA's relations with Pakistan, its ally since the CENTO-era, are strained further due to the strategic partnership with archrival India.

Stoppage or curtailment of military and economic aid has led Pakistan to seek financial bailouts from Saudi Arabia and the IMF to save its teetering economy. It is facing a serious debt crisis and on 21 June 2008, even Moody's has changed Pakistan's outlook from *stable* to *negative*[110]. Pakistan now has to lean even more heavily on China for military, economic and political support.

Even with Imran Khan installed as the new PM, political uncertainty will continue for some time until it is clear what equation the Pakistani Army will have with him. It is also too early to predict what stance he will adopt towards India on the Kashmir issue, and how he responds to US pressure to crush terrorist and radical Islamic groups. However, one thing is certain that the power of Pakistani Army in the country's affairs will not diminish.

---

[110] *Moody's changes outlook on Pakistan's rating to negative,* The Nation, 21 June 2018. https://nation.com.pk/21-Jun-2018/moodys-changes-outlook-on-pakistans-rating-to-negative

What therefore are the strategic implications for India? Those have always been obvious; at least to the military and strategic thinkers. Militancy in the Kashmir Valley is alive through infiltration of LeT and JeM terrorists, recruited and trained across the border, who in turn recruit locals for active support.

Intensive operations launched by security forces in the months preceding Ramzan 2018 had eliminated most of them, even at the cost of suffering many casualties themselves from cornered terrorists and stone-pelters. Military prudence had demanded that this momentum be maintained and the operations be persisted with until the conclusion.

However, just when the forces had gained the upper hand, the Govt ordered cessation of operations for the month of Ramzan, much to the frustration of the Forces. As had happened many times before, this respite allowed terrorists to recoup and regroup.

However, mere elimination of terrorists does not materially affect the Pakistani Army or its image, given that there is a seemingly endless supply of indoctrinated Jihadists with various terrorist organizations that it nurtures. It gets hurt and rattled only when our Army hits its posts on the LoC hard and mounting casualties there force it to plead for ceasefire.

While they never own up to eliminated terrorists, calling them *homegrown*, they are quite sensitive to casualties to their regular troops. Pakistan Army has a long history of concealing its debacles from the public, and has always painted a rosy version of *its exploits* in the 1948, 1965 and 1999 wars. It could not do so about the 1971 war, since the whole world saw how 93,000 of its troops had surrendered.

In this age of internet and 24/7 media coverage, it is no longer possible for Pakistan Army to conceal its casualties for long. Hence by inflicting robust punishment on its posts for every ceasefire violation and infiltration, not only would Indian forces send a strong signal to its Army, but also severely dent its public image. This alone will make it more amenable to a permanent solution.

Indian forces are very capable of doing so, and in fact are raring to go. However, sadly the political will is missing. Army does not get a free hand even in operational matters, despite claims to the contrary. Our casualties have been mounting due to this *soft approach*, causing deep resentment and demoralization. Soldiers are perplexed at the inexplicable '*now on and now off*' strategy.

A more robust response is imperative for *strategic signalling* too; both to Pakistan and the world. Far too long India has given an impression to the world, especially to countries in this region, of being a *pushover*. The only welcome exception in recent times was India firmly holding its ground in the Doklam standoff, which forced the Chinese to blink.

This was not the case earlier, even when India was weak in military and economic power, as well as geopolitical stature. For instance, it liberated Goa in 1961, annexed Sikkim in 1975, and militarily intervened in the Maldives to thwart a coup against its Govt in 1988. By far its boldest action was in 1971, when it truncated Pakistan to create Bangladesh, even in the face of a projected threat from USS Enterprise.

Alas, the world also saw it capitulate in the 1999 Indian Airlines hijack incident when it released five hard-core terrorists. Later, following the attack on its Parliament, India mobilized its forces in January 2002 against Pakistan, but still did not follow through. In May 2002, after the terrorist strike on an Army camp near Jammu, even then India did not retaliate. Finally, India withdrew its forces from the border in October 2002 without any action.

The audacious Mumbai terror attacks of 2008 again showed the world India's glaring internal security weaknesses. Even more damaging to India's image was a timid response, which regrettably now is only constant whining that Pakistan has not taken any action against the masterminds of that carnage.

Pakistan feels emboldened by its possession of a credible nuclear deterrent. Further, with its refusal to declare a *'no first use'* policy like India has done, and its touting battlefield nuclear weapons as a counter to India's *cold start* doctrine and massive conventional assaults, it feels it has deterred India from escalating any skirmish on the LoC.

But, this is not how sovereign, self-respecting Nations behave! Especially, when the whole world is watching! Surely, the world finds it incomprehensible that a country that supposedly is a major player in a *multipolar* world, and which expectedly would help maintain a just World Order, is either unwilling or incapable of firmly responding to onslaughts against its own National interests. The world does not respect weakness, and there are no marks for showing undue *restraint,* particularly when one's cause is just.

Israel's glaring example is there for the whole world to see. Much larger and more powerful Arab nations surround it, and yet it inflicted resounding defeats on them in all the wars it fought. True, Israel had the support of the Western world, but none of them contributed troops to fight its wars; it won them on its own strength, tenacity and ingenuity.

Even tiny Vietnam beat back the mighty USA and gave a bloody nose to the Chinese, when the latter invaded their country in 1979. North Korea doggedly pursued its nuclear and missile programme, which it believed was essential for its survival, despite global isolation, economic sanctions, and US intimidation. Ultimately, it brought Trump himself to the negotiating table in Singapore.

India is a much more powerful country economically and militarily, and has a far greater geopolitical and moral stature. *Then why does it not act as one?*

India has always maintained, and the world has acknowledged that J&K is an integral part of India due to its formal accession in 1947. The world has also long concluded that the AfPak region is the source of global terrorism, where many terrorist organizations flourish with impunity. Many of these are nurtured by the ISI as part of Pakistan's strategy of using terrorism as an instrument of state policy.

Where is the question therefore about India's legitimacy and its irrefutable right to retaliate strongly against firing and infiltration across the LoC and IB? Why must we show restraint, in defending our supreme national interests? Aren't we unduly concerned about possible international opprobrium if we escalate the conflict? Should we be so concerned even when our cause is just?

Other countries, big and small, have acted unilaterally even when they were grossly violating international norms. Russia's actions in Chechnya and Crimea, China's island reclamation and aggressive actions in South China Sea, China's brutal repression against its own people in Xinjiang, Tibet and Tiananmen Square in Beijing, USA's invasion of Iraq on dubious grounds, and its inhuman separation of the children of asylum seekers at the Mexican border; these are just a few among numerous examples.

Apart from the legitimacy of any retaliatory action, militarily too our forces have the capability to punitively deal with Pakistani provocations. Why then the hesitation of our political leadership and our policy makers? Do they take Pakistan's refusal to declare a *'no first use'* policy too seriously?

Surely, punitive artillery bombardments of Pakistani posts involved in pushing infiltrators and terrorists cannot escalate into a full-fledged nuclear exchange. Nor would India's precautionary mobilization across the IB. Would not the Pakistani leadership war-game any contemplated foolhardy option, and conclude that it would invite a devastating response? Would it not be conscious of its own lack of second-strike capability? It is high time that our leadership calls the Pakistani bluff!

On the other hand, is the political leadership too worried about the inevitable *economic costs* of even a limited escalation? However, are there no *economic costs* involved in letting the current stalemate linger? What about the *costs* due to loss of lives and injuries to security forces and civilians; the ex gratia payments etc.? What about the *opportunity costs* lost due to loss of tourism, curtailed economic activity, and lost production in J&K?

A major concern, however, could be the current state of the Indian economy that is still recovering from demonetization, GST and rising oil bill. This factor is even more critical since crucial State elections are due this year and the General elections next year. Considerations of electoral politics are therefore possibly overriding all geostrategic and military factors yet again.

Should not the body responsible to formulate and implement National Security Policy undertake a holistic analysis of political, economic, military and diplomatic dimensions, and present viable options to the top political leadership? This does not appear to be happening since quite often actions by various limbs of the Govt seem to be ill considered, incoherent and inconsistent. These aspects are discussed in more detail in the following chapter.

Meanwhile, what is the impact of our inadequate and seemingly weak-kneed responses upon other countries in the region? It does not behove our stature that even smaller countries that are within our sphere of influence, are *cocking a snook* at us.

Maldives. Its location in India's backyard makes it our legitimate security concern. It has always had strong relations with India, but ever since Yameen came to power, it has defiantly kowtowed to China and even signed on the BRI project. Tensions flared up in February 2018 when Yameen defied the Supreme Court's order to release ex-President Nasheed, and instead declared Emergency.

Eleven Chinese naval ships sailed into the Indian Ocean in a show of solidarity, but retreated after Indian Naval ships started their drills. Maldives is now heavily under Chinese influence, while relations with India are turning increasingly sour.

Even Seychelles has apparently made a U-turn in its relations with India. On 14 June 2018, it refused to ratify an agreement that it had signed with India for construction of a naval base. However, during the visit of its President in end-June, a somewhat vague statement was released that both countries would work on the naval project but at a pace that Seychelles is comfortable with. But given the fact that the country's opposition parties have declined to ratify the agreement, it remains to be seen whether President Faure is able to persuade the opposition to change its stance.

Sri Lanka. Its strategic location also deeply impacts our security concerns and therefore India is very sensitive to any inimical foreign power exercising undue influence over its Govt. Sri Lanka was getting too cosy with the Chinese and allowed them to construct Hambantota port and International airport. Relations therefore were quite strained during the Rajapaksa regime.

However, as is the experience of many countries where Chinese firms have built infrastructure projects, Sri Lanka too realized it had landed itself in a *debt trap*. Hence, the new Govt had to give control of the port to a Chinese firm on 99-year lease under a debt-for-equity deal.

While Sri Lanka has assured that the Chinese Navy will not be allowed to use the port, it nonetheless remains a security concern. India has now made a $300 million bid for operational control of the International airport on 40-year lease. Financially the deal is rather odd since the airport hardly has any flights operating from it, and would not generate much revenue. However, it will enable close surveillance over the port's activities[111].

Nepal. Despite Nepal's vital importance to India as a buffer state, and with numerous Gurkhas serving in the Indian Army, it still had to face a blockade on the Madhesi issue. Indian diplomacy has often caused heartburn among India's smaller neighbours due to its overbearing attitude.

Nepal has always had deep historic ties with India, but under its new communist Govt, it is now forging more links with China. PM Oli during his trip to China in June 2018 signed some projects under the BRI. An agreement is also in the offing for a rail link between Kerung in Tibet and Kathmandu.

Bangladesh. Relations with Bangladesh are not as fraught as they were under the Begum Khalida Zia regime, but things could change for the worse if any radical Islamist party comes to power again. The Teesta river dispute is still an issue that needs an early resolution. Given Bangladesh's strategic location, hemmed in as it is between our northeastern states and the rest of India, it is very vital that we maintain cordial and cooperative relations with it.

The Indo-Bangladesh border has largely been fenced, but incidents of infiltration do take place occasionally and are a cause

---

[111] Quartz India. *Why does India want to buy the world's emptiest airport?* https://qz.com/1146925/sri-lankas-hambantota-why-does-india-want-to-buy-the-worlds-emptiest-airport/ Accessed 23 June 2018

for tension because illegal immigrants skew the demographics of Assam and other eastern states. Of greater concern is infiltration of radical elements from terrorist organizations such as HuJI, which was responsible for the German Bakery blast in Pune. Lot of counterfeit Indian currency is also smuggled in through this route.

Myanmar. On our eastern frontier, India shed years of limited contacts with Myanmar's military junta, and warmed up to the new leader Aung San Suu Kyi; daughter of Aung San the Father of the Nation. Though her party won a huge victory in elections, she cannot be the PM since her husband was a foreigner. She now holds the newly created post of *State Counsellor*, a role akin to a Prime Minister. The military still wields a lot of power in the country.

Myanmar has drawn a lot of criticism worldwide for alleged acts of ethnic cleansing against Rohingya Muslims by the Buddhist clergy and military junta. A very large number of Rohingya Muslims have sought refuge in neighbouring countries such as Bangladesh and India, which the locals resent.

India has a big stake in deepening its relations with Myanmar. For one, it needs to ensure that Myanmar does not allow sanctuaries to insurgent groups active in our northeastern states. The ambitious *India–Myanmar–Thailand Trilateral Highway* (Fig 21) which will link Moreh in India with Mae Sot in Thailand via Myanmar is vital for boosting commerce with Southeast Asia.

Fig. 21 – Trilateral Highway Project

Taken up as part of India's *Look East* policy, the highway is expected to be completed by April 2021, and will immensely boost trade in the ASEAN-India Free Trade Area. Both India and ASEAN have plans to extend it to Laos, Cambodia and Vietnam as part of the *East-West Economic Corridor*. This will greatly enhance land-based connectivity between India and the whole of Southeast Asia. Eventually this will be much cheaper than the sea routes, apart from avoiding the congested passage through the Malacca Straits.

Afghanistan. Stability in Afghanistan is critical not just for India and the region, but for the entire world since AfPak is the nursery of global terrorism. Its rugged terrain, numerous ethnic tribes with unique culture and customs, and a long history of political turbulence, make it a dangerous, almost ungovernable region.

For over three millennia, Afghanistan has been the gateway to the Indian subcontinent for numerous migrations and invasions. Hindu Kabul Shahis had ruled the Kabul Valley and Gandhara from the 3rd up to 8th century, till Muhammad bin Qasim captured it in 712 CE for the Ummayad Caliphate[112].

Given its strategic importance, Maharaja Ranjit Singh had extended the Sikh Empire in the series of Afghan-Sikh wars from Punjab, Kashmir, Kangra and Peshawar to areas beyond the Khyber Pass. Due to the death of his leading General, Hari Singh Nalwa he could not extend it further.

In the First Anglo-Afghan war (1839-1842), the British had suffered a disastrous defeat. However, they won the Second Anglo-Afghan War (1878-1880), which culminated in the Treaty of Gandamak. Accordingly, the British withdrew from Afghanistan, allowing the Emir to rule over various Afghan tribes, but he had to cede foreign affairs to the British[113].

In 1896, the British drew the *Durand Line* that demarcated areas under the control of Afghanistan and the British. It cuts right through Pashtun tribal areas of present-day Khyber Pakhtunkhwa, towards the south through Baluchistan, and through Gilgit-Baltistan in the north. The Treaty of Rawalpindi in 1919 reaffirmed the Line after the Third Anglo-Afghan War, and finalized it in 1921[114]. While Pakistan treats it as the international boundary between their two countries, neither the Afghan Govt nor the Pashtun tribes recognize it as such.

---

[112] Dr D B. Pandey, *The Shahi Afghanistan and Punjab,* 1973, pp 1, 45-48, 80.

[113] Adamec, L.W.; Norris, J.A. (2010). *Anglo-Afghan Wars Encyclopædia Iranica.*

[114] Smith, Cynthia (August 2004). "A Selection of Historical Maps of Afghanistan – The Durand Line". United States: Library of Congress. Retrieved 24 June 2018.

The British had arbitrarily drawn a line that divided Pashtuns, Baluch other ethnic groups living on either side of the border. Later, in 1947 too they similarly drew the Radcliffe Line cutting through Punjab province of undivided India, which left thousands dead and disrupted the lives of millions during the tragic Partition. Thus, record of the British in leaving festering wounds for the posterity to suffer, has been appalling and indeed reprehensible.

The present situation remains as fluid as ever despite a rare, peaceful ceasefire during Ramzan 2018. However, while the Afghan Govt unilaterally extended it, the Taliban did not and instead responded with a series of suicide attacks. During the Eid ceasefire, Taliban had freely roamed the cities and mingled with the civil population, even with Afghan security forces. While images of such bonhomie raised hopes that the Taliban could be more amenable for peace, perhaps weary from the long conflict, it unnerved their leadership who did not extend the ceasefire.

The entire world wants a peaceful and stable Afghanistan, but Pakistan wants it to be on its terms. It wants a *friendly* regime in Kabul that does not *lean* towards India. There is a lot at stake for India too, not just because of its heavy investments in various infrastructure projects but also in the new trade route to Central Asia through Chabahar port.

Inherent contradictions due to divided ethnicities on either side of the *Durand Line* further complicate issues, especially since the Baluch and Pashtuns in Pakistan are quite restive. A key demand of the Taliban is that all foreign forces must leave Afghanistan but it is unclear how long will Trump persist with his efforts to stabilize Afghanistan.

TTP has announced Mufti Noor Wali Mehsud as the successor to Mullah Fazlullah, who was killed in a drone attack[115]. It remains to be seen if the TTP under the new leadership will step up attacks in Pakistan as a reprisal.

China too has a stake in a stable Afghanistan due to its huge investments in the CPEC. Large sections of the CPEC pass through Baluchistan, which is in the grip of an insurgency. As highlighted earlier both CPEC and BRI are critical to China in the context of its long and vulnerable SLOC.

---

[115] "Pakistan Taliban names new leader and confirms death of Mullah Fazlullah in US drone strike" The Sunday Times. Accessed 24 June 2018.
https://www.thetimes.co.uk/article/pakistan-taliban-names-new-leader-and-confirms-death-of-mullah-fazlullah-in-us-drone-strike-x67tz0gmg

BRI and CPEC. Figs. 22 and 23, along with Figs. 18, 19 and 20, clearly bring out the vulnerability of China's exports-driven economy due to its long SLOC. Any disruption of the SLOC can severely affect both, its oil imports as well as its exports.

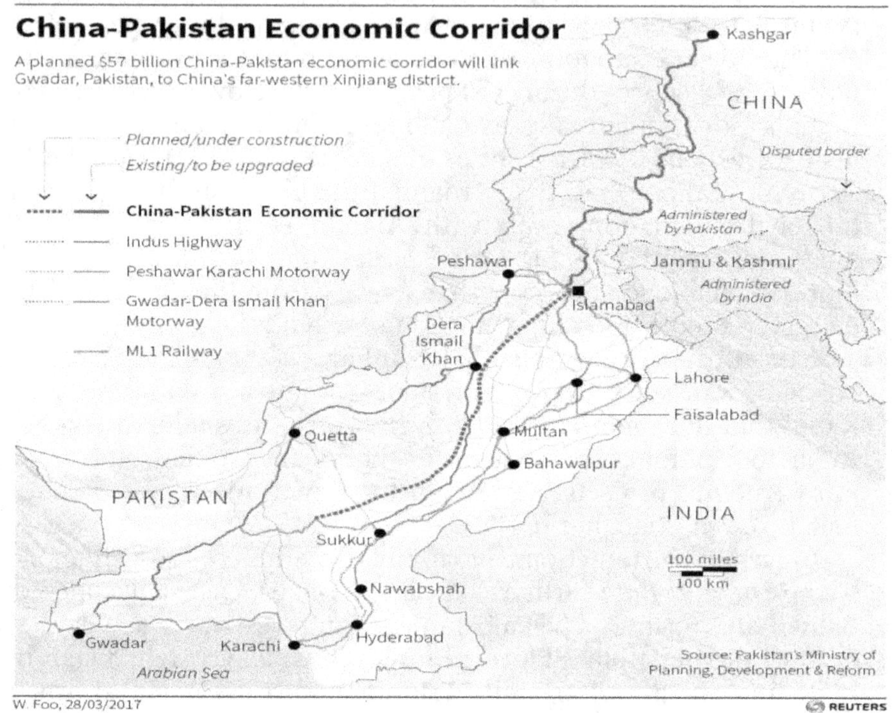

Fig. 22 – China-Pakistan Economic Corridor

Much of 21st century's geostrategic focus will therefore remain on China's ambitious *Belt and Roads Initiative* or BRI (formerly OBOR) and *China Pakistan Economic Corridor* (CPEC). With the CPEC, it hopes to reduce dependence on the vulnerable SLOC from the Red Sea and Persian Gulf, through the Indian Ocean, Malacca Straits and the dispute-prone South China Sea.

Likewise, with the BRI it seeks to better serve and further expand markets for its exports to Europe, Asia and Africa. By co-developing infrastructure projects in partnership with various countries in the BRI and CPEC, it seeks to enhance its geopolitical stature and expand its global footprint.

As a *vision statement* of a country that is aspiring for, and has been assiduously preparing to attain global leadership, the concept can hardly be faulted. Whether China will actually be able to achieve those ambitious goals remains a big question.

With its $57 billion investment in the CPEC, China has a lot at stake, especially since it passes close to the borders with Iran and Afghanistan. The Iran-Pakistan border is porous and a smuggling route for opium, heroin, arms and human trafficking. Sistan-Baluchestan is a Sunni majority province of Iran that has the same Baluch ethnicity as in Pakistan's Baluchistan.

Iran has often accused Pakistan of supporting the Sunni Baluch insurgency, initially by *Jundallah* between 2005 and 2010. After its leader was killed, erstwhile Jundallah members formed a new group Jaysh al-Adl in 2012, which continues to carry out attacks in Iran's Sistan-Baluchestan province.

The mid-section of the CPEC will be vulnerable to insurgency in Pakistan's Baluchistan province as well as from the unstable and porous Pak-Afghan border. The Baluch have long resented their political and economic exploitation by other Pakistani provinces, especially Punjab, which has left their mineral-rich province extremely impoverished and alienated.

Pakistan has assured dedicated troops to guard the CPEC, but the extent to which that can be guaranteed remains doubtful, given the widespread resentment. Already instances of kidnapping of Chinese engineers have taken place, and as greater number of Chinese are eventually deployed on various infrastructure projects, their vulnerability would increase.

The most contentious part of the CPEC is its northern section's passage through POK. There is just no question therefore of India accepting it, and despite Beijing's overtures India has firmly refused to support the BRI and the CPEC. Thus, almost the entire stretch of the CPEC in Pakistan passes through vulnerable, insurgency-affected areas.

There are serious questions about the financial implications of the project. Sri Lanka and other countries have run into a *debt-trap* due to tough Chinese financial terms for various projects. While initially loans from Chinese financial institutions are only slightly above global commercial norms, they become more stringent progressively during renegotiation of various clauses.

Renegotiation, often on spurious grounds, is also facilitated by huge bribes to host country politicians. Besides, due to *sunk-costs* in the projects, and the crunch of repaying loan instalments, host countries often have no choice.

The Chinese Govt. insists that loans be availed only from its financial institutions, and only Chinese firms execute the projects.

As highlighted earlier, Chinese oligarchs or the PLA own many of them. The Chinese Govt acquiesces with their predatory tactics to earn high profits, which keeps them happy and they in turn keep a lid on the brewing resentment due to poverty and unemployment in their respective provinces.

Such tactics also conform to larger Chinese strategic objectives of wresting control over these projects, as for instance happened with Hambantota port in Sri Lanka. Once the host Govt finds itself in a *debt-trap* due to inability to pay the loan instalment, the Chinese negotiate a *debt-for-equity* deal to swap the debt for majority control over the project.

Alarmed with the Sri Lankan experience Pakistan has cancelled the $ 14 billion *Diamer-Bhasha* dam deal under CPEC. Earlier Nepal too had cancelled a $2.5 billion deal with China for a hydropower plant under the BRI[116].

Many developing countries that were very allured by Chinese promises of aiding their economic development through so-called *mutually beneficial* partnerships under the BRI, are viewing it as neo-colonialism. This is a modern version of East India Company's land-grabbing policies.

It is not clear if Pakistani strategic thinkers are wondering if they could end up paying too heavy an economic and strategic price for the CPEC. They too should know that after all, *there are no free lunches* in the world.

Just as the CPEC, China's objectives in the BRI projects too are purely strategic, than just economic. Notwithstanding the professed intent of having a more secure and dependable alternative to its long SLOC, its *string of pearls* strategy is designed to extend its reach into the Indian Ocean up to the Red Sea and Persian Gulf.

From China's perspective, naval bases on peninsular India's deep salience into the Indian Ocean dominate its SLOC. In addition, USA has naval facilities in Kuwait, Bahrain, Qatar and UAE in the Persian Gulf, as well as at Djibouti and Diego Garcia.

Further aggravating its *"Malacca Dilemma"*, as China calls it, is the US Navy's planned base at Cocos Islands. While Diego Garcia oversees China's SLOC passing through the Malacca Straits, the new base would help the US Navy dominate China's shipping

---

[116] *"Pakistan pulls plug on dam deal over China's 'too strict' conditions in latest blow to Belt and Road plans"* South China Morning Post. Accessed 26 June 2018 http://www.scmp.com/news/china/diplomacy/ defence/article/2120261/ pakistan-pulls-plug-dam-deal-over-chinas-too-strict

traffic that bypasses Malacca Straits and goes through the deep channel Sunda Strait or the Lombok Strait[117].

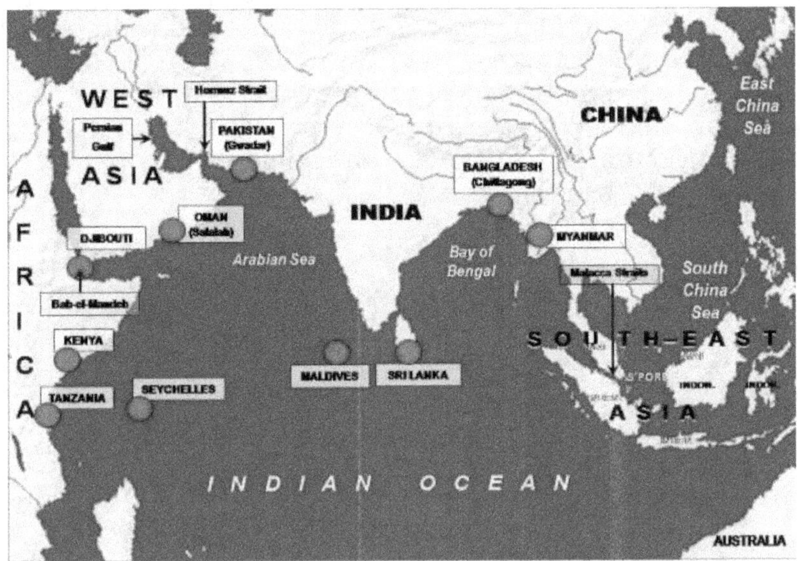

Fig, 23 – China's SLOC and access to ports in the Indian Ocean

However, this is not how India and USA see it. *String of pearls* is China's attempt at power projection into the Indian Ocean to contest US domination there. Given China's ambitions to become a global power, it is a building block for it becoming the dominant power in Asia and Africa to start with.

In the current and emerging geopolitical environment, the Sino-Indian relations are not a binary. Rising China is poised to challenge US supremacy, while India too is competing to counter Chinese ascendency. Hence, USA is hoping for a strategic alliance with India, as a counterweight to China.

India certainly welcomes a mutually beneficial partnership with USA. However, it would like to retain her strategic independence and not be sucked into Sino-US power play. India cannot be weaned away from Russia, which remains the largest seller of military equipment. Nor can it stop importing oil from Iran at US bidding.

---

[117] "The United States and the Indian Ocean Region: The Security Vector" *Future Directions*. 23 June 2016. Retrieved 27 June 2018. http://www.futuredirections.org.au/publication/united-states-indian-ocean-region-security-vector

INSTC. Even more critical for India is the *International North–South Transport Corridor* (INSTC) at Fig. 24. It is a 7,200km ship-rail-road corridor between India, Iran, Afghanistan, Armenia, Azerbaijan, Russia, Central Asia and Europe. They carried out dry runs in 2014 on two routes; Mumbai to Baku via Bandar Abbas; and Mumbai to Astrakhan via Bandar Abbas, Tehran and Bandar Anzali. To be completed in 2018, it will be a game changer for Indian trade with estimated cost reduction of $2500 per 15 tons of cargo[118].

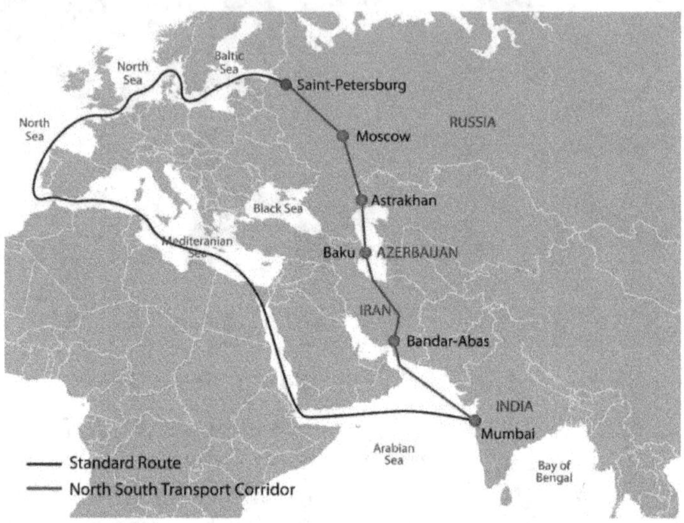

Fig. 24 - International North–South Transport Corridor

India had not entered into USA's CENTO and SEATO security pacts at the height of the Cold War, even when it was economically and militarily weak. Strategic partnership with USA? Yes. However, India must not get into an alliance that has military connotations of hostility with China, which is now India's second largest trading partner. India also cannot downgrade its traditional ties with Russia, nor can it forgo oil imports from Iran and immense benefits from the INSTC.

Despite its interest in forging a partnership with India, USA is unwilling to share cutting-edge technology. It has hardened its stance on H1B visas and has imposed tariffs on several Indian exports. It has not stated unambiguously that it will grant a waiver

---

[118] *India-Eurasia road almost ready, container dry run soon*; economictimes. indiatimes.com; Published: 3 April 2017; Accessed: 27 June 2018

from sanctions for India's purchase of S-400 Air Defence missile system from Russia, or continued oil imports from Iran.

Even though USA has distanced itself from Pakistan, it is not because of India. It is mainly due to its own frustration over Pakistan's duplicity in the war on terror and for not stamping out Taliban sanctuaries inside Pakistan.

It hardly bears emphasis therefore that the onus of resolving the Sino-Indian boundary dispute and the Indo-Pak conflict over POK and terrorism rests squarely on us alone. No alliance with USA, Russia or anyone else will do it for us.

Even when Nehru had desperately sought USAF intervention after the Chinese attack in 1962, Kennedy had refused. However, that was partially because the Chinese had cleverly timed the attack to coincide with the Cuban missile crisis, of which Mao had foreknowledge. He did not want either Kennedy or Khrushchev (who he called *renegade communist*) to help India.

Hence, it is imperative that India makes itself strong enough to confront both adversaries simultaneously, should they act in concert. In this modern age no country wants war, regardless whether one subscribes to Thomas Friedman's *Golden Arches* (McDonalds) theory or not. However, peace always has to be negotiated from a position of strength, as that alone will generate more favourable options and outcomes.

Against the foregoing review of the global and regional geopolitical environment, we can now better appreciate the extant situation apropos the Indo-Pak and Sino-Indian conflicts, and the likely portents for the future.

Indo-Pak Conflict

The current state of the Indo-Pak confrontation, especially the situation in J&K is not at all acceptable. Under cover of ceasefire violations, Pakistan continues to push in terrorists across the LoC. Their terror strikes against the military and civilians have been taking an unacceptable toll, which is causing intense anger, frustration and demoralization.

Security operations against terrorists in the hinterland always lead to a cycle of further alienation, when action has to be taken against stone-pelters who try to thwart those operations at the behest of terror outfits. This self-reinforcing cycle needs to be broken through a different strategy. More robust and muscular action is required at the LoC to stem the flow of terrorists.

Given the nature of the terrain, some terrorists do manage to sneak in despite multi-tiered deployments. However, every single ceasefire violation meant to provide cover to infiltrators, and posts suspected to facilitate infiltration, must trigger a strong punitive response with overwhelming firepower.

Even if these escalate into artillery duels, we must persist with them. Only this will send a clear signal to Pakistan that all infiltration attempts will invite severe punishment on their posts that abet them. We just cannot keep maintaining restraint, while suffering from its strategy of *bleeding us with a thousand cuts*.

Pakistan's shrill complaints, as well as its fear mongering about *further escalation* should not matter at all since the whole world is aware of its record on terrorism. Further reinforcing its sullied record was Pakistan's placement in June 2018 on the FATF *grey list* for one year at the least.

Our cause has always had legal and moral sanction and hence we need not be overly concerned about world opinion. *Unilateralism,* in any case, is the *flavour of the season*, and we must follow examples set by Trump, Putin and Xi Jinping.

The current *soft approach* and policy of restraint are just not working. India has more than adequate military capability to execute this more robust strategy. Our economy too is strong enough to withstand any temporary spike in expenditure. Pakistan's economy on the other hand is in a precarious situation, and Moody's has already downgraded it. How long can it survive on doles from Saudi Arabia, which itself is embroiled in conflict in Yemen and has its own power struggle *vis a vis* Iran?

China is unlikely to intervene given that it will be facing more assertive and even aggressive US intervention in South China Sea, now that its services as an interlocutor between USA and North Korea are no longer required. Moreover, China's main concern is the CPEC and it is therefore more likely to pressurize Pakistan not to destabilize the situation.

Sino-Indian Boundary Dispute

Barring the 1967 skirmishes in Sikkim and the 2017 Doklam standoff, situation along the LAC has remained quite stable since 1962. Despite China's claim on Arunachal Pradesh, India firmly holds the positions up to the McMahon line, which China does not recognize. That status cannot change, even though China might occasionally make *noises* about the Dalai Lama, or Indian dignitaries visiting that state.

Even in 1962, China had unilaterally withdrawn north of the McMahon Line when our troops were facing a rout. This was not done as a favour, but because it was aware that the terrain did not suit over-extension of operations across the watershed. China did not try to alter the status even when India was fully engaged in wars with Pakistan in 1965 and 1971. Now, when India is far stronger and firmly established in that sector, any major attempt to alter the status quo is unlikely, barring an odd standoff.

In the western sector, China holds Indian Territory of Aksai Chin, and the Trans-Karakoram Tract (known as Shaksgam tract) that Pakistan ceded to China in an agreement signed in 1963.

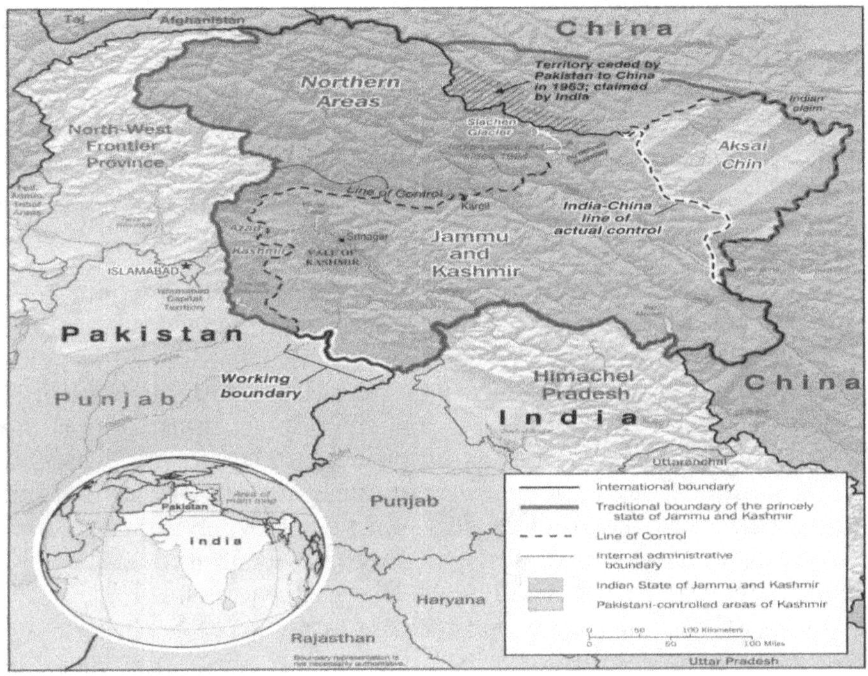

Source: US Library of Congress

Fig. 25–Pakistan and China occupied areas in J&K[119]

One can trace the origin of Aksai Chin's disputed status to the conquest of Kashmir in 1834 by Gulab Singh for the Sikh Empire. After the British defeated the Sikhs in 1846, Gulab Singh purchased Kashmir from them. His army, under Zorawar Singh captured whole of Ladakh, including Aksai Chin. However, there are different versions of the alignment of Kashmir's boundary.

The alignment determined in 1867 by WH Johnson of Survey of India (the *Johnson Line*) showed Aksai Chin as part of Kashmir.

---

[119] US Library of Congress http://hdl.loc.gov/loc.gmd/g7653j.ct000803. Accessed 29 June 2018.

However, in 1899, the British Govt ceded Aksai Chin plains in the northeast and the **Trans-Karakoram Tract** in the north to China, which is the *McCartney–MacDonald Line*[120]. After Independence India declared the *Johnson Line* as the true alignment and thus claimed Aksai Chin. *Yet another mess left by the British for posterity to deal with.*

In effect therefore, since so-called *disputed areas* in the central and eastern sectors are physically under Indian occupation, the *status quo* suits us. Only in the west, the Chinese hold Aksai Chin and the **Trans-Karakoram Tract**. This status has remained frozen in time for the past 56 years.

Question therefore arises whether the Chinese will try to alter the status now, or in the near future. Will they wage war to capture areas claimed by them in the eastern theatre? Similarly, are we prepared to liberate militarily our claimed areas in the west? Do we have the requisite military and economic strength, and geopolitical stature to do so, as of now?

China reorganized and strengthened its military under its *Four Modernizations* for over 20 years. It strengthened its economy too, which has surpassed US GDP (PPP terms), before aggressively asserting its geopolitical clout. In the interim, it kept its territorial and other disputes *frozen*, for resurrection at more opportune times using its doctrine of *unequal treaties* and *historical wrongs*.

To counter China, India needs to speed up modernization and reorganization of its military in a big way. Border infrastructure also needs strengthening, since all these have suffered and lagged behind due to inadequate defence budget allocations.

US sanctions on India because of purchase of S-400 Triumf from Russia and oil imports from Iran will come into effect from November 2018. Indications are that Washington may not grant us waivers despite our strategic partnership. How India deals with this major challenge will be interesting to watch.

India has a lot at stake in the INSTC and Chabahar port in Iran. It has been looking forward to reaping economic dividends of increased trade, at lower costs and reduced transit times, with Central Asian Republics, Russia, and Europe. Its joining the Ashbagat Agreement is also a step towards that end. Nor can it cannot forgo its time-tested Russian relationship.

Will India therefore stand up against unilateral US sanctions on Iran that do not have UNSC approval? Not only these impinge on

---

[120] Noorani, A.G. (2010), *India–China Boundary Problem 1846–1947: History and Diplomacy,* Oxford University Press India; pp. 52-53, 60, 69

India's rights as a sovereign Nation, they also critically affect our economic and strategic interests. As an emerging player in the multipolar world, *will India finally stand up and be counted?*

While India values its strategic partnership with USA, it cannot be a one-way street. USA has not delivered on many counts, be it membership of the UNSC, and NSG, or more pressure on Pakistan. So why must India meekly follow Trump's diktats on Iran? This will be a big diplomatic challenge, and India cannot afford to be found wanting.

Russia and China too have a lot at stake in Iran. While Russia and Iran together backed the Assad regime against USA, Iran is among the top five exporters of oil to China. There is therefore strategic convergence of interest with India *vis a vis* Iran. Will the three therefore together counter Trump's bullying?

In international relations, *there are no permanent friends, only permanent interests.* China and India are already considering forming an *Oil Buyer's Club* to negotiate better oil prices with OPEC. A stable Afghanistan is as much in India's interest as it is to China, apropos India's trade with Afghanistan through Chabahar and security of CPEC respectively. There are several other issues where there is a convergence of strategic interests. *Could they be harbingers of a China-India entente in future? Who knows?*

Howsoever far-fetched this might seem now; it is not beyond the realm of possibility. In past 75 years, the world has witnessed tectonic shifts on the geopolitical chessboard. This therefore merits more debate and analysis, rather than outright dismissal.

Conflicts have often resulted from suspicion and misread intent of adversaries. For example, despite India having accepted Tibetan Autonomous Region as part of China, the latter suspected India's intentions when it gave asylum to Dalai Lama and Tibetan refugees. This, along with aggressive assertions of Indian claims on Aksai Chin, was among the causes for the Chinese invasion.

While ostensibly Sino-Indian hostility is due to the boundary dispute, it has been in suspended animation since 1962. In the present context, however it is mainly due to China's perception that India has fully embraced its strategic partnership with USA to *contain* it and harm its interests. As a counter, therefore China has been allying with Pakistan to keep India under pressure.

On the other hand, if analyses by Chinese think tanks of India's actions and intentions were to indicate that India will not forgo its strategic autonomy under any circumstance, and will not be a US pawn, the picture can change. It is true that India and China are competitors in trade and geopolitical aspirations, but barring 1962, they have no history of aggressive designs over each other.

Hence, if India is unwilling to partner USA solely to contain China, the rationality of China provoking Indo-Pak hostility comes into question. This is because of the criticality of CPEC to China. It knows that India cannot support CPEC because it passes through the Northern Areas, which are under Pakistan's illegal occupation. The status of Northern Areas will therefore have to change, at the very least. China cannot feel comfortable with the current disturbed and *unsettled* status of Northern areas, through which the CPEC passes, which India can interdict if the chips are down. With its strategic stake and huge investments in the CPEC, it is quite possible that China will favour some form of resolution.

Likewise, a stable Afghanistan is important for China for CPEC's security and, more importantly, to ensure that Taliban, ISIS, Al Qaeda and other Jihadi groups do not foment militant Islamic radicalism among the Uyghurs in Xinxiang. For that, it will be essential to prevent Pakistan from giving them support and sanctuaries. Where the USA failed, China can be more effective, since Pakistan has no one else to bank upon for military, economic and diplomatic support.

As Bismarck had said, *politics is the art of the possible.* Hence, India's political leadership has to come up with more innovative and pragmatic solutions to these long-festering problems. The drift and the *status quo* cannot continue. We must do this only from a position of strength.

To Sum up therefore....

12

National Security Doctrine

As discussed in Chapter 1, connotation of National security is not just *absence of military threat* to a country's frontiers. It is far more complex and comprehensive, since it encompasses several interdependent factors in a Nation's internal and external environments. In Chapter 3 these factors were grouped under *dimensions* based on their affinity, and then integrated into the holistic *National Security Paradigm*.

Since National security needs to be analyzed in the context of the prevailing Geopolitical environment, let us first review the key *takeaways* from its analysis undertaken in Chapter 11.

- **Geopolitical Power play.** US dominance in an ostensibly *unipolar* world is under challenge from a resurgent Russia, which seeks to regain its eminence of the Soviet era. China, riding on its newfound economic power and military prowess is also challenging it, in strategic convergence with Russia. UK, embroiled in *Brexit* woes, is a mere shadow of its past. France and Germany dominate the EU, and challenge Trump's unilateralism in trade. India's economy has shown a dramatic upswing since 1991, but to become a key player in a *multipolar* world it is yet to get its act together in military strength

- **Armed Conflicts.** Major armed conflicts are confined to the Middle East at present, except for localized insurgencies or civil wars in Africa and Latin America. India-China border conflict has remained frozen since 1962, barring the skirmishes in 1967. LoC between India and Pakistan has not had a major flare-up since 1999, but frequent ceasefire violations and militancy in J&K sponsored by the latter keep tensions alive. The Taliban dominate much of the countryside in Afghanistan, but more ominous is the increased activity of ISIS and AQAP elements.

- **Economic Practices.** Much of the geopolitical power play is to gain economic ascendency over rivals. Principal *weapons* are trade and commerce, though not always on egalitarian terms. Instead, tactics such as predatory practices of MNCs, currency manipulation, tariffs, protectionist policies, and extracting exorbitant *rents* for intellectual property are used to gain unfair competitive advantage.

- **Foreign Policy.** Unlike whole of 20th century, which saw two world wars and the Cold War, and when foreign policies of nations centred mostly around security alliances, now the focus is on negotiating bilateral and multilateral trade pacts. Other means adopted to enhance geopolitical influence and economic penetration are: China's BRI, including CPEC, Trump's protectionist policies, increased focus in the Asia-Pacific region, and promoting the QUAD to counter China.

The symbiotic relationship between International Relations and International Business is thus even more pronounced in the extant global environment. Since ability of Nations to attain their strategic objectives through military means is being diminished in the current World Order, the focus will increasingly be upon boosting economic strength and dominance.

Contours of Security Doctrine in Contemporary Context

Hence, let us revisit the *National Security Paradigm* and see how its dimensions ought to be modified and integrated, so that external challenges in the emerging Geopolitical environment can be met more effectively. As a re-cap, a concise external component of the *National Security Paradigm* is at Fig. 26.

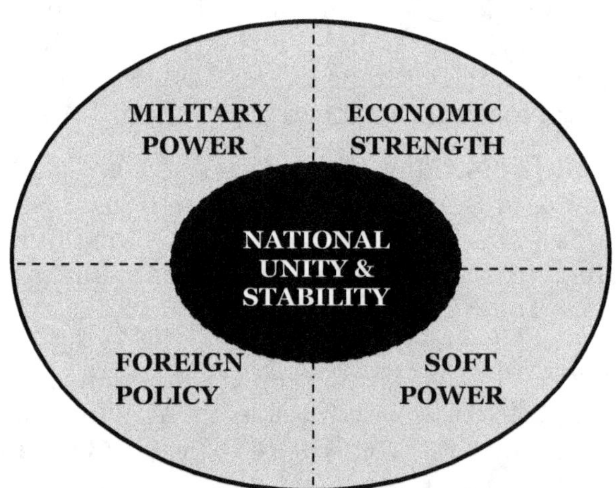

Fig. 26 – Integrated Approach to Meet External Challenges

- **National Unity and Stability.** Although this factor pertains to the Nation's *Internal Security Environment,* it is reiterated here since it is an essential *sine qua non* for meeting external security challenges more vigorously and coherently. The 21st century geopolitical power play will preponderantly centre on economic strength, and hence it is imperative that social unrest is not allowed to disrupt economic activity.

Due to social violence, strikes, *bandhs,* and damage to public property the economy inevitably incurs heavy losses. As stated earlier, the Indian economy suffered a whopping loss of USD 1.19 trillion on PPP basis (Rs 80 lakh crore) in 2017 due to violence, according to a survey of 163 countries conducted by the *Institute of Economics and Peace*[121].

Apart from loss to the economy, social violence invariably requires heavy deployment of paramilitary forces and even the Army. In the latter case, it extracts an *economic cost* due to wear, tear and damage to their equipments that have to be conserved for war. Besides, it disrupts their training as well as scheduled exercises and manoeuvres.

- **Economic Strength and Competitive Advantage.** This dimension is critical for overall national strength, and it will see intense activity. Govt will have to engage in *economic diplomacy* for bilateral and multilateral economic cooperation accords. It should offer loans to developing nations for projects built by our firms, and penetrate their markets for our goods.

Internally, Govt must enact policies that create and boost *National Competitive Advantage*[122] (explained in Chapter 13). In addition, it must enforce rules to ensure transparent trade practices, level playing field, and *ease of doing business.*

There will be dynamic changes in energy prices, currency values, financial flows, trade disputes and disruptive technological advances. Our industry and firms will have to be very agile in reacting to these changes and adapt rapidly in order to remain competitive with respect to rivals. Close coordination between various economic affairs ministries and trade associations will be essential.

To strengthen the economy the Govt will have to incentivize export-oriented and job-creating industries. There is a lot of

---

[121] *Violence costs India's GDP over $1 trillion on PPP basis, per person cost at Rs 40,000.* Economic Times, 10 June 2018. Retrieved; 2 August 2018. https://economictimes.indiatimes.com/news/economy/violence-cost-indias-gdp-over-1-trillion-on-ppp-basis-per-person-cost-at-rs-40000/artcle/64526951

[122] Michael Porter, *The Competitive Advantage of Nations,* Harvard Business Review. March-April 1990.

potential in drugs, pharmaceuticals, fashion, apparel, tourism, hospitality, premier healthcare, and a host of manufacturing and service industries. It must set up industry clusters like auto-ancillary and ITES hubs, and *Special Economic Zones.*

Coordinated efforts of the Govt and IT industry can help India *leapfrog* into a leading Service economy. It must not be just coding, back-office operations and call-centres. We must now graduate to developing *integrated system solutions* and complex IT and ITES systems for corporations. Artificial Intelligence is another frontier where we must take the lead.

The rural sector would need special emphasis to mitigate agrarian distress. There is vast scope to develop modern food-processing industry, cold storages, dry-farming technology, floriculture, fruits and vegetable exports, dairy products, handicrafts, etc; all of which will boost the rural economy.

Unfortunately, many Indian businesses do not enjoy a good reputation abroad due to delinquencies and malpractices such as poor quality, poor packaging, late deliveries and cheating. This gives a bad name to all Indian companies that do honest business, and diligently work to put India on the global map of dependable exporters. Govt must enact and, more importantly, enforce rules to curb such malpractices ruthlessly.

The foregoing was just an illustration of the immense scope and wide range of economic activities that will strengthen our economy further, and thereby help reduce poverty. It highlights the utmost need for cooperation and coordination between various limbs of the Govt, and industry and trade associations in order to achieve synergies. Only this collective effort can ensure that we seize competitive advantage over other Nations.

- **Military Power.** Vital importance of military power needs no emphasis, even though the geopolitical environment analysis indicates preponderance of economic *power play* rather than full-blown armed conflicts. Even Sweden and Switzerland retain military power, despite remaining neutral in the two World Wars. Sweden, in fact is a leading arms manufacturer.

India, in any case, has border disputes with both China and Pakistan and has had several armed conflicts with them. War might be an *option of the last resort,* but sadly, we have seen diplomacy failing quite often and India pushed into war. What is worse, barring 1971, on all other occasions we had to enter wars in a *reactive* mode; surely not an ideal situation.

Formidable military strength to meet their combined threat successfully is an imperative necessity, regardless whether a war breaks out or not. It signals an unambiguous *'don't mess with me'* deterrent to dissuade any adversary from actions that violate our territorial integrity or threaten our economic and other National interests.

➢ **Nuclear Deterrence.** To be credible it must be based on a *Triad* of delivery systems, a redoubtable second-strike capability, and streamlined command and control system.

Given that we have to contend with two nuclear-armed adversaries, we would have to factor that in, to determine the size of the stockpile. However, much more important than just the numbers is the quality, reliability, mobility, and precision of the delivery systems.

Presently we have an explicit *no first use* policy, but Pakistan has declined to make a similar declaration. Many strategic thinkers believe that we too must keep our options *open*. However, ambiguity is prone to strategic miscalculation, which can have catastrophic consequences.

Notwithstanding either of the two options, we need to call Pakistan's *bluff* about exercising the nuclear option in case of a major conventional offensive by India that threatens her existence. It is developing sub-kiloton devices purportedly to signal their usage as per the *limited nuclear war* concept.

Both Super Powers had toyed with this concept even during the Cold War but abandoned it as impractical. Likewise, we must declare unequivocally that any crossing of the nuclear threshold, even with a sub-kiloton warhead, a *dirty* bomb (a crude device), or even a *dud* (device that fails to explode), will invite a devastating nuclear riposte.

We also need to consider our nuclear policy *vis-a-vis* China too and both must be compatible. Besides, as a responsible *nuclear weapon power* our policy should be consistent with the global norms.

➢ **Conventional Military Power.** It is a fallacy that merely because we have credible nuclear capability, we would have deterred war-like actions by our adversaries. Rock-solid capability to fight full-fledged conventional wars on land, sea and air, is an absolute must.

Wars may be forced upon us by anyone of them individually, or by both adversaries in collusion. Conventional military strength is therefore the strongest constituent of military power. It is the critical bulwark; the only one we are likely to use against foreign aggression.

The fact that conventional military power is operating under a nuclear umbrella gives only notional comfort. Ultimately, when the chips are down, conventional military strength alone will count.

Militancy in J&K and cross-LoC firing and infiltration has been imposing a heavy toll on our Army and PMF. We must have a more resolute LoC policy, which explicitly states that if Pakistan violates the ceasefire or sanctity of the LoC, through firing or by abetting infiltration by so-called non-state actors, then we will give a strong punitive response.

To be truly effective, military power must be demonstrably formidable. There cannot be any quantitative, qualitative or technological gaps, which enemies' intelligence agencies would unearth in any case.

Numerically, all three Services must have the full manpower required to fight a two-front war, apart from other essential tasks. There cannot be any critical gaps, as for instance in young officers, who constitute the vital sword-arm.

They must have modern arms and equipment to fight on land, sea and air, in all terrains and all weather conditions. It must include devastating conventional firepower, mobility, strategic airlift, Special Forces, electronic warfare, undersea, amphibian, cyber warfare, communication, and the entire gamut of Naval and Air Force crafts and weapon systems.

Tenets of modern warfare necessitate *ab initio* integration of Armed Forces as per their role in different theatres, rather than coming together only before operations, as at present.

It must include integrated Higher Defence Organization to ensure unity of command, and appointment of Chief of Defence Staff to give single-point advice to political leaders.

Military power can be neither cost-effective nor self-reliant if most of the modern weapon systems have to be imported. A modern *military-industrial complex* that has the capability to deliver state-of-the-art systems must back it. I will discuss this aspect in detail in Chapter 17.

India's policy of *restraint* is often construed as *diffidence*. A perception seems to exist with our adversaries that we are too over-cautious, and they have taken advantage of that. In the geopolitical arena, too much restraint is a sign of weakness. India must demonstrably assert its WILL to act decisively and in full measure against any infringement of our sovereign National interests. Mere rhetoric will not do; it has to be backed by concrete action.

- **Institutional National Security Framework**

Bold, resolute and decisive political leadership that provides clear direction for war must reinforce military power. There must be direct, open communication between the political and top military leadership in order to develop mutual confidence and understanding that is so essential in crises.

An institutional National Security Framework is indispensable for ensuring effective national security. Currently, the NSA acts as the *czar*, who oversees all matters pertaining to national security, both in the internal and external environments.

In India, NSAs have mostly been the personal choice of the PM, and have enjoyed their full confidence. The present NSA comes with long experience in intelligence agencies, which is quite appropriate; given my contention throughout this book that internal security and stability is the most critical foundation for the external security dimension too.

However, when he oversees external security matters too, or the military's advice is either not sought or he acts as the conduit to the PM, then it is problematic. Howsoever much he may be indispensable to the PM for actual national security issues or for other *intelligence,* it is vital that the PM receives advice on military matters directly from the Chiefs.

It is pertinent to recall that the Director IB at the time of 1962 debacle, the NSA when IA plane hijack and Kandahar fiascos took place, or the present NSA for the over-centralized and late response to Pathankot airbase attack, never got the *flak*. Always the political leadership has to pay the price.

The institutional framework, where both the NSA and the CDS act as advisors to the PM for internal and external security matters respectively, is a long overdue necessity. As I will discuss in the next chapter, the two must oversee all integration and coordination in their respective domains. They must also get various contingencies analyzed and responses thereto war-gamed, and must specify the line-authority for all of them.

- **Soft Power.** This is an important, though often unrecognized and underplayed component for boosting a Nation's influence and eminence worldwide. India is truly blessed in this regard since it has a lot to offer. What it lacks is an innovative and well-coordinated plan that integrates elements of soft power with our foreign and economic policies.

  It is true that different ministries as well as non-Govt agencies are undertaking many activities, but those are in isolated silos. Some aspects that contribute to soft power and which need coordination are, cultural exchanges, music, dance, art, film, literary and culinary festivals, tourism, student exchanges, sports tournaments, foreign students studying in India, and Bollywood films.

  Indian Diaspora spread all over the world play a major role in projecting *soft power* through their accomplishments, law-abiding, friendly and peaceful deportment, and significant contributions to their host countries. All of them must believe in, and truly act as ambassadors to project a healthy image of India, its liberal democracy and its rich heritage. This is vital since in the current environment immigrants are resented in most countries due to fears of terrorism and lawlessness.

- **Foreign Policy.** Although covered last, this plays the most important role in boosting India's salience in the comity of Nations. All dimensions that ward off external challenges and contribute to the country's strength and stature ought to be in accordance with the country's well-deliberated foreign policy.

  The Ministry of External Affairs apart from carrying out its regular functions of foreign policy formulation and diplomacy must act as the nodal agency to synthesize and coordinate all relevant elements of the other three dimensions. I will discuss this too in more detail in the next chapter.

Why not a *Model for National Resurgence*

Not all elements discussed under the foregoing *dimensions* might ultimately get included in the *National Security Doctrine,* which will essentially be a concise formulation. But, I have covered them in greater detail with a purpose. I propose that we must view it more as a *Model for National Resurgence* rather than confine it to just a *National Security Doctrine.* My rationale is as follows.

The fundamental theme of this book, as highlighted in the Title and Preface itself, is to underscore the citizens' stake and role in the nation's security. The present public mindset is; *"Yes, security is important and we all need it and indeed demand it. So, aren't the Armed Forces there for external security, while police and judiciary ensure our security and the rule of law internally?"*

Chapters in Parts 1 and 2 had emphasized at great length that not only do citizens have a stake in it, but also more importantly they have an obligation too towards ensuring it. Existing *mindset* has to change. All of us also are *soldiers* in this national mission.

Citizens' participation, vigilance, and proactive involvement in all dimensions of the internal environment are imperative to ensure that all institutions perform diligently and transparently. People's votes elect the *political class,* and determine whether we get a divisive and polarizing polity, or amiable unity and social cohesion. Furthermore, it is the toil and sweat of all of us that contributes to the nation's economic strength.

If we are able to instil in our consciousness that our own thoughts and actions affect ours, as also the nation's internal security, we will disregard the shrill political rhetoric around us. If we change our mindset that *'security is Govt's business,'* and treat it as our own responsibility, we will involve ourselves more proactively in fulfilling this duty. That will be the most impactful step towards forging social cohesion, rather than frittering energy in hatred. This will free us for more productive economic activity.

Vox Populi

Once people make their *voice heard* and *make it matter,* the political class and bureaucracy will have no option but to respond and set things in order. A passive or diffident approach will get us nowhere. On the other hand, when people are able to usher change and *make things happen,* their resolve strengthens further. And this contributes to the overall *National will and ethos.*

Given the current state of our polity, *naysayers* might want to dismiss it as utopian and impractical. But, let us not forget that we ourselves have always responded admirably, whenever a rousing call was given by the leaders in times of crises, be it in 1962, 1965, 1971 or 1999. We have also risen and asserted ourselves to vote out leaders, howsoever strong, when they curbed our democratic freedoms, or they did not deliver upon their electoral promises.

Even though the Nation has been wracked intermittently with communal and caste mayhem due to divisive politics, yet we are the same people who have rejoiced together whenever our scientists notched brilliant successes in space, nuclear technology etc, and our sportspersons won team or individual laurels.

Power of the people must therefore never be underrated. It has always been effective in all democracies around the world and it has worked time and again in our own country. What is required is enlightened and motivating leadership to harness it.

Visionary and Charismatic Leadership

The boundless energy and enthusiasm of the people needs to be channelized for nation building through visionary and charismatic leadership. Throughout history, many such leaders have pulled their Nations out of the throes of disaster or led them to attain glorious heights.

In the 20th century alone, Churchill's rousing *"blood, toil, tears, and sweat"* speech had fortified the will of his countrymen who were reeling from the disaster of Dunkirk, and relentless German air assaults during the *Battle of Britain*. Roosevelt led USA in the most trying times of the *Great Depression* and World War 2.

Mao led the communist army to victory over the Kuomintang, which created the present Chinese state. However, he is also known for the infamous *Great Leap Forward,* which as per some estimates caused 45 million deaths. It was Deng's leadership that turned around China into the strong economic and military power that it is today through his *Four Modernizations* plan.

Nehru's stirring *tryst with destiny* speech at the dawn of our Independence, was truly inspiring, and led to the creation of healthy democratic institutions as well as building the *temples of modern India.* In the same vein Shastri's clarion call of *Jai Jawan, Jai Kisan* fortified people's resolve at a time of acute food shortage and the 1965 war.

Indira Gandhi's steely resolve and strong leadership had led to the dismemberment of Pakistan. Likewise, Vajpayee showed bold decisiveness in allowing the employment of our Air Force in J&K

during the undeclared Kargil war of 1999. It assisted our Army to take back so valiantly all the peaks and territory that Pakistan had occupied surreptitiously.

Visionary leaders exhort people to rise above communal, caste, regional and lingual differences. They give people *super-ordinate* goals and motivate them towards Nation building. On their own part, they rise above divisive politics for electoral gains, and lead by their personal example of dedication and probity.

Hence, charismatic and motivating leadership that is able to rouse people and channelize their surging enthusiasm will achieve *National resurgence.*

Why is it Important – *the Lost Decades*

Model for National Resurgence is the *Aim Plus* that goes a step further than just a *National Security Doctrine.* It enhances the latter with the addition of two vital elements; *visionary leadership* and *people's active and enthusiastic participation.* It is as much a *Vision Statement,* as it is a blueprint for collective action.

My principal aim behind the proposed enhancement is that we have to *catch up* with our main adversary, China. This is because of *The Lost Decades* when we lost the plot and the momentum of Nation-building. Not only was our economic growth sluggish, but even more regrettably our Armed Forces were neglected and lagged far behind in filling critical manpower and equipment voids as well as weapon system modernization.

Political instability and a series of serious social, communal and economic crises were responsible for stagnating growth and lack of social cohesion. The history and causes thereof were covered in Part 2, and hence do not merit repetition here.

What is more pertinent now is that the Nation has to redouble efforts to make up for the lost time and opportunities. Geopolitical challenges of the 21st century are also far more demanding and only concerted efforts of the nation can enable us to meet them.

Thus, critical components of *leadership* and *people's participation* were missing from the earlier formulation. With the addition of these aspects, it is my conviction that a sincere and resolute implementation of this model can help us to *catch up,* and lead us to *National Resurgence.*

Model for National Resurgence Explained

Model for National Resurgence is identical to the *National Security Paradigm.* It has the same dimensions in the nation's internal and external environments. Only *visionary leadership* and *people's active and enthusiastic participation* have been integrated into it. A stylized version of the model is at Fig. 27.

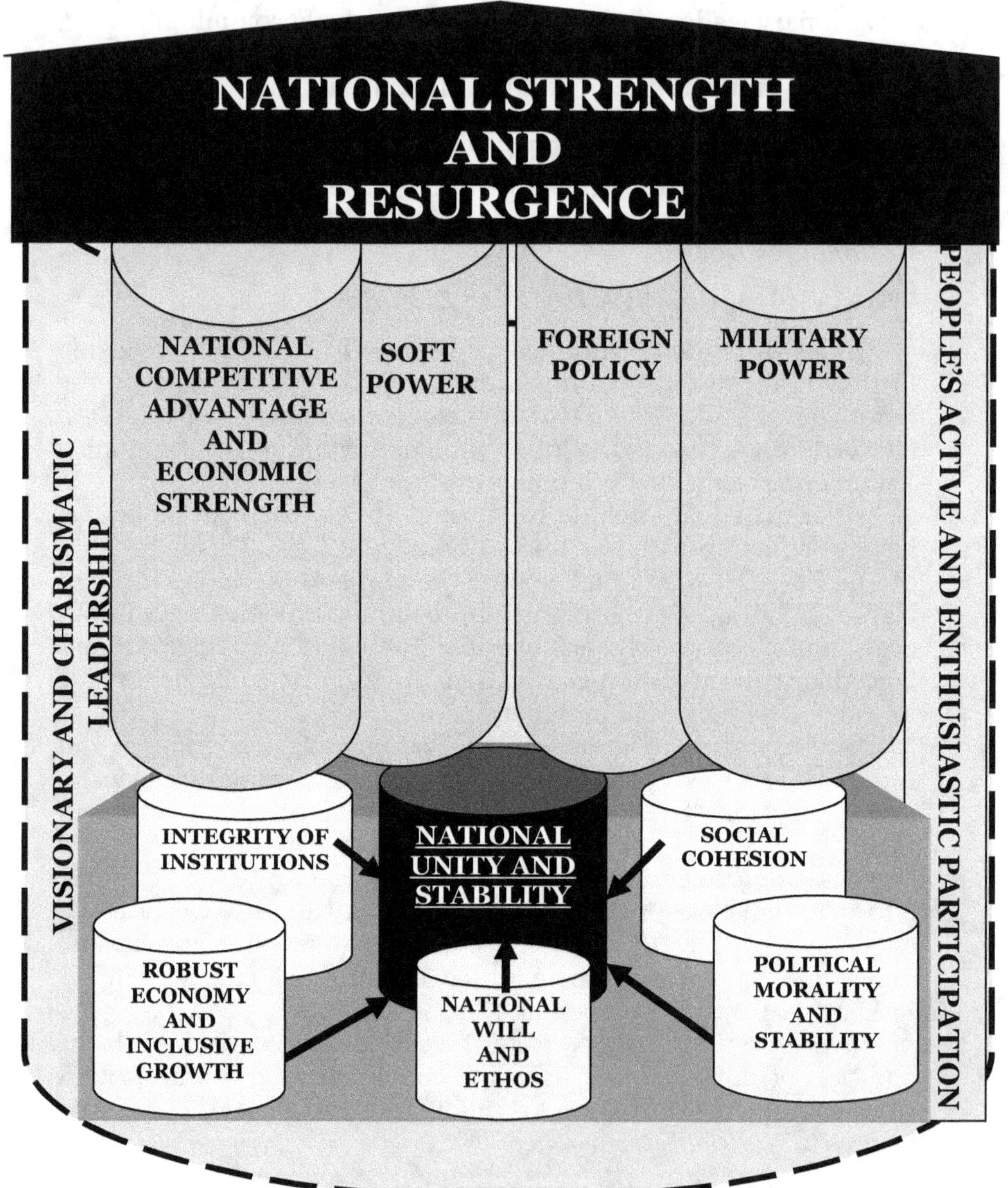

Fig. 27 –National Security and Resurgence Model

Inherent fissiparous tendencies and communal, caste, and class fault-lines of a highly diverse Nation as India, if exacerbated due to electoral or religious rhetoric can keep the inner core in turmoil. We have to keep all those tendencies dormant by ensuring that elements in each of the five dimensions described in Fig 1, function optimally and in complete harmony.

That alone will lead to *National unity and stability*. That is where citizens' active involvement, vigilance and intellect come in, so that they are not swayed by that divisive rhetoric. People have to realize that such polarization and the resulting mayhem only hurts their own lives and livelihood. Besides, all such violence leaves indelible scars on the Nation's psyche, and future generations will find it very hard to reconcile with them.

National unity and stability thus provides the solid foundation and is the most essential prerequisite for the Nation's external security, economic strength and eminence. It is indeed the very fountainhead for *National resurgence.*

On this solid foundation, it will be possible to build all four elements of the superstructure in our external environment, with complete assurance and full support from the internal dimensions. The most important among these is *National competitive advantage and economic strength. Military power* reinforces it, and assures complete protection.

The important element of *soft power* embellishes the nation's image and eminence among other nations. *Foreign policy* acts as the glue that binds all the dimensions, so that they seamlessly and in an integrated manner contribute to overall national strength and stature.

We need to use *soft power* to give ourselves a badly needed image makeover. Many in the World perceive us a Nation with lot of potential, but often bumbling in exploiting it to the hilt. This is due to lack of unity and sense of purpose, and an unfortunate proclivity for self-serving dishonesty.

The foregoing Model for National Resurgence is a conceptual framework, whereas the *National Security Doctrine* has to be a more formal and concise articulation. Some countries use the label *National Security Strategy* to describe it. Nonetheless, all countries have some form of National security document and plan to safeguard national interests. Due to the ever-changing geopolitical environment, it is necessary to update it periodically so that the doctrine remains in sync.

From World War 2 up to Obama's presidency, USA has had eight major formulations on National security. China articulated its approach to National security in the form of White Papers three times just in the past decade. So have Russia, UK and other major powers in the contemporary *multipolar* world[123].

Ironically and quite regrettably, however, we still do not have a *National Security Doctrine.* Not just that, India is yet to produce even a *White Paper* on National security. It is incomprehensible how the top political leadership could have ignored such a vital aspect in all these years.

The security establishment tries to justify its inaction with the reasoning that *'it is better to hide our strategies in a cloak of ambiguity rather than spell our intentions upfront'.* However, this is nothing but an absurd argument to mask apparent apathy.

This is because the world over, countries make their strategic intent and national aspirations very apparent to friends and foes alike. They particularly make their *red lines* obvious, so as to dissuade adversaries from crossing them. Only specific strategies need to be kept secret.

Before we discuss possible contents of the *National Security Doctrine,* it will be useful to clarify some issues of Constitutional responsibility and accountability.

Whose Responsibility is it?

Who is responsible for our security; yours, mine, of all citizens and indeed the Nation itself? Who is the Supreme Commander? On whose orders does the security establishment function? In all democracies and even in Constitutional Monarchies, it vests in just one person. This may be either *de facto* or vested in that person notionally.

In the Presidential form of Govt, as in the USA, the President is the Commander-in-Chief and the Chief Executive of the Nation. *The buck stops at his table.* He has the authority, the responsibility, and the ultimate accountability.

In the Presidential form of Govt, although the President has the authority to appoint members of his Cabinet, Advisors, Heads of Intelligence and other agencies etc, the ultimate responsibility is his alone. Thus, Kennedy is blamed to this day for the *Bay of Pigs* fiasco, as much as he is lauded for his resolute handling of the *Cuban Missile Crisis,* which forced Khrushchev to blink.

---

[123] *'Having a national security doctrine helps avoid ambiguity about dealing with a crisis and to avoid repeating the mistakes of the past'.* AVM Arjun Subramaniam, Article, The Print (28 August 2017). https://theprint.in/opinion/eagle-eye-time-india-formulate-national-security-doctrine/8225/

In the Westminster system of Parliamentary democracy and in Constitutional monarchies the Supreme Commander notionally is the President (King/Queen in the latter). However, the Prime Minister, who is the Chief Executive, exercises the real power. In this system, although the Prime Minister is only the *first among equals* and the principle of *collective responsibility of the Cabinet* applies, but in actual practice, *he calls the shots*. Of course, this depends on the personalities involved.

Thus, relative to the Presidential form there is an element of diffused responsibility. Unless authority and responsibilities are clearly defined, there is scope for some ambiguity and confusion. In our system of Parliamentary democracy, therefore it is even more important that all National security issues be handled in a formally structured and institutionalized manner.

It is the PM's prerogative to consult anyone individually, the NSA, Service Chiefs, Director RAW, and IB *etc,* depending upon his style of functioning. However, the Cabinet must clear all vital decisions. The institutional mechanism must record such decisions for posterity, especially the various inputs and thought processes that led to them. This is not with a view to apportioning blame or fixing accountability. The intent is to evaluate continually how the system worked in crises, so that it could be refined.

Most importantly, the institutional mechanism must visualize all possible contingencies, and unambiguously lay down the *line authority* in different crises. In the volatile geopolitical environment, especially when we are confronting not just two nuclear-armed adversaries but also terrorists and non-state actors, the authority has to take split-second decisions. To ensure there is no *decision paralysis,* it will essential to formulate clear-cut SOPs.

This is not at all far-fetched. Unfortunately, we have faced such situations before, and the Nation has suffered due to either late reactions or ill-considered ones. Some such instances were: not taking appropriate action when the hijacked IA plane was on the tarmac in Amritsar; releasing five very high profile terrorists in Kandahar; ineffectual mobilization after the Parliament attack; withdrawing the Army after several months' stay at the border without taking any action; and incompetent handling of Mumbai terror attacks.

These are just a few examples where, either there was no institutionalized response system, or it failed miserably; although alibis and obfuscation of facts by Govts might claim differently. No lessons were learnt, and apparently, no institutional mechanisms have been put in place even now. This is borne out by the late and incoherent response to the Pathankot airbase attack, as also some other flashpoints in J&K that elicited late or muddled reactions.

A comprehensive, properly crafted *National Security Doctrine* will obviate such lapses. However, its scope is not restricted only to SOPs, nor is it just another bureaucratic exercise. It is much more profound and far-reaching than that.

What must it include?

National Security Doctrine being an Executive responsibility, it would broadly reflect the PM's *vision* for the Nation. While the PM articulates it, such a *vision* will evolve through deliberations, both within the Party, other political parties and leading intellectuals.

It will be presumptuous on my part to second-guess what details the PM would want to incorporate therein; but the following aspects should merit inclusion.

• **Vision.** Foremost, the preamble should include what the vision for the Nation. What ought to be our National aspirations, given our history, heritage, ethos, collective genius and potential? What goals must we set for ourselves based on our strength and economic prosperity? How do we see our eminence and stature in the comity of Nations, now and in the foreseeable future?

• **Core National Interests.** Which are our core and inviolable National interests that would have to be safeguarded at all costs?

• **Apex Body.** Top-tier of the security establishment responsible for formulating the doctrine, and orchestrating its implementation in the external and internal dimensions.

• **Institutional Framework.** Overall institutional framework for the security establishment; its structure; secretariat; separate divisions for external and internal security; periodicity of review meetings; coordination; briefings; dissemination of summaries.

• **Input Channels.** Which agencies will report and provide inputs to respective divisions; frequency and form thereof.

• **Crisis Management Groups.** Contingency plans to manage different crisis situations; e.g. external threat, border incidents; terror strikes, hijacking; natural disasters; riots etc. Composition of groups and authority for ordering action, as well as earmarking of units and other resources.

- **External Environment**

  ➢**Military Power.** It will obviously be central to countering all external threats. The previous section elaborated these aspects.

  ➢**Economic Strength.** As already highlighted, 21st Century geopolitical power play will mostly be in the economic arena.

  ➢Concerted action to build up economic strength by focusing upon sectors where the Nation has the capacity to build up *National Competitive Advantage.*

  ➢Vigilant action and activism in WTO against unfair trade practices; protection of SLOC; assured supplies of oil and gas; forging economic partnerships to further strategic interests.

  ➢The National Security Doctrine must identify and incorporate the nation's economic interests.

  ➢**Soft Power.** Projecting India's heritage, values, democratic traditions, eminence and moral standing among nations.

  ➢**Foreign Policy.** Integrating and coordinating activities in all the four external dimensions. Project a confident National image and coherent responses in all multinational forums.

- **Internal Environment**

  ➢**Internal Security Forces.** In recent times, a plethora of forces and agencies has come up to deal with internal security issues. In some cases, they overlap in terms of role and jurisdiction. Thus, there has to be an apex body that coordinates all internal security aspects with the agencies.

  ➢**Intelligence Agencies.** A number of intelligence agencies have also come up at the Centre and State levels. It is essential to delineate and coordinate their roles, jurisdictions, and reporting channels.

  ➢**Insurgencies.** The Centre and States that are still afflicted with insurgencies and the Naxalite problem must ensure close coordination and cooperation. A political solution is essential in conjunction with economic development of affected areas.

  ➢**National Disaster Management.** This must be brought within the purview of the *National Security Doctrine,* and the role of the body responsible for the same must be clearly defined.

➤**Narcotics, Arms, Counterfeit Currency Smuggling.** These activities are closely linked to terrorist activities and often have networked couriers, safe houses and informants.

➤**Cyber Security.** This vital dimension of security too must be integrated.

How must it be formulated?

National Security Doctrine being an Executive responsibility, the Directive for formulating it must come from the Prime Minister himself. The *Vision Statement* and key directives about forming a *Core Group* and the timeline must also come from him.

The process itself is a matter of detail and the *Core Group* can adopt a suitable methodology to draft a cogent, well-analyzed *National Security Doctrine*[124].

Since this is a critical void, in the interim the establishment must prepare and circulate White Papers on *Foreign Policy, Military Power, Economic Interests,* and *Internal Security* among all stakeholders for their detailed comments and inputs.

---

[124] *"If India starts now, it can finally have a national security doctrine by 2022.* AVM Arjun Subramaniam, The print 7 sep 2017. https://theprint.in/opinion/if-india-starts-now-it-can-finally-have-a-national-security-doctrine by2022/8961

13

Integration and Orchestration

The Nation's economic clout, duly secured with adequate military strength, will be the principal means to attain our geopolitical ambitions. Boosting economic strength is imperative since besides providing decent livelihood to the people and helping to keep social turmoil and disaffection under check, it releases resources for strengthening our defence capability.

The global economic environment is highly competitive and hence it is the arena for intense economic and geopolitical rivalry. Given the high stakes, powerful Nations often skew the *playing field* to secure unfair advantage by employing various stratagems. It is of utmost importance therefore, that we remain vigilant and do not allow our own competitiveness to be eroded.

Building and Sustaining National Competitive Advantage

Concept of *National Competitive Advantage* mentioned in the previous chapter needs elaboration to appreciate its importance. What are its determinants? What actions the Govt and industry must take to identify and promote them?

No nation can possibly have a competitive advantage (in simple terms, *lower costs*) in all its products, compared to rivals. This was the basis for Adam Smith's *Theory of Absolute Advantage* and Ricardo's *Theory of Comparative Advantage*, which advised nations to produce only those items where they had a comparative advantage, and import those where they did not have it.

Michael Porter in his seminal piece in Harvard Business Review turned the extant economic theory on its head, by arguing that national prosperity is *created* and not *inherited*. It does not flow from the nation's natural endowments, its labour pool, interest rates or its currency valuations[125].

Instead, he argued, *"A nation's competitiveness depends on the capacity of its industry to innovate and upgrade. Companies gain advantage against the world's best competitors because of pressure and challenge. They benefit from having strong domestic rivals, aggressive home-based suppliers, and demanding local customers"*. He drew these inferences from a

---

[125] Michael Porter, *The Competitive Advantage of Nations,* Harvard Business Review. March-April 1990.

four-year study of the patterns of success of firms in ten-leading trading nations.

Porter summarized his conclusions in the form of a model known as Porter's *Diamond of National Competitive Advantage*. Apart from its four nodes, as listed below, there were two extrinsic elements; *Govt.* and *Chance* (fortunate stroke; serendipity).

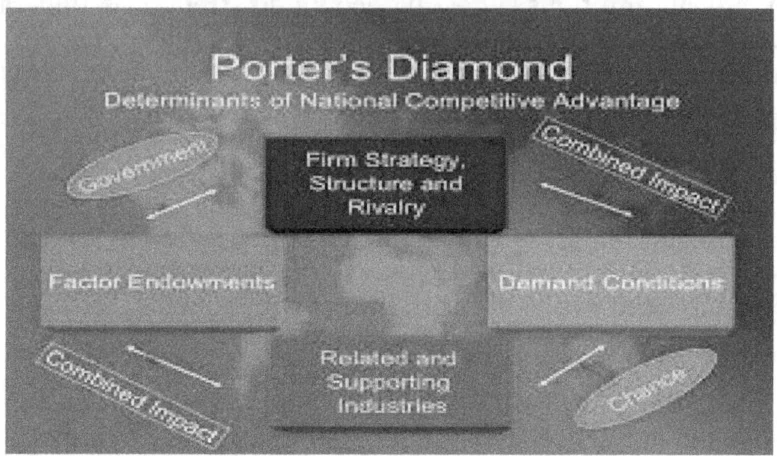

Fig. 28 – Diamond of National Competitive Advantage

- ***Factor Endowments***. Factors of production like skilled labour or infrastructure. Not much emphasis is on natural resources, which can be imported. It is more on individual and team skills essential to compete in a given industry, which the rivals will find time-consuming, difficult and costly to imitate.

- ***Demand Conditions.*** How is home-market demand for the industry's product or service? More *demanding* consumers will force firms to innovate and improve quality.

- ***Related and Supporting Industries.*** Are internationally competitive suppliers and other related industries available in the nation?

- ***Firm Strategy, Structure, and Rivalry.*** How is the environment in the nation on creation of new companies, their organization and management, as well as the nature and extent of domestic rivalry?

In essence, the model's key focus is upon innovation, and the development of unique skills, processes, and procedures by firms. Intensity of competition among rival firms impels them to add new features, apart from improving the content and quality of their products. This helps to boost competitiveness of the industry overall, in the global marketplace. He cited several examples of Japanese firms, which became world-beaters because of their persistent emphasis upon innovativeness.

Govt policies play a key role by ensuring a *level playing field* for the competing firms. Govt must never allow monopolies or even duopolies to dominate the market. Nor must the Govt allow *crony capitalism* that creates market imperfections, for its electoral or other gains. It must not stunt innovation and healthy competition by granting licenses, contracts or financial bailouts from Public sector banks to undeserving and uncompetitive firms.

Govt has to play a nurturing role instead. It should identify sectors and industries that potentially have the ability to achieve a competitive advantage globally. They must be provided with all the opportunities to develop; by providing access to its research laboratories, opening skill centres, developing infrastructure, facilitating essential imports and technical collaborations etc. The Govt must also provide subsidies and protection, wherever those are admissible under the WTO norms for *infant* (new) *industries*.

Several of our sectors and industries have the potential to be globally competitive. Among the sectors listed in Chapter 12, IT and ITES, drugs, premier healthcare, fashion, cars and tourism have greater capacity to move up to next level of sophistication.

We have an extremely fragmented supply chain that adds *transaction costs* and *margins* at each tier. Hence, even for the domestic economy, integration and consolidation of food-grains, dairy, and food processing sectors on a pan-India scale will greatly benefit farmers and consumers. As highlighted earlier, increased focus on rural, employment-generating sectors is indispensable for alleviating agrarian distress.

Integration at the Macro Level

Effective implementation and institutionalization of *National Security Doctrine* and its enhanced model of *National Resurgence* is extremely critical. In fact, this will be far more challenging than the task of merely formulating it. Even the most carefully devised plans fail due to shoddy execution. Causes thereof could be many, such as lack of adequate *buy in* and commitment, low motivation, and even bureaucratic wrangles and subjectivity.

An insightful Chief Executive ought to be fully conscious how our system functions. Since, ultimately it is his responsibility he must use his leadership acumen to instil profuse enthusiasm and dedication for this task. More importantly, he will have to delineate specific roles, assign responsibilities, lay deadlines, get regular feedback, and personally monitor its progress.

In my conceptualization, there is an overlap between *National Security* and *National Resurgence*. As stated earlier, *National Resurgence* builds on the solid foundation of *National Security*. *National Resurgence* seeks to leverage the assured security of the internal and external environments, and then takes coordinated actions to boost our economic strength and competitiveness. This is to make up for *the lost decades,* when we fell behind in attaining our aspirations.

The composite model below seeks to depict the overlap between *National Security* and *National Resurgence*.

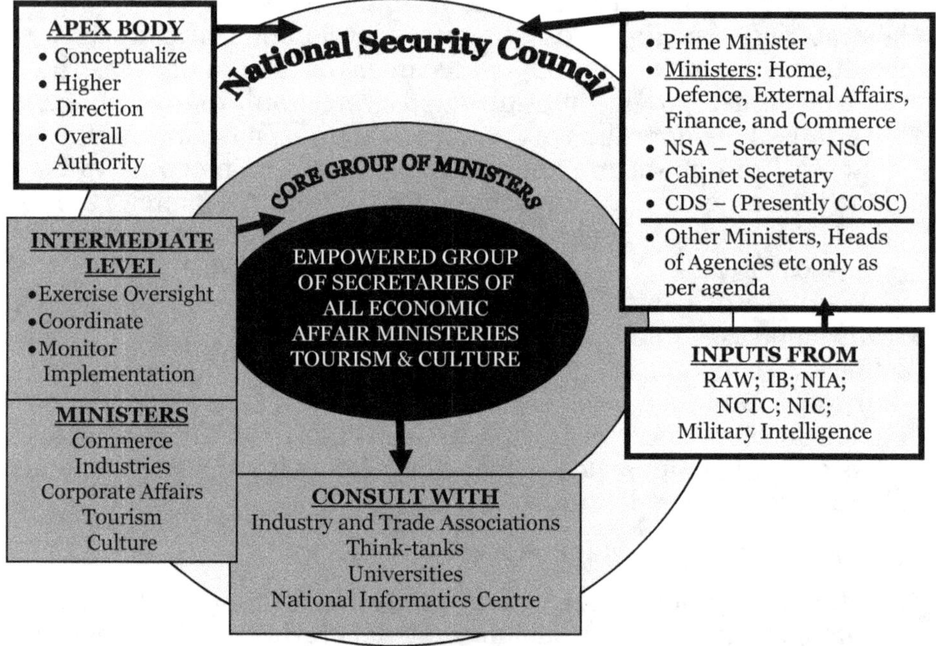

Fig. 29 – Integration and Coordination

Orchestration

I have consciously chosen *'orchestration'* to underline the vital importance of close coordination and harmonized actions by all ministries, departments and agencies within the Govt, as also with various external bodies and associations shown above. Only such *fine-tuning* will achieve the requisite effectiveness of this intricate plan, and enable developing and leveraging of synergies.

Highly complex Govt bureaucracies, giant conglomerates and multinational corporations; all of them have to deal with the same bugbear of *complex interdependence*, which inhibits their capacity for timely and well-coordinated actions. Creating a new structure solely to ensure better coordination serves no purpose. It only ends up adding another layer of bureaucracy, without any commensurate increase in effectiveness.

Hence, Management Gurus recommend *flattening* of multi-tiered hierarchies and rigid structures. Instead, organizations must depend more on task-oriented working groups, lateral and vertical information-sharing, regular coordination meetings, and greater emphasis on *personal touch* and informal interactions. Hence, many MNCs organize periodical retreats where CEOs down to junior managers meet in informal settings; even play party games, to tear down and *humanize* hierarchical barriers.

All this is especially important in our context. This is due to our proclivity to think in terms of hidebound hierarchies, domains, designations and *parent* Service (IAS, IPS, Army, Navy, Air Force, PMF, Cadre etc) Turf battles are not uncommon anywhere in the world; they occur even in nature. However, nowhere else people carry them to such extremes, in utter disregard of larger National interests.

Such a mindset is the negative fallout from our ancient heritage of feudal parochialism and fiefdoms, which was described in the chapter on *National will and ethos*. To this day, we identify foremost in terms of our religion, caste, province, language etc, and not as an Indian first.

As per Hofstede's postulation about cultural differences that I described earlier, we think more of our *individual* interests rather than in *collective* terms. That is why it takes much more effort for us to forge *esprit de corps* and bond as a team. Strangely, as a Nation, we have brilliant world-renowned solo artists, but we are not known for quality symphonies or orchestras?

To laypersons, this might sound as exaggerated or too unlikely, given that the task is vital for national security. Most people who have served in the Govt or have dealt with bureaucrats would say, *not quite so*. Above-cited traits and proclivities influence affiliations, loyalties, interpersonal relations and even official interactions much more, than task-oriented objectivity.

Thus, the *pecking order* matters much more in deciding the venue for a meeting and the person who is to chair it, than the fact as to what the task is and who is the *point-person*. People flaunt their designations and even pay-bands unabashedly to assert their eminence and authority, rather than fulfil their responsibility in a spirit of cooperative team effort.

Such petty things do not matter anywhere in the world. For instance, in the event of a major crisis in a small town when additional outside resources are rushed in, the local point-person assigns tasks to them. This is regardless whether he is junior to the person leading the reinforcements. No one questions it and they all perform diligently.

Regrettably, such deep-rooted tendencies and mindsets inhibit team spirit from the word go. If these or not checked, and if even the higher-ups have the same inclination, then it will sound the death-knell of teamwork and lead only to blame-games.

Leaders at all levels must not be *in denial* about the prevalence of this malaise. Mindful that it exists, they have to anticipate and pre-empt it. They must use leadership skills to motivate people, and firmly curb such tendencies if they crop up, in order to forge healthy team spirit.

Importance of close interface with industry associations for formulating suitable economic and trade policies is self-evident. This will help evolve a coherent plan to identify sectors that can leverage *economies of scale* and *economies of scope*. To achieve global competitive advantage we must nurture them.

Similarly, close interaction with leading Think tanks and top research universities will be immensely beneficial. Bureaucracies in all nations, overburdened with routine work, find little time for creative thinking and long-term perspective planning. Hence, they must sponsor and delegate in-depth studies and specific projects to these organizations. The National Informatics Centre must collect, collate and analyze data on issues that are relevant for planning and monitoring purposes.

Integration of Services

The Armed Forces have always had a truly secular ethos, where they serve as well-knit teams regardless of religion, ethnicity or caste. However, a very large number of civilians work alongside in Armed Forces HQs, MES, and Defence Accounts etc, who have not had the opportunity to imbibe the same ethos. Differences in their organizational cultures often create functional problems, which mar harmony and efficiency. I will discuss this aspect in more detail in the chapter *on Integrated Manpower Policy.*

Similar issues crop up wherever Paramilitary forces (PMF) or Central Armed Police Forces (CAPF) operate with the Army. Regrettably, due to the feudal mindset of treating them as their *fiefdoms,* bureaucracy has adamantly refused to put them under command of the Army wherever they are a part of the Army's operations. This creates incoherence and seriously impedes the Army's operational effectiveness.

Even worse, due to bureaucracy's tinkering with grades and pay-bands through Pay Commission awards, there is a lot of acrimony. This is because many designations in those organizations now claim seniority over their erstwhile seniors due to the altered *inter se* parity. This serious anomaly has drastic repercussions even during peacetime, and is virtually a recipe for disaster in the operational environment.

A vital and imperative necessity is integration of the Services into task-oriented Theatre Commands. Armed Forces of all major powers, including China, adopted this concept long back and have successfully internalized the sweeping changes over the years. Not only has their system stabilized now, it has been tested and refined in operations and manoeuvres.

Such reorganization is a very complex process that will take a lot of time to complete, after receipt of the order. Procrastination has already put our Armed Forces to a great disadvantage. It has further compounded serious problems stemming from the huge backlog of weapon modernization and critical shortages.

Strategic think tanks and the Defence Forces fully agree about the necessity, structural form, and modalities of integration. The delay is on the part of the political dispensation and bureaucracy. They are also dragging their feet on another critical and long overdue issue; appointing a *Chief of Defence Staff* (CDS).

Nowhere in the world, have issues of tri-Service integration into Theatre Commands and Chief of Defence Staff been *flogged* as much as in India. This is because elsewhere they are deemed so straightforward and logical that they are treated as *a given*, and hence beyond debate.

This is because a *single point authority* is indispensable for any organization to ensure that it functions effectively and efficiently. Such a person, who wields the *authority,* also carries complete *responsibility* of the organization and is fully *accountable*.

Unfortunately, our Armed Forces do not have such a *single point authority*. Instead, we are persisting with the antiquated system of a *rotating Chairman of Chiefs of Staff Committee*. Quite incongruously, he has the *accountability*, but does not have the requisite *authority*. Quite weirdly, in our system the Defence Secretary is supposed to be *responsible*, which begs the question, will he ever be held *accountable*?

Can there be a more absurd situation? If present arrangement of a rotating Chairman is so *effective*, then why not a rotating Prime Minister among top three Cabinet Ministers; or a rotating CEO from the COO, CFO and CTO of a firm? Militaries all over the world therefore switched to the system of a permanent *Chief of Defence Staff* long back. Hence, the appointment of the CDS brooks no further delay.

The CDS will have to be responsible for tri-Service integration, since only such a *single point authority* will be able to ensure smooth reorganization. It will be obvious to anyone that when there are integrated Theatre Commands, such integration must take place at the highest level too. It will be downright bizarre for the integrated *body* to be topped with a hydra-headed entity; i.e. current system of independent Chiefs and a rotating Chairman.

This is an onerous task. The most critical challenge for the CDS will be to ensure *emotional integration*. He will have to show extraordinary leadership to inculcate new tri-service work culture, and institutionalize new norms. He will have to transform the ethos of three separate Services into an integrated military ethos.

Why the Resistance?

All along, bureaucrats have doggedly employed various ploys to thwart the appointment of a CDS. Any guesses needed about their motivation? Bureaucracy's prejudice and deep-rooted rivalry is a major reason why the Armed Forces have always been getting *short-changed* in every respect. This is the prime reason for the increasing civil-military divide, which is acquiring dangerous proportions.

That, this is not just a paranoid misperception of the military will be obvious from the following fact. Manekshaw received his pay arrears cheque after 35 years virtually on his deathbed, and that too only at the behest of President Kalam. You could say, *'Unlikely! Senior bureaucrats can't be so petty!'* Really? Is there any other plausible explanation?

Soon after Independence they got the post of C-in-C abolished and had the Services downgraded in the warrant of precedence. They did so by stoking paranoia in politicians by citing the military coups that were taking place in many countries including Pakistan.

After the glorious victory of our Armed Forces in 1971, Indira Gandhi reportedly wanted to appoint Manekshaw as CDS. However, the bureaucrats prevailed upon her against doing so.

Pakistan's occupation of Kargil peaks in 1999, and the heroic operations to recapture those heights had brought out several glaring shortcomings. Serious lacunae in our intelligence and defence structures had landed us in that grave situation, which portended even more terrible strategic consequences. It was only the stupendous grit, valour and sacrifice of our troops that saved the day.

Govt appointed the *Kargil Review Committee* (KRC) under the eminent strategic thinker, Late K Subrahmanyam to analyze the causes. It submitted an insightful report on issues like National Security Council, Intelligence set-up, Apex Decision-making, National Security Management, Nuclear Policy, Defence Budget, Modernization, Declaratory Policy on LOC, among others[126].

The Group of Ministers (GoM) appointed to examine the KRC's recommendations as also its four Task Forces reiterated the same. The bureaucracy simply *sat over them*. In 2011, reports of KRC, GoM and the Task Forces were dusted and dug out, but another committee was set up to examine them. This committee headed by Naresh Chandra included several former military commanders, intelligence chiefs, diplomats, and strategic analysts.

In its report submitted in May 2012, it recommended a fulltime National Security Adviser (NSA), CDS, National Intelligence Grid, National Counter Terrorism Centre (NCTC), deputation of military officers to MoD, and a National Defence University. The only *eyebrow raising* point was to amend the *Prevention of Corruption Act* to protect officials for '*errors in judgement*' in arms purchases.

The bureaucracy cleverly *cherry-picked* items that suited them, such as appointment of NSA and setting up of NIA and NCTC but put the rest in cold storage. CDS appointment was one of them.

It is significant that the doyen among India's strategic thinkers K Subrahmanyam, had clearly anticipated the bureaucracy's stout resistance, and had explicitly said so in the formal report itself. It stated that; "*political, bureaucratic, intelligence and military establishments have a vested interest in the status quo*".

This was no ordinary remark. It had an unambiguous and very ominous message. It was all the more remarkable that it was part of a formal report tabled in the Parliament.

---

[126] Kargil Review Committee Report: Executive Summary.25 February 2000. http://nuclearweaponarchive.org/India/KargilRCA.html. Retrieved 12 July 2018

Given the theme of the book, I do not wish to digress by delving into specific instances of those self-seeking *political, bureaucratic, intelligence and military interests*. The book's primary intent is to enlighten citizens about various dimensions of National security, internal and external. I want to be motivational in my approach so that we proactively fulfil our obligation towards strengthening it.

I also do not want to fan cynicism in the public mind about the system. In any case, the widespread *malaise* is evident from the scandals that keep breaking out regularly. It would, however be unwise to ignore it, as if it does not exist. It will also be a disservice if we do not initiate the necessary remedial measures. Hence, the following are only few broad examples of the nature and extent of malfeasance.

Domains such as Ordnance Factories Board, Defence Estates Service, Military Engineering Service, Armed Forces HQ Service, and Military Farms, which have civilians paid from the Defence budget, continue to thrive. This is despite the fact that reports of the CAG and many Parliamentary committees contain very severe strictures against them.

Many such domains serve virtually as *fiefdoms* of the MoD and flourish without any accountability. This is because they are a source for numerous *perks and benefits* for the political class and officialdom. They are also a means of extending patronage through award of contracts and jobs in these establishments.

The alleged *politico-bureaucratic-military* nexus would not want to alter the *status quo* in respect of multi-billion dollar arms deals. Scandals that have erupted in the public domain be they Bofors, Westland choppers or the last-minute switch in the Rafale deal are only a tip of the proverbial iceberg. Numerous others have managed to slip under the radar.

For the Armed Forces, such scandals are a *double-whammy*. After years of negotiation if deals are abandoned, it adds further delays to the huge backlog of weapon replacements and overdue modernization. Over-caution of honest officials in their decision-making results in even more delays.

Even worse for the Armed Forces is the bad name they earn in such scandals, even though they are not involved in the financial aspects. That is the domain of politicians and bureaucrats. However, military officers fall *willy-nilly* into the murky *swamp,* when they have to tinker with the Qualitative requirements or Comparative evaluation reports. Given the multi-billion dollar stakes, the nexus employs ruses such as *persuasion,* temptation, coercion or blackmail.

This is an extremely dangerous trend for our military ethos and the high standards of ethics and values, which are the hallmark of our Armed Forces. If unchecked, this would leave lasting damage to our values for future generation of soldiers.

A powerful nexus of politicians, bureaucrats and builders has been eyeing vast tracts of military land in cantonments for civilian use and development. Such lands are a virtual goldmine. This nexus received a boost from the MoD's recent controversial order to open up cantonment roads, in total disregard of security of the weapons systems, radars, equipment and ammunition therein. Besides, several recent terror strikes on military units have targeted living quarters of soldiers and families, to hold them hostage and secure the release of imprisoned terrorists.

It is very unfortunate that lust for lucre has infected even the highest echelons of the military as in the Augusta Westland and *Adarsh* scams. This cannot but have a deleterious effect on the morale and ethical standards down the line. Is it any wonder then that the KRC wrote in its report that alleged *politico-bureaucratic-military* nexus does not want to alter the status quo?

It must however be emphasized that despite the prevailing environment there can be no generalizations. Numerous upright politicians, bureaucrats, and military officers perform their duties diligently and honestly. Those in the nexus are a small exception. Sadly, however, the *exceptions* are increasing progressively.

In Sum

To sum up therefore, integration, coordination and synergistic functioning of all three Services, CAPFs and various intelligence agencies is imperative to ensure security in the internal as well as external environments. This will require a radical change in our existing mindsets, so that we cease to think and identify only with the silos of parent organizations. We will attain synergies only if we think as teams and focus on our common tasks and goals.

There is no scope for any more delay in Defence reorganization and filling up of manpower gaps, especially of junior officers. Likewise, critical shortages of modern weapon systems in all three Services have now reached precarious levels, and the Govt must address this issue urgently.

Economic strength and National competitiveness is the primary means of attaining National resurgence. It will come through focus on innovation, fair competition, and the coordinated actions of the Govt, industry, and collective genius of the people. Nurturing role of the Govt and promoting genuine competition will be critical.

Industry and firms too will have to eschew the shortcuts of *cultivating* politicians and bureaucrats for unfair advantage. They must focus on product and service quality, and ethical business practices to build brand equity and their reputation with foreign firms and consumers. Spirit of entrepreneurship, the zeal for global presence, and innovativeness will be truly vital.

The top leadership and leaders at intermediate levels have the most important role. This is because it is a monumental task with a lofty goal. Far more than the policy, technical or organizational issues will be the leadership challenge.

As highlighted throughout, changing deep-seated mindsets is very difficult. Inspiring and motivating everyone to work as a team and work towards the super-ordinate goal will help achieve this. Only then, they will be able to integrate and orchestrate this phenomenal effort for National resurgence.

14

The Soldier

Soldier! (Used generically to also include *sailors* and *airmen*) The word itself evokes images of integrity, valour, honour and pride. Soldiering is no ordinary profession - certainly not meant for anyone weak in body, spirit or character. No wonder then, that throughout history Nations have eulogized soldiers, lauded their sacrifices, and built grand memorials in their honour.

Such *izzat aur iqbal* (honour and glory) sustains soldiers, and motivates them to persevere against the toughest odds. It rouses them to make even the *supreme sacrifice* flinchingly; reassured in the belief that a grateful Nation would look after the dear ones they leave behind.

'It's the man behind the gun that matters' is not a mere cliché. It is a cardinal dictum as old as warfare itself. Hence, the *soldier* is the most important constituent of military power that protects the nation from external aggression. Any analysis of the Nation's military prowess is meaningless without focusing upon the *soldier.*

He fires the guns, handles the weapon systems, flies the aircraft and operates the naval ships. Even more importantly, his courage, motivation, tenacity, and perseverance alone win battles.

What makes the *soldier* tick? How does *he* brave the most terrible odds and selflessly carries on regardless? What motivates him? What elements in the politico-bureaucratic environment can potentially demoralize him? It is important to understand these vital aspects to appreciate the psyche of the *soldier.*

Motivation and morale of the *soldier* hold the key to his fighting spirit. Military history is replete with examples where fewer, but better-motivated soldiers, have routed larger numbers of better-armed opponents.

By far the strongest motivation that impels youth to join the military is to defend the motherland. Tales of valour of heroes in our heritage fortify his conviction that he is fighting for a noble cause. Further motivation comes from his value system, as well as from the adulation he receives from the environment.

In Chapter 5 heroes from our ancient history, and gallantry awards earned in both World Wars were covered. Our soldiers have fought even more magnificently in all the post-Independence wars and conflicts. Even in the 1962 War, when they had to go into battle ill equipped and ill clad, they fought valiantly.

Since Independence, over 22,600 soldiers have lost their lives and earned numerous gallantry awards. These include 21 Param Vir Chakras (PVC) and 50 Ashok Chakras[127].

We must commemorate the outstanding bravery of our post-independence heroes so that they too become part of our folklore to inspire future generations of soldiers. Rather than confine these to regimental histories, we must eulogize their valour more widely through movies, TV serials and memorials to inspire youth.

The next few paragraphs list the prominent, decorated heroes of post-Independence wars. However, I must emphasize that besides those who received decorations for valour, there were innumerable other veterans of those conflicts whose heroism, fortitude, and sacrifice was not any less.

Exceptional valour of soldiers like Maj Somnath Sharma, PVC (P), Lt Col DR Rai, MVC (P) and Brig Mohammad Usman, MVC (P) saved Kashmir from Pakistani invaders during 1947-48.

Truly inspirational is the exemplary courage of heroes such as Maj Shaitan Singh, PVC (P) and Sub Joginder Singh, PVC (P) in fighting off the Chinese in 1962, in spite of their mortal wounds.

Our Armed Forces inflicted severe punishment on Pakistani forces in 1965 through the bravery of such heroes as CQMH Abdul Hamid, PVC (P), Lt Col AB Tarapore PVC (P), Wg Cdr PP Singh, MVC, and Sqn Ldr P Gautam, MVC among many others.

Liberation of Bangladesh is the most glorious achievement of our Armed Forces until date, which totally altered the geopolitical landscape. The victory came in just 15 days, with our Army fighting Pakistan also in the West, as well as holding defences in the North and East against the Chinese.

Our Navy inflicted immense damage on Karachi harbour, while our Air Force wiped out their Air Force in the East and inflicted crippling blows in the West. Moreover, we simply shrugged off the intimidation when USA sent the nuclear-powered USS Enterprise.

This became possible with the superb political and military leadership, meticulous planning, and coordinated operations by all three Services. Above all it was the tremendous valour of heroes such as 2/Lt Arun Khetarpal PVC (P), Maj Hoshiar Singh PVC, L/Nk Albert Ekka, PVC (P), Flt Lt NS Sekhon, PVC (P), Capt (IN) MN Mulla, MVC (P) and Cdr BB Yadav, MVC, among many others that made this epoch-making feat possible.

---

[127] Param Vir Chakra (PVC) is the wartime highest gallantry award, which is equivalent to the British Victoria Cross. Ashok Chakra is the highest award for conspicuous bravery or self-sacrifice otherwise than in the face of enemy.

Since then Pakistan has fanned insurgency in J&K to avenge its humiliation. The battlefield extends to the Siachen glacier, where our Army holds Saltoro Ridge west of the glacier, and Bilafond La, Sia La and Gyong La passes even further west. At 21,000-22,000 ft these are the highest manned posts in the world.

Courage and tenacity of our soldiers who fight at such heights in Minus 50° Celsius, where existence itself is a superhuman feat, is truly magnificent. However, Nb Sub Bana Singh went beyond the superhuman when he captured the fortress-like Qaid post (renamed Bana Post in his honour), for which he won the PVC.

Pakistan made another gambit in 1999 by surreptitiously occupying posts in Kargil, which both sides used to vacate during winter. Just few men holding the high peaks can halt battalions on the precipitous approaches. Our soldiers displayed indomitable courage, to recapture all those posts. Among the many heroes were Capt Vikram Batra, PVC (P), Lt Manoj Pandey, PVC (P), Rifleman Sanjay Kumar, PVC and Grenadier Yogendra Singh Yadav, PVC.

It is essential to view the splendid performance of our soldiers against the fact that they have always had to face better-armed and better-equipped forces. Regrettably, there is little appreciation of their sacrifices and extremely tough service conditions. This is galling since gallantry of our soldiers surpasses other armies who have superior weapons and technology.

Comparison with Other Armies

The powerful US Army could not achieve its objectives in the Korean War. Later, it made an ignominious retreat from Viet-Nam, despite facing a smaller army that had just basic weaponry and limited resources. Despite deploying high technology and phenomenal firepower in Afghanistan, it has not met with success.

US Army is chary of putting *boots on ground* for close quarter combat. This was in evidence in Tora Bora Mountains where Osama bin Laden was cornered. Their reliance instead on massive 15,000 lb *Daisy Cutter* bombs, allowed Osama to escape to safe sanctuaries in Pakistan.[128]

The mighty Soviet Army was not able to vanquish the weaker Chinese Army during clashes along the *Ussuri* River in 1969[129]. In

---

[128] Krause, Peter John Paul. *The Last Good Chance: A Reassessment of U.S. Operations at Tora Bora.* Security Studies, Volume 17, p. 644-684, 2008.

[129] Kuisong, Yang. *"The Sino-Soviet Border Clash of 1969: From Zhenbao Island to Sino-American Rapprochement,"* Cold War History (2000): 21-52.

1988, the Soviets had to make a humiliating withdrawal from Afghanistan after years of occupation of that country.

In 1967, China suffered humiliation at the hands of our Army when its troops had to retreat from Sikkim (then an Indian protectorate) at Nathu La and Cho La after suffering significant casualties.[130]

In 1979, China, despite having world's largest army, received a drubbing from the much smaller Vietnamese Army in their border war. China had to make a face-saving unilateral withdrawal by claiming that it had *achieved all its strategic objectives*[131].

Ethical values are imperative for any military's ethos. Morality and rectitude must permeate their conduct, or else they would be just brigands. Such moral anchor provides the inner strength for gallantry in the face of death, and prevents brutality even in heat of battle. More importantly, soldiers' innate righteousness and his *military upbringing* would never let them commit wanton killing, rape and decapitation of innocent civilians.

In practice however, soldiers' conduct differs vastly. It depends upon the ethos and traditions of respective militaries. Aberrations abound by way of wartime excesses, ethnic cleansing, and genocide. It would be instructive to compare the conduct of other armies and our own soldiers in this regard.

As previously described, in 1968, US Army had carried out the infamous *My Lai massacre*[132] in South Vietnam in which they shot 400 unarmed men, women and children, gang-raped women, and mutilated bodies. After global outrage, they charged only 26 soldiers, but only a Lieutenant received a life sentence, of which he served only three and half years under house arrest.

---

[130] Chengappa, Bidanda M. (2004). *India-China relations: post conflict phase to post cold war period.* A.P.H. Pub. Corp. P. 63.

[131] Zhang Xiaoming, *"China's 1979 War with Vietnam: A Reassessment",* China Quarterly, Issue no. 184 (December 2005), pp. 851–874. Actual numbers are thought to have been 200,000 with 400 – 550 tanks. Zhang writes that: "Existing scholarship tends towards an estimate of as many as 25,000 PLA killed in action and another 37,000 wounded. Recently available Chinese sources categorize the PLA's losses as 6,594 dead and some 21,000 injured, giving a total of 24,000 casualties from an invasion force of 200,000."

[132] Greiner, Bernd. *War without Fronts: The USA in Vietnam.* New Haven, Connecticut: Yale University Press, 2009.

Who can forget the horrendous genocide[133] in Bangladesh in 1971, when Pakistan Army killed three million people and raped 400,000 women? Its soldiers systematically executed own citizens and confined Bengali women in Army camps as sex-slaves. They massacred leading professors, doctors and authors in an organized plan to eliminate Bengali intellectuals.

Pakistan's alliance with USA under CENTO and SEATO, and its facilitating US detente with China, shielded it from international tribunals. Even 195 Pakistani soldiers including five Generals, who were directly responsible for the massacre returned to Pakistan in exchange for its formal recognition of Bangladesh.[134]

Soldiers and militias are accountable for atrocities committed even during undeclared conflicts, civil wars, anti-terror operations and insurgencies. UN-mandated tribunals investigated crimes against humanity in Serbia, Cambodia, Rwanda and Sierra Leone.

A permanent body, the *International Criminal Court*, set up in July 2002 is currently investigating 11 cases of mass killings and rapes in Uganda, Congo, Darfur, Libya, Georgia and Central African Republic among others.

Record of our own soldiers in this regard has been impeccable. Remarkably, while there were coups galore in many countries, including in our neighbourhood, there was not even a whiff about them in India. There have never been accusations of excesses against Indian Armed Forces during all the wars, counter-insurgency operations, and UN peacekeeping missions.

An eloquent testimony to our moral conduct is that while the Pakistani Army committed genocide in Bangladesh against its own people, India treated 93,000 Pakistani POWs in the most humane manner for two years. Contrast this with the reprehensible inhuman treatment of prisoners by the most powerful and professional US Army in the notorious *Abu-Ghraib* prison.[135]

Then what distinguishes the Indian soldier from other armies? What is the source of his indomitable courage and fighting spirit that sets him apart? How does he continue defending the motherland, doggedly braving better-equipped enemies without ever complaining about his own limited resources?

---

[133] Sisson, Richard, Leo E. Rose. *War and Secession: Pakistan, India, and the Creation of Bangladesh.* University of California Press, 1992.

[134] S. Linton, 'Completing the circle: accountability for the crimes of the 1971 Bangladesh war of liberation', Criminal Law Forum (2010) 21:191–311, p. 203.

[135] Seymour Hersh *Chain of Command: Road from 9/11 to Abu Ghraib.* New York: Harper Collins. 2004

Apart from roots in Indian heritage, which provide the moral anchor, it is his conviction that the Nation depends upon him and the people love and respect him for his selfless service. Such *izzat aur iqbal* boosts his self-worth and motivates him to persevere even against the toughest odds.

Discordant Notes and Warning Signs

Regrettably, the very source of strength of our soldiers, their *izzat aur iqbal,* has been taking a beating for quite some time. It is leaving them increasingly disillusioned and frustrated. Their angst is not against citizens, who hold them in high esteem. It is mainly against the ruling elite - the political class and the bureaucracy.

Our centuries-old heritage still motivates soldiers, but with the general decline in societal mores, its impact has been waning over the years. This is in keeping with trends even within our society, where lot of cynicism and distrust pervades due to steep decline in ethical and moral values in all occupations.

In our highly materialistic society where *get-rich-quick* by means fair or foul, is *the way to go,* can the Armed Forces alone remain an island of purity? To its credit, our military leadership perceptively foresaw such eventuality and took steps to counter it.

"It's not a question of 'IF,' but rather 'WHEN' the Armed Forces will catch the contagion of corruption and declining values afflicting our society. They just can't remain insulated." Late Nani Palkhivala sounded this stark warning in 1991, when I interviewed him for the film *'Pause to Ponder – Ethics, Values and the Soldier'*[136]. The Army War College had produced that film on the directions of Army HQ.

When I interviewed Late JRD Tata for the film, he was more scathing in his criticism of the political class and bureaucracy. His opening remark was, *"The fact that I am speaking to a Colonel of the Indian Army I can safely assume that you are a person I can automatically trust. Sadly, I can't say the same about any politician or bureaucrat".* Such was the level of respect the doyen of Indian industry had for our Armed Forces.

Their prophecy has unfortunately proved true since there has been a marked decline in standards of probity even within the Armed Forces. What started as a trickle alas has turned into a

---

[136] *"Pause to Ponder – Ethics, Values and the Soldier."* Army War College, 1992. This 60 minute motivational film, produced by Army War College, was scripted and anchored by me and was shot by *Green Oscar* winning filmmaker, Mike Pandey.

stream. In the early years, blatant corruption was quite rare, and offenders received severe punishments. Breaches were generally by way of misuse of Govt property or transport.

During the seventies and eighties a big concern of COs and Sub-unit commanders was to ensure that *tricks* suggested by Auditors themselves do not become routine malpractices. *Modus operandi* of Auditors was to raise numerous objections, even frivolous ones, and then *settle them* in return for sugar, kerosene, rations or Rum.

Since higher HQ, frown upon unsettled audit objections, COs overlooked such malpractices *'for the sake of the unit'*. They were nonetheless vigilant that subordinates did not indulge in such practices for their personal benefit.

Over the years, the *quid pro quo* has grown more alarming and the *demands* too exorbitant. The *contagion* is more widespread, apace with the rapidly declining societal value systems.

A cynical perception has taken root that notwithstanding the platitudes leaders routinely mouth about *integrity*, they are not averse to corruption themselves whenever there is an opportunity. Even the stigma against offenders and punishments now seems to be diminishing.

Scandals involving General rank officers, apart from tarnishing the military's image, have breached the bond of trust between the *leaders and the led*. Regrettably, two former Army Chiefs and a Naval Chief were involved in the *Adarsh* scam, and a former Air Chief is out on bail in an acquisition scandal. A serving Army Chief had an ugly spat with the Government, and in a deplorable action hauled it before the Supreme Court.

The hallowed institution of Service Chiefs seems to have lost its sheen, and in public perception, they are as mired in murky deals as other limbs of our polity. The *rank and file*, who have always viewed Service Chiefs as demigods, is very disillusioned. There is growing resentment that Service Chiefs who ought to stand up for them and safeguard their interests, are failing to do so. The perception is that in trying to ingratiate themselves to the powers that be, they are forgetting all about the Chetwode motto and oath.

Soldiers are beginning to question the double standards *vis-a-vis* civilian counterparts. There is a mismatch in treating death in line of duty of soldiers, CAPFs or police personnel. In instances of tragic deaths of the latter, even due to own negligence, they have received gallantry awards and high *ex gratia* payments.

On the other hand, truly heroic acts of martyred soldiers earn fewer awards and lower compensation. Sadly, their wards have to run from pillar to post even to receive them. Soldiers invariably receive punishments even for negligence or minor offences. They feel aggrieved when civilians get away with gross misconduct and blatant corruption, and brazenly lead ostentatious lifestyles.

Deteriorating Civil-Military Relations

The politico-bureaucratic combine primarily is responsible for dealing the severe blow to motivation and morale of soldiers. They are more educated, better informed, and perceptive compared to yesteryears. They are painfully aware how they have been getting a raw deal from the ruling combine, be it in pay and allowances, disability awards, or pensions.

Successive pay commissions and cadre reviews have slyly tinkered with the *inter se* parity of civilian and military grades - all to the military's detriment. This causes intense acrimony and creates serious functional problems, especially where the military and civil services function together.

All these issues, as well as the OROP (one rank, one pension) agitation, have been discussed *ad infinitum* in the public domain. Most citizens are fully aware of them, as also with the fact how critically these are affecting soldiers' morale.

According to Maslow's [137] *'hierarchy of needs'* fulfilment of *esteem* and *self-actualization needs* is the strongest driving force that contributes to high motivation. However, those needs are met only after basic *physiological* and *safety* needs have been satisfied.

Can we expect a soldier to be so highly motivated as to embrace even martyrdom, if he is constantly agitated about his unjust treatment? He might even take his own death or incapacitation into stride, but how will he give his best if he is unsure about the welfare of his family that he will leave behind?

It was an alarming revelation when during the Golden Jubilee celebrations of my Regiment last year some veteran and serving JCOs opened up about their sentiments on this issue. In rustic Punjabi they candidly spoke words to the effect, *'Saab Ji, during Regiment's tenure in J&K we were more hesitant about needless "pange" (bold risks), than when we took the new Bofors guns up the treacherous, snowy terrain in Sikkim for the very first time.'*

---

[137] Abraham Maslow's 1943 paper *"A Theory of Human Motivation"* theorized about a hierarchy of human needs; with "physiological" needs at the bottom, and moving up through "safety", "love and belongingness", "esteem", up to "self-actualization and self-transcendence". As lower level needs get fulfilled, humans get motivated to fulfil the higher level need for "self-actualization".

'Seeing on TV 70-80 year old veterans and Veer-Naris at Jantar Mantar, agitating month after month, we thought if this can happen even to retired Generals and widows of martyrs, then what will be the fate of our families if we were dead?'

Many veterans have heard similar emotions in unit reunions. Can such over-caution produce *heroic actions beyond the call of duty?* How will a CO order his men on a *suicidal mission* without agonizing about plight of their kin, since he cannot guarantee that the wards would get their dues in time?

A very disturbing development is the lodging of FIRs against soldiers for performing their duty in militancy-hit J&K and states affected by insurgencies. This is despite their showing tremendous restraint against terrorists and stone-pelting civilians, which have resulted in numerous deaths and injuries to soldiers themselves. In an unprecedented move, many soldiers have approached the Supreme Court to seek justice and a clear ruling against this.

Over past several months, assault on soldiers' pride and motivation has incensed them immensely. Tasking the Army to clear trash left by tourists in hilly areas, or cleaning up a highly polluted lake, hurt his sensibilities. A Chief Minister warned the striking civic staff that he would call the Army to clear piling garbage from city streets.

The deplorable precedent was actually set when soldiers had to lay yoga-mats on *Rajpath*. It was a demeaning task for proud combatants who dream of marching proudly on *Rajpath* in their resplendent uniforms on Republic Day.

Army engineers were ordered to reconstruct collapsed railway over-bridges in Mumbai. Citizens wondered why railways did not do so themselves, when they have the expertise and resources to lay railway tracks and built bridges even in the mountains.

The military has always helped the civil administration during riots and natural disasters. Although it is an *option of last resort,* it has become a practice now even when sufficient civil resources are available. Soldiers are a readily available workforce to erect giant stages for quasi-religious organizations, rescue kids from bore-wells, or prepare helipads.

When the RM should firmly curb the increasing propensity of civil authorities to call the Army even for menial tasks, ironically she herself orders many of them. It is mostly to shield Govts from public anger at lapses, where her party is in power.

The previous chapter had described how a powerful nexus of politicians, builders and Defence Estates officials, with eyes on prime defence land, got Cantt roads opened to public access. This is a recipe for disaster from the obvious security threats. It will also seriously have a deleterious effect on military discipline.

A challenge for military leaders is to keep soldiers insulated from the evils afflicting our society. With free civilian access into Cantts, they will now have greater exposure to drugs, gambling, clandestine sale of petrol and rations, subversive activities, *honey trapping* and blackmail. This will sow perpetual hostility with civilians due to accidents, eve teasing and squabbles.

Soldiers are very angry due to crude utterances of some politicians. A Minister said that soldiers joining the Army *are meant to die,* and politicians cannot always be present to receive their dead bodies. Another legislator crossed all limits of decency when he passed highly derogatory remarks against soldiers' wives.

It is unfortunate that this disparaging tone was set by the PM himself from ramparts of the Red Fort in his Independence Day speech. Instead of lauding the Armed Forces for their sacrifices, he delivered a homily. Speaking in the context of OROP, his public rebuke to the effect; *the Nation can afford to give just this much, as it has to be done by depriving the poor*, caused intense anguish to soldiers, veterans and their kin. His address seemed a signal to the bureaucracy and media not to heed soldiers' pleas for justice.

Our President and PM pay homage at War Memorials during their visits abroad. Surely, citizens would notice the stark incongruity that there is no such memorial to honour thousands of our soldiers martyred in conflicts since Independence.

Isn't it ironical that the *Amar Jawan Jyoti*, which was only a temporary memorial built after the 1971 war, stands under India Gate – a memorial built by the British to honour Indian soldiers killed during World War 1? If our Colonial masters could honour the martyrdom of Indian soldiers in their wars, why has India not eulogized our own soldiers in our own wars?

Strength of our military is not so much in armaments, as it is in the morale and fighting spirit of soldiers. They draw sustenance from people's love, respect and support. Our soldiers are innately simple, undemanding, and can withstand lot of hardships with fortitude. However, they are very sensitive when wronged or slighted – much more so when their pride is hurt.

Resentment on a host of such issues has now coalesced into an all-pervasive angst. Many experts have been warning about its perilous portents. Due to harsh service conditions, Armed forces are no longer the *career of choice*. Despite relaxed selection standards, vacancies remain undersubscribed.

Paradoxically, when there is vast unemployment in the country, Armed Forces are short of 60,000 personnel. The RM provided the following details in the Lok Sabha. The Army tops the list with a shortage of 27,864 personnel (including 7,679 officers), followed by the Navy with 16,255, and the Air Force with 15,503[138].

Shortage of junior officers is much more worrying as they are indispensable for combat. Units have just 30% of the authorized strength, which immensely over-burdens remaining officers and adversely affects command, operational readiness and training.

When they compare themselves with civilian services, soldiers wonder; *is it really worth serving?* Soldiers' bruised self-esteem, *sense of injustice* and extreme stress is manifesting itself in large increase in suicides, fratricides and stress disorders. Cases of insubordination, indiscipline, desertions and absence without leave too are on the increase.

In addition, there is an alarming increase in the requests for premature retirement from officers as well as other ranks, which aggravates the already critical personnel shortages. Along with the huge backlog of weapon modernization and critical shortage of munitions, this has led defence preparedness to an abysmal low.

Our country is painfully aware that communal passions once unleashed can be disastrous. Our Armed Forces had a terrible experience in 1984, but the sagacity and wisdom of Sikh leaders at all levels of the military hierarchy had prevented a disaster. However, the trauma of Op Blue Star and the horrendous anti-Sikh riots after Indira Gandhi's assassination reverberated for many years, as the following episode will show.

I had the privilege of assuming command of the first Bofors regiment in 1987. It is a renowned unit comprising purely Sikh troops, unlike mixed-class units. It was located in Punjab at time of Op Blue Star and my predecessor, a Sikh officer, with great diligence had ensured that there was no ugly incident.

Soon after I took over, the Regiment received orders to move to high-altitude sector of Sikkim. A year later the Army Commander, who had commanded Op Blue Star and who was on the hit list, was to visit my regiment. He was to spend few hours with the troops, and then fly out for reconnaissance of the LAC.

I was aghast when there was a *suggestion* that the perimeter cordon will be from another unit. Although it was couched in

---

[138] *Armed forces facing shortage of 60000 personnel: Govt.* The Indian Express 27 December 2017. Retrieved 21 July 2018. https:// indianexpress.com/article/ india/armed-forces-facing-shortage-of-nearly-60000-personnel-govt-5001467

diplomatic doublespeak, I went ballistic. They dropped the idea. Can anyone realize the anguish it caused? How stigmatized my proud and valiant Sikh soldiers felt, for no fault of theirs?

I bring this up because lately politics have accentuated religious and caste polarization. Number of communal incidents and lynching have increased manifold, as has caste-based violence. This is very dangerous, since our soldiers come from all religions, castes and ethnicities. They are bound to be upset by inflammatory rhetoric of political, religious, and community leaders of all hues.

Armed Forces are a model of secularism in thought, word and deed, wherein religion, caste or creed of comrades has never mattered. The manner in which the political class is recklessly polarizing society for electoral gains is bound to affect them too.

In 1991, following communal violence due to *Rath Yatra*, my dissertation titled, *'Impact of the Internal Security Environment on our Armed Forces'* analysed this problem, and had some stark conclusions[139]. Unfortunately, our society experienced even more polarizing events and agitations since then.

Chances that this will seriously affect our soldiers are very real now, due to growing angst among them. This poses a big challenge for our military leadership. It has to ensure that the prevailing milieu does not affect the only institution, which our citizens unequivocally admire. It takes decades to build strong traditions, but once damaged much longer to restore them.

Upon taking oath of allegiance on entering service, soldiers enter into a compact with the Nation, which exhorts them to *fight valiantly for the country*. In return, the Nation affirms, *"fear not for your kin. Should you attain martyrdom; we shall look after them as our own"*. This assurance, people's love, and their own *dharma* infuse them with courage that is so vital to win battles.

Our Armed Forces have invariably fulfilled their part of that compact. It is time the Nation too fulfils its part. It is now up to the citizens to nudge the Govt, and ensure that it fulfils all its obligations towards soldiers.

If this does not happen, the supply of motivated young men and women willing to lay down their lives in the Nation's defence will progressively dwindle.

---

[139] Deepak Sethi 1991. 'Impact of the Internal Security Environment on our Armed Forces', *The Combat Journal,* Vol.18 No. 2, 1991. Extracted from the dissertation of same title, submitted to the College of Defence Management.

15

The Defence Budget

Defence preparedness comes at a cost. The onerous task of defending the Nation against external aggression extracts a very heavy price; not just in terms of the blood, toil, and sweat of its soldiers, but also for the weapons and equipment required by them in order to fight effectively. The Nation's military strength depends as much on the valour of its soldiers and the leadership of commanders, as it does on the sophistication of their weaponry.

Historically, marauders of the likes of Mahmud of Ghazni financed their campaigns by plunder, and let their hordes retain some of the spoils as salary. Kings and Emperors too maintained huge armies mostly by usurping the riches of the conquered lands.

In the Colonial era, the colonies primarily bore the burden by providing money and soldiers for the wars of colonial masters. In the present-day world however, *the modus operandi* has become more subtle. Military-industrial complexes of Major Powers rake in billions of dollars through sales of arms, while their MNCs generate phenomenal revenues in Third World countries through neo-colonialist, predatory trade practices.

Rest of the world has to find resources for defence by striking a judicious balance between *guns* and *butter*. It is a tough choice. As highlighted earlier, India had been left impoverished at the time of Independence, with virtually no industrial development. Hence, scarce resources had to be devoted mostly for Nation-building, while diplomacy and policy of Non-alignment were to avoid war.

When diplomacy failed and we had to face Chinese aggression in 1962, the glaring neglect suffered by the Armed Forces showed up in the humiliating debacle. It drove home the stark truth that although *butter* is undoubtedly very important, neglecting *guns* beyond a minimum threshold can end up in disaster.

With passage of time, we seem to have forgotten that lesson. Since ultimately it all boils down to the defence budget, let us examine India's defence spending compared to adversaries. This comparison is as per data compiled by *Stockholm International Peace Research Institute* (SIPRI) for all countries worldwide.

Fig 30 shows the amounts spent on defence in 2017 by India, China and Pakistan. The amounts are in billions of US dollars at constant 2017 prices and exchange rates. Figures in red column represent the amounts as a percentage of GDP.

Pertinently, according to SIPRI Pakistan's spending data does not include Capital expenditure, which is the major Head for weapon purchases. Hence, if Capital expenditure is also included, it spends much more than 3.5% of the GDP.

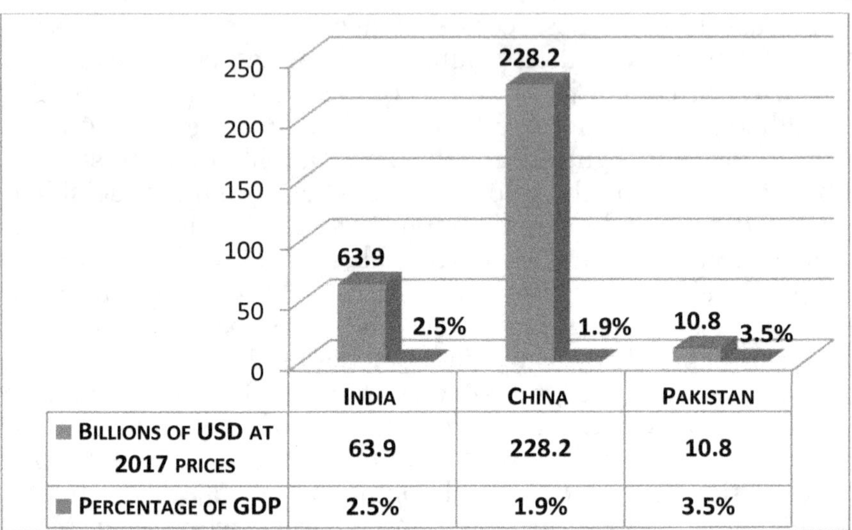

	INDIA	CHINA	PAKISTAN
BILLIONS OF USD AT 2017 PRICES	63.9	228.2	10.8
PERCENTAGE OF GDP	2.5%	1.9%	3.5%

Source: SIPRI Database

Fig. 30 – Defence Spending India, China, Pakistan – 2017

On the other hand, in the 2018 budget India's defence spending has come down even further to about 1.5% of the GDP. The sheer incongruity of our budgetary allocation is even more glaring given the fact that our Armed Forces are required to fight a two-front war with both China and Pakistan. Both adversaries together spend USD 239 billion, as against just USD 63.9 billion by India.

It is true that China's spending is commensurate with its Super power ambitions. However, its current budgetary allocations do not reflect the fact that it has already completed modernization of its Armed Forces, spread over the past 25 years. A key component of Deng's *Four Modernizations* launched in 1978 was the modernization of its Armed Forces.

China had undertaken this comprehensive and radical overhaul of the entire military as a *mission*. Most strategic analysts believe there was separate allocation of funds for the same, which were not included in the budget. China had adopted a holistic approach for the modernization, which rested on three pillars:

• Development, procurement, acquisition, and fielding of new weapon systems, technologies, and combat capabilities.

- Institutional and systemic reforms.
- Development of new war-fighting doctrines.

China's spending on research and development, paramilitary forces, strategic forces, and on acquisition of imported weapon systems is not included in the regular budget. Estimates of China's defence-related expenditures thus have a very wide variation even among most reputed Think tanks. For instance, the Table below shows how estimates of China's defence budget differ 537% from the officially declared figure of USD 35 billion[140].

Table 9.1 Competing statistics on China's military expenditure, 2006
(billions of US dollars)

Source	Expenditure
Official budget[a]	35.0
SIPRI estimate[b]	51.9
DoD low estimate[c]	80.0
DoD high estimate[c]	115.0
IISS estimate (PPP)[d]	122.0
SIPRI estimate (PPP)[e]	188.2

PPP = purchasing power parity

a. US Department of Defense (DoD), *Military Power of the People's Republic of China 2006*, Annual Report to Congress (Washington), www.defenselink.mil, 7.

b. Stockholm International Peace Research Institute, SIPRI Military Expenditure Database, http://milexdata.sipri.org.

c. M. D. Maples, "Current and Projected National Security Threats to the United States" (statement for the Record, US Senate Armed Services Committee, Washington, February 27, 2007).

d. International Institute for Strategic Studies (IISS), *The Military Balance 2007* (London), 346.

e. Stockholm International Peace Research Institute, *SIPRI Yearbook 2007* (Oxford University Press, 2007), 270.

India, with the current level of allocations, is nowhere near catching up with China in modernizing its Armed Forces. Nor has India initiated even critical reorganization and systemic reforms.

---

[140] *China's Military Modernization*, Peterson Institute for International Economics
https://piie.com/publications/chapters_preview/4174/09iie4174.pdf

Before analyzing the defence budget in absolute terms, as well as on *percentage of GDP* basis, let us first understand the distinction between Revenue expenditure and Capital expenditure.

- **Revenue Expenditure.** This is the largest component, which makes up around 67% of the defence budget. The Major heads of expenditure under it are:

  - Pay and allowances – approx 60%.
  - Ordnance stores such as equipment, clothing, indigenous ammunition etc. – approx 12%.
  - Works. This is for maintenance of existing infrastructure and not for new projects – approx 12%.
  - Supplies. Dry and fresh rations etc. – approx 4%.
  - Transportation. For rail, road, and air move of personnel, equipment and stores; operational and training moves of units; turnover of units; fuel expenditure etc – approx 12%.

- **Capital Expenditure.** It forms about 33% of the total defence budget, and finances new acquisitions. This part primarily contributes to defence modernization. It is under three Heads:

  - About 80% of the Capital expenditure is for acquisition of new imported weapon systems and equipment. The Ministry of Defence controls this Head entirely.
  - About 10% is for new buildings and infrastructure. The Engineer-in-Chief Branch controls this expenditure.
  - The MGO receives about 10% for procuring equipment, vehicles etc. from the Ordnance Factories Board.

Pay and allowances under the Revenue Head are for military combatants as well as of civilians working in various defence establishments, such as Armed Forces HQ Service, Military Engineering Service, Controller General of Defence Accounts, Canteen Stores Department etc. Likewise, the Defence Budget also caters for the expenditure incurred by the Defence Research and Development Organization and the Ordnance Factories Board.

Pensions do not form part of the Defence Budget now, although prior to 1990 these were included in it. Due to the financial crisis in 1990-91, when India had to approach the IMF for a loan, it became necessary to exclude them as they were inflating the Defence Budget and conveyed a wrong impression. This could have become a reason for the IMF to decline the loan or demand stringent structural reforms, which could have included reduction in the Defence expenditure.

Budgetary Trends

The graphic at Fig. 31 shows India's Defence Budget from 2010 to 2018. It reflects a steady increase in the total expenditure, mainly because of higher Revenue expenditure. These actually cater for inflation, and the increase in pay and allowances due to Pay Commission awards.

Capital expenditure, which is the more critical imperative for defence modernization, has remained virtually stagnant. In fact, it has shown a decline in 2016-17 and 2017-18. In real terms, the decline is much worse since prices of imported weapon systems have increased steeply year-to-year. Moreover, depreciation of the Rupee against the USD reduced its purchasing power substantially over this period.

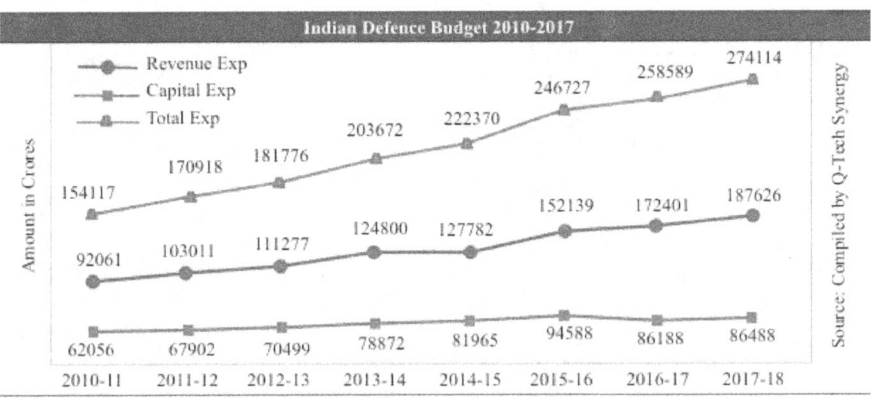

Fig. 31 – Indian Defence Budget from 2010 to 2018

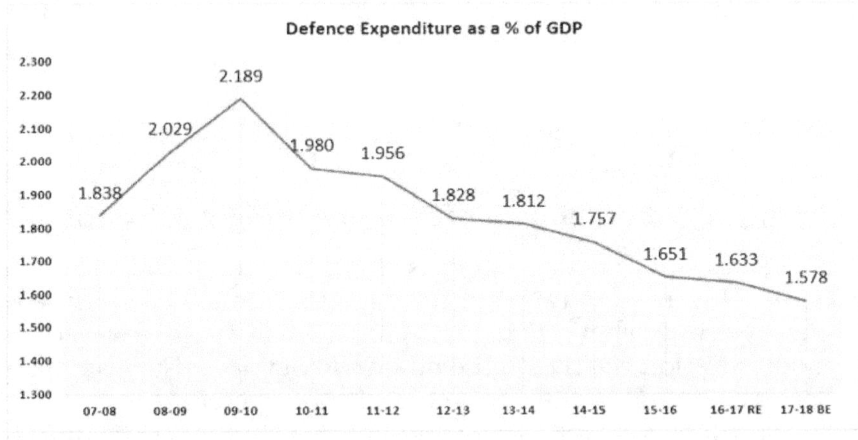

Fig. 32 – Defence Expenditure as a Percentage of GDP

Fig. 32 shows Defence expenditure from 2007-08 to 2017-18 as a percentage of the GDP. This paints an even more dismal picture, since it shows a steady decline from the peak of 2.189% in 2009-10 to just 1.578% in the current year. While it is true that the GDP too increased during this period, it is equally true that the purchasing power of the Rupee relative to USD decreased during this time. Imported weapon systems too became more expensive.

Figs. 30 and 32 show different figures of Defence expenditure, as a percentage of GDP. Fig. 30 shows the expenditure as 2.5% of the GDP, which is from the SIPRI database where the practice is to include defence pensions. Percentage of 1.578 in Fig. 32 is as per the current Indian practice of not including pensions of combatants and civilians in the Defence budget.

Dept	Revenue allocation	Capital allocation (₹ cr)	Total allocation	Revenue to capital ratio
Army	92,601	20,661	1,13,262	82:18
Navy	12,387	22,592	34,979	35:65
Air force	20,507	31,818	52,325	39:61
Joint staff	1,589	829	2,418	65:35
DRDO	5,985	5,975	11,960	50:50
OFB*	1,343	530	1,873	70:30
Land & works		6,872	6872	
Others		311	311	

Fig. 33 –Breakdown of Defence Budget Allocation

Long overdue modernization is the dire need of all the three Services. However, as ratios of Revenue to Capital expenditure of all three Services show (Fig. 33), the Army has the largest backlog in modernization relative to the other two Services. Navy's Capital budget allocation is the highest at 65%, whereas Air Force is marginally lower at 61%. The Army's allocation for modernization is just 18% of its total allotment.

Budget Percentage

It is pertinent to highlight that statistics on Defence spending of Nations, as a percentage of their GDP, is more an academic notion than a realistic reflection of their actual security needs. It is a global template, which shows comparative Defence spending of Nations, *vis-a-vis* Human development and welfare expenditures.

How much this percentage translates into absolute amounts obviously depends on the size of the Nation's GDP. For instance, a Nation with a USD 2 trillion GDP spending 3% on Defence, will actually be spending much less than a Nation that spends only 2% of its USD 4 trillion GDP.

Such a percentage has little relevance unless it also takes into account the security threats faced by a Nation, and the level of its economic development and score on HDI (Human Development Index) parameters. Why would Sweden and Switzerland, which have traditionally been neutral and whose populations score high on the HDI, spend a large percentage of their GDP on Defence?

On the other hand, Pakistan spending a higher percentage of its GDP on the military, when the bulk of its population lives in dire poverty can signify only two things. One, that it is obsessed with avenging its 1971 humiliation at any cost. Two, given its Power structure and its fragile democracy; *what the Military demands, the Military gets*.

India, on the other hand, has to strike a judicious balance between *guns* and *butter*, as emphasized earlier. We cannot afford to neglect either of the two. More importantly, if the top political leadership, based on defined National interests and Geostrategic analyses, determines that our military could face a two-front war, then it must provide it the requisite wherewithal.

Percentages, in such a case, do not matter. If spending just 1% of the GDP, gives our military adequate capability to confront a collusive war by China and Pakistan, then it is GREAT. If even 4% of GDP does not give the military, the barest minimum required, then it will not be of much value.

Modernization Backlog and Budget Options

It will be painfully apparent that Capital budget allocation, which provides funds for Defence modernization, has been grossly inadequate for a long time. This has created a huge backlog for all three Services. Given the equally critical imperatives of increasing social spending for alleviating agrarian distress, boosting our dismal HDI figures, and creating employment opportunities, there is not much scope for substantial increases in the Defence budget in the near future. The Nation cannot cut down on these measures, as it would aggravate socio-economic tensions and unrest, which in turn would be detrimental for internal cohesion and stability.

It is equally imperative to clear the perilously large backlog by innovative, *out of the box* solutions. We need to take them up in *mission mode*, akin to *Modernizations* initiated by Deng in China.

Foremost, it is essential to take up the modernization as a time-bound seven-year *mission*. The timeframe is short, yet essential, since we have to *catch up* with China. It must have a separate allocation in the Union budget that is outside the regular Defence budget. Some avenues for raising funds for the *Defence Modernization Mission* could be:

- Divestment of equity in select Defence PSUs and Ordnance factories, for joint ventures with reputed Private Sector firms having a good track record in producing defence systems.
- Issue *National Defence Bonds* for subscription by public.
- Invest offsets from foreign OEMs exclusively into the *Mission*.
- Develop Defence manufacturing hubs with extensive Private sector participation to achieve greater indigenization.
- Reduce *Revenue* component of the Defence budget through a new *Integrated Manpower Policy*, as per details in Chapter 16.
- A massive effort to develop a *Military-Industrial complex,* with large-scale Private sector participation, which can generate large revenues from Defence exports. Details in Chapter 17.

Marshalling funds for the massive investments required for the *Defence Modernization Mission* is certainly difficult, but not impossible. The Nation has been able to generate enormous resources for numerous grandiose schemes in the past. Many of those, though well intentioned, proved a dismal failure and resulted in a colossal waste of funds, such as the plan to cleanse River Ganges. Other ambitious populist missions might have been successful in giving electoral dividends, but with little else to show.

The *Defence Modernization Mission* is critical for the Nation's defence capability. Modernization of our Armed Forces has long been overdue, and can brook no further delay. We have to generate resources and complete the mission in time. There is no other option.

16

Integrated Manpower Policy

From the analysis of our military capability thus far, we can draw two major deductions. First, *the soldier,* who is indeed the foundation of the Nation's military might, is presently under a lot of physical and emotional stress, which is seriously undermining his morale and consequently our overall military capability. Two, there are critical gaps and huge backlogs in the modernization of our Armed Forces. The budget, primarily, is a major constraint on both counts.

Deficiency of Personnel

The Armed Forces are deficient of 60,000 personnel according to the RM's statement in Parliament. It is pertinent to note that this shortage is as per the extant authorization, which itself has been *pared down to bare bones* over the years as an economy measure. Since the shortage is entirely among young soldiers and junior officers, it has badly eroded the true fighting prowess.

Even then, the borders still have to be defended 24/7, counter-terrorism operations have to go on, training obviously cannot be curtailed, and troops have to rush in aid of civil authorities when called for emergency, or even *sundry* tasks. Commitments are so heavy that invariably each *soldier* ends up performing the duties of two to three comrades. Often, he cannot even get leave.

Howsoever motivated our *soldiers* might be, such overload of work in highly stressful situations throughout the year is bound to take its toll. However, such is our military ethos that no commander would ever admit that his soldiers are overstressed or demoralized, or express reservations about taking on an additional responsibility. Nonetheless, high incidence of stress disorders, cases of indiscipline, fratricide, overstaying leave, desertions, and inordinately high pleas for discharge, speak for themselves.

As highlighted earlier, of late the external eco-system too has been eroding soldiers' morale. Soldiers have felt incensed over the assault on their pride by undignified and un-soldierly tasks assigned to them, and utterly reprehensible comments of some politicians. They also feel dismayed by the grossly unfair treatment meted to them *vis-a-vis* civilian counterparts in pay, allowances, service conditions, status, and grade disparities.

Paradoxically, despite rampant unemployment in the country, the Armed Forces are not getting enough able-bodied, capable, and motivated soldiers, thus leading to such large deficiencies. Have our youth suddenly run short of valour and patriotism? Neither is the private sector brimming with new jobs, nor is the agricultural sector in any great shape. Then, what is the reason for such a large shortage?

Regrettably, the Govt and its agencies do not have a culture of commissioning scientific studies to analyze underlying causes, which may help evolve remedial measures and sound policies. However, the reason for shortages could well be in the eco-system.

Could visuals or media reports of *soldiers* cleaning up polluted lakes and mountain tourism spots, or laying Yoga mats, de-motivate aspiring youth? Likewise, visuals of elderly veterans and *Veer-Naris* protesting for rightful dues, or the angst of serving *soldiers* over the raw deal from the politico-bureaucratic combine can hardly enthuse our youth to enlist. Even scenes of martyred soldiers regularly returning in body bags will fail to stir patriotic emotions, when politicians shy away from even the charade of comforting their grieving families.

The Govt has dropped the proposal to raise a *Mountain Strike Corps*. Obviously, it has done so to cut costs, and not due to any rethinking on operational necessity. Strategy experts had debated its need at great length, and only then mooted the proposal. Yet again, budget constraints have trumped operational imperatives.

Notwithstanding above-cited causes, making up the entire shortfall of *soldiers,* especially junior officers in all three Services cannot brook any more delay. It is imperative that the govt addresses the root causes of the growing angst, take urgent steps to rectify anomalies, and most importantly, assuage the bruised self-respect of our soldiers. That alone will rebuild morale among serving soldiers, and attract our youth to join the military.

Our military capability has hit its nadir, and strategic experts are already raising alarm about the pre-1962 type neglect of our Armed Forces, which can only portend disaster. It is essential for the Govt to find requisite budgetary resources to fill the manpower and modernization gaps.

Budget Implications

Expenditure under Revenue head, accounts for 67% of the Defence budget. Pay and allowances of *soldiers* and of civilians in various Services under the MoD, take up over 60% of this amount. Pensions currently are not a part of the Defence budget, but still this is a huge expense in the Union budget. This is a lifelong commitment to *soldiers* who have given the best years of their lives in serving the Nation in the toughest of conditions.

A soldier typically enters at 18 years of age, and serves for 18 years, which is the minimum pensionable service. Commitment to pay pension starts when he is about 36-37 years old. He then starts looking for employment afresh, which is not easy given his age and extant high unemployment rates.

For the Govt, the pension burden keeps burgeoning, which it has to provide until the soldier's death, and thereafter to his kin as Family pension. This will increase further when existing deficiency of *soldiers* is made up. With increasing life expectancy, eventually the burden may even become unsustainable.

BROAD CONTOURS OF MANPOWER POLICY

Reconciling additional manpower and the interlinked financial load of pay and life-long pensions, with the severe budgetary constraints seems intractable. Yet, there is no option but to find some solution, howsoever infeasible it might seem.

The option I propose is neither too *radical* nor *infeasible*. However, the biggest roadblocks it could face will be absence of politico-bureaucratic will, and opposition from *fiefdoms* that seek to perpetuate the *status quo*.

Personnel below Officer Rank (PBOR)

Shortage of PBOR keeps fluctuating since the recruitment rate has not been constant over the years, which causes *bunching*. When a larger batch upon completing colour service proceeds on pension, it causes a greater shortfall, which new recruits in a standard batch cannot fill entirely. Moreover, since recruitment takes place at many centres for different arms and services, deficiencies are not uniform across the board.

It is necessary to rationalize *recruitment rates* and correlate them with *wastage rates* to ensure more even *flow*. Several statistical techniques are available that can develop algorithms to reduce *bunching*, and ensure low variation in vacancies of various services. Recruiting directorates must adopt them.

It is imperative to reduce the workload and commitments of PBOR, which is causing growing stress levels. The increasing propensity to deploy soldiers for tasks that civilian agencies ought to perform has to be curbed drastically. While *aid to civil power* in emergencies is a legitimate duty, to treat *soldiers* as a readily available work force is unconscionable and abhorrent.

The MoD is duty bound to curb this practice, but it is complicit in overburdening soldiers even when no emergency or dire need exists. Top military leadership, which must protest against this, is abdicating its duty by acquiescing with unwarranted demands.

Within the Armed Forces, despite strict orders against undue ostentation, senior officers seldom take stern deterrent actions. These measures, both external and internal will help ease the extra burden on our *soldiers* until shortages are made up.

Terms of Service of PBOR

- Terms of service of regular entrants into all three Services need some modifications, with the following intent: *to ensure a younger profile; retain only the fittest, most capable, and motivated personnel at various levels of career progression; provide alternative employment at each stage of the review process; and rationalization of military pensions.*
- Upon joining units after basic military training, soldiers must undergo *review* at five, ten and fifteen years of service. There would be separate parameters for each stage, but must include physical and mental toughness, professional competence, service and discipline profile, military and education courses attended, future prospects, and aptitude.
- *Soldiers* not retained after each *review*, must be sidestepped to alternative employment based on their preference and aptitude.
- Importantly, this sidestepping is not a *rejection per se*. It is an opportunity for *soldiers* to make the lateral move, based on their family circumstances, personal choice, aptitude, and overall organizational interest.
- Upon their lateral move, the terms of service of the new organization will govern their pay, allowances and pension. They will earn gratuity for each year of military service.
- Those nominated for lateral move at 15 years service, will earn pension as per rules of the new organization, and that too only upon serving in it up to its pensionable service.

Burgeoning Pension Budget

To resolve the pension burden the Govt has to treat *soldiers* at par with its civilian employees, and provide them with assured alternative employment until the age applicable to civilians. This is its moral responsibility too, as it cannot leave in a lurch middle-aged *soldiers* who have served the country valiantly during their prime and withstood the hardships of military life.

On completion of colour service, once soldiers are absorbed into alternative employment, then civilian terms of service and pension would apply to them. They will receive gratuity and not military pension. If a soldier declines to accept alternative employment due to family circumstances, then too he will not get military pension, but may get gratuity and a *golden handshake.*

Assured Alternative Employment

- Major avenues for employment of *soldiers* sidestepped at various stages of the *review* process are; CAPFs, Ordnance factories, Defence PSUs, and various Services under the MoD that are tenable by civilians.
- It will be obvious to anyone that such *soldiers* would be a great asset to these organizations due to their immense practical knowledge and experience in handling those weapons and equipment in all types of terrain and weather conditions.
- For example, can there be any doubt about value of Cavalrymen in HVF, Gunners in GCF, Infantrymen in small arms factories, EME personnel in Vehicle factory or BEL, Sailors in Mazagon and Garden Reach, or Airmen in HAL? These were just a few examples, and *soldiers* would be assets anywhere.
- Civilian employees serve in many services under the MoD such as AFHQ Service, MES, CGDA, CSD, Record offices etc. *Soldiers* can, and do perform all such tasks very efficiently.
- In fact, they would be better suited for such tasks due to their knowledge and experience of the military environment, and thus obviate need for orientation training to civilians.
- As per their new terms of service, such *soldiers* would be beyond the pale of Trade union activity.
- Private sector firms forming part of the *Military-Industrial Complex* (discussed in the next chapter), will find such *soldiers* invaluable for their enterprises.

Critical Shortfall of Young Officers

By far the most critical problem facing the Armed Forces is the very high shortfall of young officers. Young leaders are the true strength of all militaries and their most vital battle-winning factor. Our military academies regrettably, are just not attracting the right material in sufficient numbers.

The officer cadre in the military is no longer the career of choice for our youth who have the required calibre. This is not just due to more lucrative career options now being available in the *Civvy*

Street, but also because of the deteriorating image of service conditions and growing civil-military discord. Even Service officers, who have a family tradition of military service, sadly are no longer sending their sons to the Armed Forces.

It will be disastrous for the Armed Forces to lower intake standards merely to fill up vacancies. The Govt will have to think seriously about ameliorating service conditions to attract the right material. Increased intake of women officers into non-combat services does help to let male counterparts join the combat arms. However, there is a need for a more enduring solution.

Benefits that will accrue

To summarize, the following benefits will accrue to the Govt's budget situation, Armed Forces, and the entire Defence structure.

- Rationalization of pensions will reduce the load on the budget.
- Reduction in workload and commitments on extraneous tasks will reduce stress levels of overburdened soldiers.
- Ensure younger profile of the Armed Forces.
- Retention of only fit, competent, and motivated personnel will improve overall fighting capability.
- Boost morale of serving soldiers due to removal of anxiety about post-retirement rehabilitation.
- Availability of physically fit, disciplined, dedicated, motivated, and professionally competent workers to Ordnance factories, Defence PSUs, Services under MoD, and private sector firms in the defence sector.
- Change in work culture of these organizations due to *soldiers'* ethos of dedicated service and their abjuring Trade unionism.

Management of Change

The *Integrated Manpower Policy* will have to be executed with deliberation and sensitivity. Knowledge and experience of *Change Management* experts, who routinely oversee large organizational restructurings in the corporate world, would be useful.

The Nation would recall how vehemently trade unions and bank employees had opposed the introduction of computers. It was not just the canard spread about job losses, but also their reluctance to learn a new skill, which kept fuelling that agitation.

There is bound to be a lot of resistance to the lateral placement of *soldiers* in CAPFs, MoD's civilian services, Ordnance factories and Defence PSUs. However, this will be more for subjective reasons than because of any real threat to the efficiency of these organizations or career prospects of the employees. The age-old scourge of *vested interests,* which the Kargil Review Committee[141] was constrained to include in its report to the Parliament, would not allow the status quo to be altered.

However, given the serious budget situation that is preventing the Govt from funding the defence modernization plans and filling up manpower shortages, it will have little option except to push this through. While the Govt must address genuine concerns of stakeholders, it will have to deal firmly with the obstructive and dilatory tactics of the interested parties.

Imperatives of National security will have to override all other considerations.

---

[141] Kargil Review Committee Report: Executive Summary.25 February 2000. http://nuclearweaponarchive.org/India/KargilRCA.html. Retrieved 12 July 2018

17

Military-Industrial Complex

No Nation that aspires to be a significant player in a *multipolar* world can do so with imported weapon systems, even if those are *state of the art*. Modern history is replete with examples how only formidable *military-industrial complexes* of United States, Soviet Union, UK, France, China, and earlier Nazi Germany and Imperial Japan, enabled them to become strong military powers.

Development of armaments is a race. Any Nation that fails to keep pace, risks serious harm to its security. No wonder, Nations spend hundreds of billions of dollars on research, development and manufacture of exotic, *sci-fi* type weapons to stay ahead. For most Nations this expense is a dire necessity due to their security situation, and lack of adequate defence infrastructure. However, for Major Powers that have developed strong military-industrial complexes, it is an investment, which earns humungous profits.

Multi-Trillion Dollar Industry

It is a pity, and a sign of our decadent times and priorities that the world spends much more on producing *killing machines*, than on human welfare. According to SIPRI, world's total military expenditure rose to $1,739 billion in 2017, which is 2.2% of the global GDP. This represents an expenditure of $230 per person on armaments; far above the food consumption of billions[142].

This enormous spending is no drain on the economies of such countries as their military-industrial complexes are self-sustaining. In fact, they contribute handsomely to their National exchequers. Not only do they recover all expenditure on R&D and manufacture through global sales, they even make huge profits.

For the Major Powers it is a *win-win* situation. Their Defence industry creates a lot of employment for high-skill engineers and technicians, which boosts the skill levels of the workforce at large. Many firms fund research projects in leading universities and tap the talent therein for their own R&D programmes. This benefits the universities, the students, the firms themselves, and improves the general scientific temper of the community.

---

[142] *Global military spending remains high at $1.7 trillion,* SIPRI 02 May 2018. https://www.sipri.org/media/press-release/2018/global-military-spending-remains-high-17-trillion. Accessed: 22 August 2018.

These corporations spawn a large web of ancillary industries and suppliers, and such clusters spin-off numerous benefits to the local economies by way of revenue, local businesses, and technical institutes. Taxes on multi-billion dollar profits raked in by these corporate houses fill up the coffers at the State and National level.

Even if the likelihood of full-fledged conventional wars has reduced in the Post-War era, these firms will stay in business and flourish as long as there is conflict in the world. They have all types of fare on their menu; lethal small arms and machine guns for rebels, mercenaries, and terrorists; tanks, guns, ships, and aircraft for Nations in conflict, and even for those who purchase them more as symbols of power and status.

And then, there is India; currently the world's largest importer of weapon systems. It has not developed adequate capability to produce cutting-edge weapons for defence against adversaries China and Pakistan, despite fighting five wars with them.

India's Defence Industry

For a Nation, wherein the British set up the first Ordnance factory as early as 1787, and increased the number to 18 by 1947, it is astonishing that we still do not have a modern *military-industrial complex*. It is equally perplexing that although Ordnance factories now total 40, we still face shortages of many products these factories are supposed to provide.

Our National leaders had the foresight to set up Defence PSUs such as HAL, BEL, and Mazagon docks as well as factories for production of tanks, guns and vehicles soon after Independence, despite the resource crunch. Yet, even with decades of experience, they have not been able to attain global standards of R&D and product excellence. Nor have they provided the Indian Armed Forces with quality systems that obviate the need for imports.

Low Productivity of Public Sector Units

What ails Indian Ordnance factories and Defence PSUs? The same ills afflict them too, as they do with all Govt offices, establishments and PSUs; overstaffing, lack of accountability, and an indifferent, self-serving work culture.

Protectionism inevitably spells the death-knell of innovation, excellence and productivity, be it in the corporate world or other endeavours. Public sector defence units enjoy *protection* because they have *captive buyers* in the Armed Forces, who have no option but to accept whatever is dished out to them. If they were to face competition, and get orders based only on superior product features and reliability, then their productivity could improve substantially. It is essential that both, financial as well as product quality parameters should govern the evaluation of these units.

This will impose greater responsibility and accountability on Managers who will have to adhere to the corporate dictum, *perform or perish.* Unfortunately, our antiquated labour laws, trade unions, and grossly selfish political and bureaucratic interests have engendered a *work culture* that is very antithetical to productivity.

This malaise is not peculiar to India alone. It is ingrained in the human nature itself, and that is why a system based on *rewards* and *accountability* always extracts better performance. Govt units and bureaucracies all over the world, consequently, suffer from much lower productivity compared to the corporate world.

Private Sector

The Private sector, which is the engine of growth, productivity, and innovation in any Nation, has unfortunately not been involved in our Defence industry at a significant scale. On the other hand, military-industrial complexes of all Major Powers, barring those of Socialist economies of Russia and China, revolve almost entirely around Private sector enterprises.

Bureaucratic red tape, political interference, and sloth in the workforce do not hinder free markets. Importantly, competition keeps them *lean and mean,* and they have to *fight* for orders based more on excellence of the weapon systems than on *captive* buyers.

For instance, for decades our Armed Forces had to purchase Shaktiman and Nissan trucks made by the Vehicle factory under license from foreign developers. For all those years that our generation of soldiers had to *suffer them,* we did not see even marginal improvements. There was just no incentive for the Govt factory to put in that extra effort.

India has several excellent corporate houses that compete in the highly demanding global marketplace with quality products. A vast pool of skilled engineers and technicians is already doing excellent work for them, and many more are readily available. Given appropriate policy decisions, they have all the potential to turn India into a major developer and producer of sophisticated weapon systems.

Firms, such as Tatas and Mahindras have been providing high quality vehicles for quite some time. We produce high tensile steel, which is the core of the defence industry. Likewise, Bharat Forge is now considered a world-class supplier of metal forgings that go into tank and gun barrels. Our large pool of talented software experts and system designers can contribute immensely to developing hi-tech systems and avionics for the Armed Forces.

It is imperative that our Private sector is involved in a big way at the earliest to give a fillip to our Defence industry. It should form the nucleus of our military-industrial complex and become its engine of its growth. Indian Ordnance Factories and Defence PSUs, which have colossal investments in them, will play have to play a complementary and even a competitive role in this, as I will elaborate hereafter.

Modernization and Budgetary Imperatives Revisited

Discussion in preceding two chapters underscored the utterly dire situation as regards our defence capability, both in terms of manpower shortage and defence modernization. Defence budget is the major constraint for both. Any substantial accretion is unlikely, given the need for funding poverty alleviation and even *populist* schemes in an election year.

Our Defence industry therefore has to be self-sustaining, which is the model followed by all Major powers. Revenues generated from Defence exports will be the only feasible way of meeting our Capital budget requirements. Defence exports by both Private and Public sector units would require at least as much, if not more emphasis than just meeting domestic requirements. That is where all the money will come from.

After formulation and dissemination of policies, this effort will obviously take a long time to attain *critical mass*. Entry into the highly competitive arms export market will have a long gestation period and needs sustained effort. Based on market research of requirements of potential buyers, firms will have to develop products, arrange demonstrations and Defence expos to market them, and only then will they be able to begin production. There is no such thing as buying *off the shelf* even in advanced countries. For these reasons, we must kick-start the process without delay.

The Way Forward

Policy Framework. Formulation of a comprehensive policy and related guidelines for Private sector participation will obviously be the first step. Reportedly, a policy is in the offing, but not many details are available in the public domain. Nonetheless, the policy must take into account the following principles.

It will be obvious that Private sector firms will have to make enormous investments in infrastructure and equipment, without any guarantee of ultimately bagging the contract. As discussed, this venture is critical for the Nation on several counts. Hence, Govt will have to *invite* Private sector participation, *encourage* them to make the huge investments, *facilitate* their entry with speedy clearances, and *nurture* them through *teething problems,* till they become major revenue earners. They must export their weapon systems, subject of course to security issues.

An important principle in the policy must be to ensure *competition*. There should never be a single vendor situation, as it would create monopoly pricing, stifle innovation, and limit user choices. It will tantamount to encouraging *protectionism*, which is the bane of our Ordnance factories. To uphold this principle the Govt must invite, and even pay two to three potential developers to produce prototypes for the users to test out comprehensively.

Pre-qualification. Govt's initial *Request for Proposals* (RFPs) should be to pre-qualify corporate houses that seek to enter the defence exports industry. It must adopt very stringent criteria based on their existing industry and product line, track record, technical capability, infrastructure, management expertise, and financial resources.

The RFPs must focus only on firms that have the potential to develop, produce, and export *complete systems*. The Govt must deal with only this single entity for all aspects of the weapon system, and hold it accountable. Firms may select own vendors for producing components, but will be accountable for their quality.

Financial Position. This must be a vital parameter in the pre-qualification process. It must evaluate firm's overall *financial health*, equity and working capital, reserves, and importantly, its debt and liabilities to lenders and Public sector banks. Firms will have to raise finance for such projects, which should preferably come from in-house corporate reserves, global capital markets, or public issues of equity.

Corporate houses entering the armaments sector will likely establish a *Defence subsidiary* (DS) for this endeavour. Financial *due diligence* must be carried out not just of the DS, but also of the parent company. Contractual agreements must put the liability squarely on the parent firm in case of default, to avoid *Kingfisher Airlines* like situations.

Ordnance Factories and Defence PSUs

The biggest challenge will be to *stir up* the huge behemoth of our Ordnance factories and Defence PSUs into making greater contribution to our Defence industry. With hundreds of crores invested in this virtual *white elephant,* it is imperative that radical policy and structural measures are initiated to turn them around.

This must be done in spite of inevitable opposition from the workers, managers, bureaucrats, and politicians, all of whom have a major stake in perpetuating the existing state of affairs. However, given the high stakes involved our leadership will have to find the *political will* to remedy the situation.

Such profound changes have to be thought through with great deliberation, and implemented in a calibrated manner with utmost sensitivity to avoid a counterproductive backlash. Broad features of one possible option are discussed below.

There will be a need to establish joint ventures (JVs) between specific Ordnance factories or Defence PSU units, with selected Private sector DSs. It will have to be processed on a case-by-case basis since there cannot be a *one size fits all* solution. The basis will be the preference of the DS, as to which Ordnance factory or PSU will complement its own resources for the new JV.

Level of equity participation will determine what component of the plant, machinery, and infrastructure of the public sector unit will be transferred to the JV for the value of equity purchased. This could either be through setting up an entirely new plant, or bifurcation of the existing PSU for the new JV.

The central idea behind this is to eliminate monopoly situations, and make the parent PSU and the JV compete for orders from the Armed Forces for that equipment, armament, or ammunition. The PSU may transfer to the JV some engineers and technicians along with the plant, who will thus have the requisite institutional and technical knowledge to get the venture going. Remaining workforce will be hired by the DS, and will be governed by the corporation's terms of service. Several major advantages will accrue, such as:

- The private sector DS will be investing in the JV, which will get the plant, machinery and infrastructure of equivalent value from the PSU. Since it will be from an *up and running* unit, the JV can hit the ground running.
- Such divestment will provide a lot of money for the budget.
- Competition between the parent PSU and the JV will boost productivity and encourage innovation.
- The corporate work culture of the employees in the JV will bring about a positive change among PSU workers too, especially since both units will now be competing for orders.

- Armed Forces will benefit from better quality products, with newer features.

Intensive Efforts to Boost Exports

Success of this entire endeavour depends solely on the ability of the Indian defence industry, both in the private and public sectors, to generate export revenues on a massive scale. The Govt and the pre-qualified corporate houses will have to pull out all stops in this regard. A joint Apex body to formulate new strategies, coordinate between Govt agencies and private sector, and remove roadblocks will be necessary to oversee this *mission*.

This will necessitate holding Defence Expos on a grand scale in all potential markets, especially in Asia, Africa, Latin America, and the Middle East. Military attaches in our embassies abroad can play a very important role in assessing the potential requirements in those countries, and help them connect with firms back home.

As stated earlier, this will require very large investments from the private sector and it will take many years for them to bear fruit. Until export revenues start streaming in, Govt will have to provide them with all possible support, by way of suitable regulations, tariff structure, export subsidies and access to Govt's own R&D establishments.

Joint Ventures with Foreign Firms

Development of armaments is extremely expensive and a high-risk investment. Leading Global arms manufactures are loathe to share that knowledge, and very reluctant to agree to technology transfer. However, we have a significant advantage by way of low labour costs, good industrial base, infrastructure, and skilled manpower.

Private sector firms and even PSUs wherever possible, must go for joint ventures and technical collaboration in a big way, to produce weapon systems in India. Such manufacturing hubs will not only generate employment, but also more importantly, facilitate immense knowledge dissemination to the firms and the general industrial environment.

Technology transfer must remain a very high priority, as it will help upgrade features of systems for our domestic use, and make our weapon systems meant for export markets more attractive by adding new features. This must not be confined to just peripheral technologies, but will have to be more substantive.

Weapon System Imports

The following might be like showing a *red rag to a bull,* but nonetheless I firmly believe that import of new weapon systems, if still necessary for our Armed Forces, must be channelized through the Private sector Defence firms. These firms are quite adept at negotiations with foreign firms. Acquisitions, mergers, JVs, and collaborations with foreign entities are almost a matter of routine for them.

They are in a much better position to bargain, not just the costs but also critical technology transfers. While negotiating arms purchases, they can leverage their capabilities to manufacture *under license,* sophisticated systems for them at much lower costs. Their ability to forge such long-term relationships with foreign firms will help us upgrade our weapons technology on a continual basis.

This will also eliminate the sword of *scandals* that hangs over all arms deals negotiated by the Govt, which have wreaked havoc with the defence preparedness of our Armed Forces for decades. Ideally, two or three private sector defence firms must negotiate separately with competing foreign arms manufacturers, and then make product offerings of their entire package to the Govt. The Armed Forces can then pick whichever package is best overall.

All advanced Nations follow this model, and there is no reason we should not adopt it too. Only the politico-bureaucratic combine would be averse to it.

Defence Research & Development Organization (DRDO)

Apart from the Ordnance Factories, the DRDO is another much derided, money-guzzling *white elephant.* It gets a major share of the Defence budget, but sadly nothing much to boast about by way of results and productivity.

Tales of its appalling and utterly indefensible cost and time over-runs abound, and this organization has been vilified by the Armed Forces, strategic experts, as well as the general public alike. However, such is its power and influence as a fiefdom and under the MoD, that the Armed Forces are invariably compelled to accept whatever stuff it dishes out. And that too, without a question being asked about the delays, quality, and cost.

DRDO is ever eager to bag projects (and thus virtually get a blank cheque from the MoD), and makes lofty promises of meeting all GSQRs and *delivering* within the time allotted. However, there are any numbers of *horror stories* in the public domain about scandalous delays, be it fighter aircrafts, tanks or missiles.

It needs drastic restructuring, and more importantly a radical departure from its current lack of performance and financial accountability. *It has to be subject to competition from Private sector defence manufacturers.* It must be made to follow the principle *perform or perish,* and its funding should be contingent only upon its productivity in terms of quality, cost, and time.

The DRDO should not get GSQRs automatically, and be the sole agency to receive funds for development. They must compete with private vendors. Far too long they have enjoyed the privilege of being a monopoly and this must change. The Private sector has the capacity to deliver, as the following example will show.

Two private sector firms had produced prototypes of medium guns, which were evaluated by the Army and one of them has been awarded the contract. Both were very good guns by all accounts, which is a far cry from the lack of non-performance of the DRDO and Ordnance factories.

A strong military-industrial complex is indispensable for all Nations that aspire to be at the *Global High Table*, and who want to be a significant player in a *multipolar* world. Not only would it help resolve the severe budgetary constraints that are holding back utterly needed Defence modernization, but would also fill manpower and technology gaps. There will also be spin-off benefits for unemployment and knowledge transfers.

Only the requisite *political will* can force the recalcitrant bureaucracy from being impediments to urgently needed radical changes. That alone would help fulfil this *mission.*

18

Foreign Policy

While a Nation's *military power*, and in the present-day context, predominantly its *economic strength* are critical for meeting external challenges, *foreign policy* weaves these elements together to present a more coherent response. For a Nation that now counts among the leading players in a *multipolar* world, it is vital that we manoeuvre the volatile geopolitical landscape deftly.

By integrating our core National interests and aspirations, as defined in the *National Security Doctrine,* foreign policy devises and coordinates strategies to attain those goals. It conceptualizes the contributions *economic strength, military power,* and *soft power* must make towards that end, and synthesizes them in order to build up synergy.

Analysis of the geopolitical environment in Chapter 11 covered most of the important politico-economic, geostrategic and security aspects that are relevant to India. The following discussion seeks to summarize only some of the key aspects that ought to influence our foreign policy formulations.

United States

The post-9/11 era and the Global war on terrorism triggered a radical shift in Indo-US relations, which before then were reeling under sanctions imposed after India's nuclear tests. The growing entente secured for India the critical US *waiver*, which cleared the way for her entry into the nuclear club. USA has now accorded India the status of a *strategic partner,* and as a spin-off, it could sell arms worth $17 billion to India since 2007.

USA would like to see India ensconced more firmly on its side, in its bid to contain a rising China. It wants India to join the QUAD along with Japan and Australia, without any reservations. However, the perceived growing Indo-US proximity sets off a different dynamic in India's relations with Russia, China and Pakistan that India cannot, and must not ignore.

Whatever is the state of the *strategic partnership*, the State Department, Pentagon, and strategic think tanks are under no illusion that India would unequivocally side with USA in the event of a full-blown Sino-US confrontation. If India could steer clear of Big Power rivalry during the Cold War, when it was much weaker economically and militarily, there is no reason why it should foreclose its options now.

Indo-US relations must stay transactional, especially given the current unpredictability of the Trump presidency. There is a lot of mutual benefit for both, and India must nurture the relationship. However, there is no need for India to forgo its strategic independence and become a client state.

Russia

It hardly bears emphasis that Russia has been our all-weather friend. Its support at the critical juncture of the 1971 war, when USA was trying to intimidate us by sending USS Enterprise, allowed us to accomplish our magnificent victory. It has been the biggest seller of advanced weaponry to all three Services. The nuclear submarine leased by Russia constitutes the vital third leg of our Triad.

Growing Indo-US entente had inevitably created a perception of some coldness in Indo-Russian relations, which coincided with signs of the latter warming up to Pakistan. It seems, more recently Russia has been reassured about our continuing commitment to the relationship, which is certainly in India's interest.

Russia seems well on the way to reclaiming its Super Power status. In any case, it is the dominant power in the eastern hemisphere. Presently, there is strategic convergence between Russia and China despite their history of territorial and ideological disputes. China, which keeps alive the bogey of *historic wrongs* done to it, has apparently decided to forget Imperial Russia's acquisitions on China's eastern seaboard, for the time being.

There is no clash of strategic interests between Russia and India. Even though in International Relations *there are no permanent friends,* there is no reason for India to cool-off on our time-tested friendship. The *International North-South Transport Corridor* (INSTC), which links Central Asia, Europe and Russia to the Persian Gulf, and thence to India, promises immense economic benefits. It is yet another reason why we should nurture this relationship.

From a long-term strategic perspective, the global fulcrum of military and economic power has shifted to the East. While it is true, several strategic permutations would emerge in the ever-changing geopolitical dynamic, it is all the more important that we maintain our strategic independence. We must pursue a foreign policy guided solely by our supreme National interests. Let us not be caught on the wrong side of the strategic divide.

Europe

India has strong economic relations with all European nations, but post-*Brexit* India will have to negotiate separate economic agreements with UK. Indo-European economic and political relationships gain even more importance in the context of political uncertainties in USA, and Trump's trade war with the EU.

While there are no contentious political issues between India and the EU, we must strengthen our economic relationship with them much more to counter China's strong presence in that market. There is a lot of untapped potential, especially for more collaborations and Joint ventures.

India has good infrastructure, ample supplies of raw material and steel, and low-wage, technically qualified workers. India's geographical location dominates major SLOC to the huge Asian, African, Persian Gulf and European markets. There is no reason why India cannot become another *factory of the world,* which will have substantial labour and transportation cost advantages *vis-a-vis* China.

China

Sino-Indian boundary dispute has remained frozen since 1962 and it must remain so for several reasons. The status quo in the Eastern sector suits us since we hold territory up to our claim line. In the west, the Chinese hold Aksai Chin and the Karakoram tract. Notwithstanding the ambiguity about respective historical claim lines, for the present it is neither feasible nor desirable to attempt changing it.

Strengthening our economy and our defence capability should remain our immediate top priority. It took China more than two decades following its *Four Modernizations,* to attain its present strength. During that period, it maintained a low profile and started becoming more assertive in the geopolitical arena only after it had reorganized its Armed Forces and had provided them with ample modern weaponry. We have yet to make up for the *Lost Decades,* and fill up the critical gaps.

In geopolitics, it is not possible to predict anything with certainty. One can only assess probabilities. A full-blown border war is unlikely since it suits neither China nor India, considering our respective strategic and economic compulsions and priorities. It did not happen in Sikkim in 1967, the 1971 war, the Sumdrong Chu episode, and the more recent Doklam face-off. Despite the backlog in defence modernization, India is much stronger now, which would dissuade China from any misadventure.

Indian foreign policy therefore must persist with the diplomatic route to resolve the boundary dispute, howsoever long that might take. Meanwhile, we must have trade and closer cooperation with China on economic issues of mutual interest in WTO and other forums, to increase economic interdependence.

Our diplomacy must send appropriate signals that despite our strategic partnership with USA, we are not committed to any overt or covert hostile actions against China. That might make China less inclined to go overboard, in propping up Pakistan as a counter. We must be balanced and confident in safeguarding our National interests; neither too diffident nor unduly acrimonious.

Pakistan

Dealing with Pakistan will be more intractable given the long history of wars and acrimony. What course our diplomacy should take, depends entirely on the political will and choice of our top leadership. The present state of *drift* must not go on.

With the new PM in power, it will take at least few months before a clear picture emerges about the stance of Pakistan's political establishment and military. However, with India too being in election mode, political rhetoric, grandstanding, and vituperative *Media circus* will muddy the waters. Such an acrimonious environment will reduce the possibility of any major diplomatic initiative.

Meanwhile, militarily on the LoC we need to give a more muscular response to all attempts at infiltration and cross-LoC firing. Experience has shown that the only way to deter Pakistan is by meting out swift and strong ripostes to all its transgressions. Its policy of *bleeding us,* by keeping the inflicted casualties below a certain threshold, must be thwarted most resolutely.

Other Neighbouring Countries

Although I am covering them last, this aspect is the most vital and challenging task for our diplomacy. Unfortunately, we do not have a consistent record of maintaining friendly relations with all our neighbours. They often resent our purported overbearing *big brother* attitude, and interference in their internal affairs.

This is *a cross*, which all large countries *have to bear*. Smaller neighbours of any large country inherently nurse that feeling, justifiably or otherwise. Our political leaders and diplomats therefore must be conscious of such perceptual mindset, and must deal with their foreign counterparts with greater sensitivity.

Regrettably, our leaders and diplomats are generally far too obsequious while dealing with those from the advanced Nations, and overly condescending with our smaller neighbours. Obviously, they must rectify their predisposition in both cases.

Maintaining good neighbourly relations is very crucial for our own security, since otherwise our adversaries are bound to *fish in troubled waters* and foment trouble. Mutual trust, respect and cooperation are cornerstones to a healthy relationship, and must be followed to ensure stability on our borders.

Undoubtedly, our National interests remain paramount, and our neighbours would be quite cognizant about that. At the same time, we too must be mindful about their interests and not indulge in coercive diplomacy. There should be regular diplomatic interactions and differences, if any, must be resolved speedily.

As the larger country, India must show magnanimity and deference to their interests. Greater economic interactions, not just on equitable, but on terms that are more generous would go a long way towards cementing the relationship. Such generosity is actually an *investment* for our own security and stability.

Economic diplomacy would pay even greater dividends in our own neighbourhood, relative to Afro-Asian Nations. Our public and private sector firms must be encouraged to make investments in them, and forge economic partnerships for mutual benefit.

India needs to pay greater emphasis upon developing closer politico-economic cooperation with Myanmar for both strategic as well as economic dividends. The *Trilateral Highway Project* through Myanmar is our doorway to Southeast Asia, which will require much closer cooperation with it. Similarly, a better understanding with Myanmar is imperative due to the Rohingya crisis and future repatriation of their refugees.

Economic Diplomacy

As previously highlighted, 21st century geopolitical power-play will be predominantly economic in nature. China's BRI is a well-crafted strategy to promote strategic interests through economic linkages. However, avaricious predatory lending practices of its state–owned enterprises have created a backlash in many host countries, and led to cancellation of several projects.

This presents India with an opportunity to leverage discontent in those countries, and offer economic partnerships on more fair and transparent terms. While our Private sector firms would obviously take decisions based on the commercial viability of such ventures, they must be encouraged and incentivized by the Govt. Many strategic and politico-economic benefits would accrue from such partnerships in Third World markets.

There are many well-established Public sector firms such as BHEL, HMT, and ONGC-Videsh etc, who are more amenable to Govt *diktat*, and who must be nudged to enter such partnerships on a large scale. They must establish JVs in Third World countries to produce and market their products in those markets.

In an era of very rapid technological advancements, life cycles of products as well as industrial processes have become very short. The world over, the race is on to constantly upgrade, acquire and disseminate knowledge among partners and subsidiaries. There is a technological hierarchy in this process. Advanced Nations invest heavily in R&D to develop cutting-edge technologies. These firms recover their costs through the high prices of innovative products.

Once the technology is standardized, they seek to lower costs by licensed production in low-wage countries. Thus, it is a continual cycle. India occupies a vital intermediate position in this hierarchy. Indian firms, in both private and public sectors, must enter into strategic partnerships and collaborations with firms in advanced countries to acquire the latest technology, and then produce those products for them in India at lower costs.

They must enter into similar partnerships *downstream* too. JVs with Third World firms that are at the lower rung, can produce the more standardized and matured products in those countries. Such *migration* of Foreign Direct Investment (FDI) and technology, from the advanced to the intermediate, and thence to Third World countries, is now the new normal[143].

In this manner, Indian *economic diplomacy* must create our own version of BRI in the vast markets of Central Asian Republics, SE Asia, Middle East, Gulf states and Africa. There will give high political, economic, and strategic dividends.

Soft Power

As the principal Node for coordinating all external dimensions, Foreign policy must integrate all elements of Soft Power too. As

---

[143] Deepak Sethi, Stephen Guisinger, David Ford, and Steven Phelan, 2002. 'Seeking Greener Pastures: A Theoretical and Empirical Investigation into the Changing Trend of Foreign Direct Investment Flows in Response to Institutional and Strategic Factors'. *International Business Review,* 11 (6), pp. 685-705.

stressed while discussing the *National Security Doctrine* in Chapter 12, all components of Soft Power need integration into a coherent plan. Presently, many of those activities happen only sporadically, and hence it is difficult to develop synergies.

India has tremendous potential to leverage its central, geographical location in the Afro-Asian landmass and Indian Ocean, and become the hub of a multitude of cultural and economic activities. Apart from all activities covered in Chapter 12, two areas need more attention. Conferences and symposia organized in multifarious fields will boost interactions with Afro-Asian and SAARC nations, with added spin-offs for the tourism and hospitality industries.

There is immense scope to expand quality higher education to allow much more participation from neighbouring and Afro-Asian countries. These institutions should sponsor competitive scholarships for such students, on lines of prestigious scholarship programmes in USA and UK etc.

Corporate Sector

The corporate sector can make invaluable contributions to boosting Soft Power. They can conduct and sponsor conferences, symposia, higher education scholarships, sports tournaments, trade and Defence Expos, and a host of similar activities. In doing so, they too will reap many commercial and publicity benefits from them; after all, there are no free lunches.

To give a fillip to greater corporate participation, the Govt should consider these activities as part of their obligation towards *Corporate Social Responsibility*. Govt can also go for joint sponsorships with them, or consider allowing them rebates in corporate taxes.

The corporate sector in the developed countries makes handsome contributions by offering competitive scholarships and internships to deserving foreign students. This helps them to not only attract bright talent from abroad, but also boosts their image in those countries, which helps their business. Our corporate sector too has similar programmes, but those need to be expanded much more to neighbouring and Third World countries.

Maintaining a clean image and following ethical business practices is extremely important. Unfortunately, some of our firms have a bad reputation in this regard. It is vital to remedy that image. Our corporate sector doing business abroad is virtually an ambassador of the country. It must desist from unethical practices and *short-cuts* only with an eye on profits.

In effect, therefore, foreign policy and diplomacy apply the softer and more agreeable approach towards resolving intractable issues between countries. In the contemporary world negotiating and forging economic relationships occupies the centre stage.

While representing the *velvet glove* for the external dimension, internally they synthesize and coordinate all other elements that constitute National power, both hard and soft. This aspect of their role is critical to prevent various Govt and corporate entities from working at cross-purposes.

19

In Essence therefore...

National security is *multi-dimensional*. In the present-day world, it no longer signifies *absence of military threats,* as was its earlier connotation. Threats to a Nation's security abound in the contemporary geopolitical environment. They could be overt or covert, may manifest in the external or internal dimensions, be from hostile *Westphalia* States or non-State actors, and could be either outright military or economic, or might emerge through devious geopolitical and hegemonic manoeuvrings.

Security against such threats therefore, also has to be multi-dimensional to *cover all bases.* The *National Security Paradigm* proposed in Chapter 3 is a comprehensive generic conceptual model that integrates all dimensions in the Nation's internal and external environments, which have a bearing on National security.

You, I, and indeed all people, both citizens or otherwise, have a vital stake in National security. It is the duty of the State to ensure our security, and guarantee our lives, property, and all our freedoms as enshrined in the Constitution.

However as *citizens,* we have an obligation too, in contributing to National security in our own way, in our respective fields. Thus, all citizens are in fact *soldiers* in this noble mission. Citizens' *rights* and *duties* apropos National security are thus inextricably intertwined.

In many respects, our task as *citizen soldiers* is far more profound and sweeps across the *time and space continuum,* than that of even *military men and women.* As this book has stressed repeatedly, one of its central themes is that internal security, stability, social cohesion, inclusive growth, and institutional integrity are vital prerequisites to developing a more formidable capability against external threats. And who plays a key role in all this? It is WE THE PEOPLE.

Readers might wonder why I have not included the dimension of *Political stability and morality.* Is it not important? In fact, it is the most important element, since its *health* critically affects the *health, integrity, and proper functioning* of all other dimensions.

Regrettably, however, detailed analyses of internal dimensions of the *National Security Paradigm* in Part 2 amply highlighted that in the current environment it is our *Achilles heel.* It is true that there is political stability, unlike the era of short-lived Govts shown in Table 1. However, *political stability sans morality* is tantamount to *stability of the graveyard.* The rot is all across the political spectrum, and no party is immune to it.

As Chapter 11 highlighted political expediency and malfeasance has spread the virus to all our institutions, which are actually supposed to be the watchdogs of democracy. Deeply entrenched politico-bureaucratic interests, together with sections of the corporate world that thrive on the bounties bestowed upon them, are actually *ruling the roost.*

In the Nation's internal environment, brazen electoral politics is recklessly creating religious and caste fissures. A compliant Media is actually fanning, rather than cautioning people against it. While the economy has recovered somewhat from the twin shocks of demonetization and poorly implemented GST, agrarian distress and unemployment are causing social and economic hardships.

Peoples' anger and frustration are manifesting themselves in increasing incidence of violence, lynching and lawlessness. No respite appears to be in sight, given that approaching State and National elections will vitiate the atmosphere further.

That brings me back to the point about the role of the *people.* Foremost, it is imperative that *we the people* stay insulated from divisive politics. All violence ultimately ends up causing deaths, injuries, destruction of property, and widespread distress to us only. Having been victims of so many riots, we have to stay united and not fall prey to the polarizing rhetoric of politicians.

Next, *we the people* have to assert ourselves and endeavour to usher in *the change* that gets rid of the corruption-ridden system that is eating into the *body politic.* TALL ORDER? Certainly. But, we owe it ourselves and to our future generations to fight for our Second Independence. If freedom fighters and millions of ordinary people could throw the British out, surely we the *citizen soldiers* can show the same resolve to cleanse the system.

It will require us to go out and vote. Vote we must, but not on religious, caste, provincial, or other parochial considerations, but based only on the candidate's integrity, competence and record. At no cost, must we vote for candidates with a criminal record, regardless of party affiliation. Nor should we vote for candidates or parties having divisive, hate-mongering, or parochial ideology.

Far too long, political parties have preyed upon populist or parochial sentiments, and once voted to power, have shed all pretence of political morality. They are the source of the endemic corruption in the system, which like cancer has spread to all our democratic institutions.

Nowhere in the world are radical improvements in the system brought about by political parties, which prefer to perpetuate the status quo. Such changes are triggered only by the pent up frustration of the people against the political mess. That is the call, which our people have to make.

The title of the book addresses *Citizens and Soldiers,* who together ought to keep the Nation's tryst with destiny. While the people – the *citizen soldiers* will strive for stability, social cohesion and economic growth in the internal environment, *soldiers* in the Armed Forces will guard the Nation against external threats.

Analyses of dimensions in the external environment carried out in Part 3, highlights two critical shortcomings. These are absence of a *National Security Doctrine* and Strategy, and the severe budgetary constraints. All other weaknesses stem from these two.

Lack of a *National Security Doctrine* is absolutely indefensible. How can a country that aspires to be a major player in a *multipolar* world, not even define what its core national interests are, and evolve a well-deliberated coherent doctrine and strategy to safeguard them and promote them? Little wonder then that in its absence we have just lurched from one crisis to another, with only incoherent and *ad hoc* responses.

National Security Doctrine is among the most important executive responsibilities of the top political leadership. That is where the buck stops, and it cannot abdicate its responsibility by letting the NSA or anyone else act on its behalf. It does not happen anywhere in the world.

After comprehensive analyses of all dimensions, once the doctrine is evolved and formally adopted, the execution of the formulated strategy must be entrusted to an Apex body. This could be the *National Security Council,* comprising the PM and key ministers, the Cabinet Secretary, the NSA and CDS, as shown in Fig. 28.

The *National Security Council* must have the requisite authority and resources to implement the formulated National security strategy. It should have analyzed all military, diplomatic and economic scenarios, and clearly designate the line authority and institutional mechanism for their implementation.

Severe budgetary constraints have led to a dangerous backlog of defence modernization, infrastructure, and critical manpower shortages. As Chapter 17 had stressed there is no alternative except to develop a military-industrial complex in line with all advanced nations. This alone can make generate resources for defence modernization, and through large-scale weapon exports make the entire defence establishment self-sustaining.

It will require extensive participation by the private sector, and suitable Govt policies to encourage them to make the heavy initial investments. A radical restructuring of the Ordnance factories, Defence PSUs and DRDO is imperative to turn them around and make them productive. Divestment of many of the units to the Private sector defence firms and joint ventures with them will be the way to go.

With China, we need to boost trade and economic interactions, and not disturb the status quo at the LAC. In the meanwhile, we must pursue rapid economic growth, and build robust defence capability through restructuring and modernization.

Against Pakistan, we have to counter transgressions on the LoC and ISI sponsored terrorist acts more firmly. Partnership with USA is welcome, but without foregoing our strategic independence, and not at the cost of our relationship with Russia.

In sum therefore, *we the people*, the *Citizens and Soldiers* have to step up to resolutely strive for change. We have to exorcize the corruption-ridden politico-bureaucratic system to save democracy, our institutions, and indeed our socio-economic fabric. The power of vote, exercised judiciously, can certainly achieve it.

National Resurgence

As stated earlier, *National Resurgence* is the next step of the mission of *Citizens and Soldiers to keep our tryst with destiny*. An all encompassing and coherent *National Security Doctrine* and Strategy will help provide the solid foundation for it.

Wholehearted involvement of *the people* is a pre-requisite for social harmony and a stable internal environment. Once we have their motivated commitment, it will be possible to channelize their energy and enthusiasm to attain the goal of *National Resurgence*.

In academia, research papers typically end with the section on *Avenues for Further Research*. Hence, *National Resurgence* is the next goal - the *aim-plus* to pursue beyond National security.

While it will require more debates and detailed analyses, the key thrust areas would be *stringent, fast-tracked actions against political-bureaucratic-corporate sleaze, restoring institutional integrity, strict law enforcement, inculcating law-abiding conduct among people, eschewing parochialism, Nationalistic fervour,* and above all, *strengthening National Will and ethos*.

This could well be the subject matter for the next book.

ABOUT THE AUTHOR

Deepak Sethi earned his PhD in International Business Strategy, Organizational Studies, and Management from the *University of Texas at Dallas* in 2001. He also holds the Master of Management Sciences and Master of Science degrees, as well as Post-graduate Diploma in Management from leading universities in India. Since 2001, he has been a professor at the *University of Texas at Dallas, Oakland University* in Michigan, and *Old Dominion University* in Norfolk.

Dr Sethi's research has been published in top academic journals such as Journal *of International Business Studies, International Business Review, Journal of International Management, European Business Review,* and the *Asia Pacific Journal of Management.* He writes extensively on geopolitical and International Business issues, focusing especially upon South Asia, China, and the USA.

Prior to entering academia in the United States, he served in the Indian Army for 31 years, and took early retirement in the rank of Brigadier General in 1997. A veteran of the India-Pakistan War of 1971, he later commanded an Artillery Regiment in a high-altitude sector on the India-China border, and an Artillery Brigade on the border with Pakistan.

During his military career, he also held several important Staff and Teaching appointments, and has been the Editor of *The Artillery Journal.* He scripted, anchored, and produced a motivational film for the Army; *Pause to Ponder: Ethics Values and the Soldier,* for which he interviewed Bharat Ratna JRD Tata and Nani Palkhivala among others.

He is a recipient of the *Chief of Army Staff Commendation* from the Indian Army, and *Best Dissertation Award* from the College of Defence Management.

He published his memoir, *He Opens another Door* in 2013, and *"Operation Jantar Mantar"* in September 2015.

www.ingramcontent.com/pod-product-compliance
Lightning Source LLC
Chambersburg PA
CBHW070824250726
48662CB00003B/1081